Contents

List of Figures and Tables

Figure

Tables

Abbreviations

ABM	Anti-Ballistic Missile
ACA	Arms Control Association
AEC	Atomic Energy Commission
BARC	Bhabha Atomic Research Centre
BGR	Barbour, Griffith, & Rogers
BJP	Bharatiya Janata Party
CIGNL	Contractors International Group on Nuclear Liability
CII	Confederation of Indian Industry
CPI	Communist Party of India
CPI(M)	Communist Party of India (Marxist)
CSC	Convention on Supplementary Compensation for Nuclear Damage
CTBT	Comprehensive Nuclear Test Ban Treaty
DAE	Department of Atomic Energy
DMK	Dravida Munnetra Kazhagam
DRDO	Defence Research and Development Organisation
ENR	Enrichment and Reprocessing
EU	European Union
FARA	Foreign Agents Registration Act
FMCT	Fissile Material Cut-off Treaty

GDP	Gross Domestic Product
GNEP	Global Nuclear Energy Partnership
HFAC	House Foreign Affairs Committee
HIRC	House International Relations Committee
HR	House Resolution
HTCG	High Technology Cooperation Group
IAEA	International Atomic Energy Agency
IDSA	Institute for Defence Studies and Analyses
ITER	International Thermonuclear Experimental Reactor
ISIS	Institute for Science and International Security
ISRO	Indian Space Research Organisation
LWR	Light Water Reactor
MEA	Ministry of External Affairs
MPs	Members of Parliament
MTCR	Missile Technology Control Regime
MW	Megawatt
NDA	National Democratic Alliance
NNPA	Nuclear Non-Proliferation Act
NNSA	National Nuclear Security Administration
NPAS	Nuclear Proliferation Assessment Statement
NPCIL	Nuclear Power Corporation of India Limited
NPT	Nuclear Non-Proliferation Treaty
NRC	Nuclear Regulatory Commission
NSC	National Security Council
NSG	Nuclear Suppliers Group
NSSP	Next Steps in Strategic Partnership
PHWR	Pressurized Heavy Water Reactors
PMO	Prime Minister's Office
PNND	Parliamentarians for Nuclear Non-proliferation and Disarmament (PNND)
PSI	Proliferation Security Initiative
QFRs	Questions for the Record
SCOMET	Special Chemicals, Organisms, Materials, Equipment and Technology
SFRC	Senate Foreign Relations Committee
SP	Samajwadi Party
UK	United Kingdom

UN	United Nations
UNPA	United National Progressive Alliance
UPA	United Progressive Alliance
US	United States
USIBC	US–India Business Council
USIFC	US–India Friendship Council
USINPAC	US–India Political Action Committee
WMD	Weapons of Mass Destruction

Preface

THIS is a study of a very complex nuclear negotiation. The study examines how the United States and India negotiated a historic and politically contentious civilian nuclear agreement. The agreement changed long-standing US laws and non-proliferation regime guidelines to recognize India's nuclear status: through the agreement, India became the sixth country in the world that could retain nuclear weapons and still participate in civilian nuclear commerce. The Bush administration announced the agreement in July 2005 and completed it in late 2008.

Despite its importance, there are few comprehensive analyses of the US–India nuclear agreement. This book fills this gap in scholarship by thoroughly examining the politics of the agreement. More significantly, it draws upon the well-established framework of two-level games, that combines diplomacy with domestic politics, to explain key puzzles in the US–India nuclear dialogue. This framework explains why Washington and New Delhi could not reach a nuclear agreement in the early 2000s and why, even after they announced an agreement in 2005, they could not complete it until 2008. Such an analysis also offers lessons for US nuclear negotiations with other countries and for the broader US strategic dialogue with India.

A number of individuals and organizations assisted with this manuscript. The Woodrow Wilson Center's fellowship program, its superb staff, its South Asia program directed by Bob Hathaway, and many friends and colleagues at the Center provided a rich intellectual environment and vital research support at the early stages of this project. The American Political Science Association's Centennial Center, the University of Cincinnati's sabbatical program, and its Taft Research Center offered additional support. Further, a number of experts and participants in the nuclear dialogue offered their insights in research interviews and in comments on the draft manuscript: these were off the record and, without identifying them by name, I am especially grateful for their contributions. The reviewers of this manuscript also offered insightful comments. Doug Jackson at the Wilson Center provided much research support, and several political science colleagues offered helpful suggestions, including Jacques Hymans, Jacob Wilson, Ivan Ivanov, Joel Wolfe, and Rina Williams. I also acknowledge a long-standing debt to Barclay Ward, Sumit Ganguly and Stephen Cohen. They introduced me to the fields of nuclear affairs and South Asian security; they have been the best of mentors over the years; and they offered vital fellowship recommendations for and useful comments on this manuscript. Finally, I would like to thank all who assisted at Cambridge University Press with the publication of this book.

CHAPTER ONE

The Argument

THIS book examines how the United States and India settled decades of nuclear differences through a civilian nuclear agreement. The agreement was central to the US effort to build a strategic partnership with India in the early years of the twenty-first century. To further this partnership, New Delhi urged Washington to recognize its nuclear status and to lift a long-standing embargo on civilian nuclear cooperation with India. Washington agreed in July 2005, when President George W. Bush committed to attaining 'full civilian nuclear energy cooperation and trade with India' (The White House, 2005).

Washington and New Delhi then planned to complete the technical and legal requirements for nuclear cooperation ahead of the president's March 2006 visit to India. US–India talks on these issues were advancing in late 2005. India's national security advisor then informed the US ambassador that India's government had 'pulled out all the stops' to finalize the outstanding issues and that India was expecting to quickly 'close the deal'.[1] Yet, both sides could not close their nuclear deal until October 2008, when President Bush finally signed legislation permitting nuclear trade with India.

Why was the Bush administration unable to complete the nuclear agreement with India in 2005, 2006 and 2007, and why was it eventually able to do so in 2008? This book adopts a two-level framework, linking diplomacy with domestic politics, to explain these outcomes. Domestic politics substantially impeded – and may have entirely prevented – US nuclear accommodation with India; when domestic obstacles were overcome, US–India negotiations advanced; and even after negotiations advanced, domestic factors placed conditions on and affected the scope of US–India nuclear cooperation. In the end, US–India negotiations only advanced when the conditions for nuclear cooperation satisfied key domestic constituents in both countries. This chapter elaborates upon this argument. The chapter begins by reviewing the historical significance of the US–India nuclear agreement and the scholarly contributions of this study, and goes on to discuss its explanatory framework.

The Significance of the Case

The US–India nuclear agreement was a major event in US foreign policy, in world politics, and in India's foreign policy. First, the agreement was the most significant American attempt to forge strategic relations with India. During the Cold War, Washington and New Delhi had substantial differences over US support for Pakistan, India's tilt towards the Soviet Union, and India remaining outside the Nuclear Non-Proliferation Treaty (NPT).[2] India's nuclear program continued to impede US–India rapprochement after the Cold War. The Bush administration concluded that, to establish enduring strategic ties with India, it needed to cut this 'Gordian knot'. It proceeded to accommodate India through the civilian nuclear agreement, which comprehensively addressed, and went far beyond prior US attempts to incrementally settle, the issue of India's nuclear status.

Second, the agreement undermined decades of US nuclear non-proliferation policy. Containing the spread of nuclear weapons through a strong non-proliferation regime had long been a core US foreign policy priority. To reinforce the regime, Washington developed the full-scope safeguards rule for civilian nuclear exports. This rule, embedded in the 1978 Nuclear Non-Proliferation Act (NNPA), and adopted by the international Nuclear Suppliers Group (NSG) in 1992, banned civilian nuclear trade with countries that had not signed the NPT and placed all their nuclear facilities under safeguards. The rule was thereby a significant incentive for countries to renounce nuclear weapons and join the NPT; conversely, it was a disincentive for them to remain outside the NPT. Yet, in 2005, the Bush administration exempted India from this rule despite concerns that, once the rule was bent for one country (that is, India), it could be similarly bent for others, thereby undermining the non-proliferation regime. In essence, Washington conceded ground on one vital national interest – that of upholding a fundamental rule in the nuclear non-proliferation regime – to further another foreign policy objective: that of developing strategic relations with India.

Third, the nuclear agreement was a significant event in world politics. It bent critical rules of a major international regime – the full-scope safeguards rule of the nuclear non-proliferation regime – to accommodate just one country. Simply put, the agreement moved India closer to the five NPT-recognized nuclear weapons countries, because India then became the sixth country that could keep nuclear weapons and still participate in international nuclear commerce.

Fourth, the nuclear agreement was a very important event in India's foreign policy. Through the agreement, New Delhi sought to gain international recognition of its nuclear and major power status, access a clean source of energy for its growing economy, and advance strategic ties with the US. It was also the first time that an Indian government risked its domestic political survival for a foreign policy initiative: never before had an Indian government faced a parliamentary no-confidence vote because of an international agreement.

The Contributions of this Study

This study of the US–India nuclear agreement makes three contributions to scholarship. First, despite its historical significance, there are few comprehensive analyses of the nuclear agreement. This book fills this gap in the literature by examining, in considerable depth, negotiations for the agreement and by providing new details on this important case. Second, it offers a better analytical framework, combining diplomacy with domestic politics, to explain the case. Third, the analytical framework has broader applications beyond this case: it can usefully inform nuclear dialogues with other states and also adds to scholarship on nuclear security.

On this last issue, scholarship on nuclear affairs has examined extensively the causes of nuclear proliferation and the question of why states seek nuclear weapons and nuclear technology. Some scholars note that security reasons, domestic pressures, and prestige considerations influence national nuclear decisions (Sagan, 1996–97). Others highlight the psychology of proliferation and the beliefs of national leaders in a state's nuclear decision

(Hymans, 2006). Still others stress political–economic considerations and note that governments prioritizing economic liberalization and integration with the international community would favour nuclear restraints (Solingen, 2007). Scholars have also analysed the normative constraints to acquiring nuclear weapons (Rublee, 2009) and the transfer of technologies that help states acquire nuclear weapons (Fuhrman, 2012; Kroenig, 2010).

Overall, such scholarship provides valuable insights into the causes of proliferation. These insights can guide nuclear diplomacy with particular countries: knowing the basic causal factors behind a national nuclear program can be useful in negotiations involving that program. Yet, these insights do not substantially explain the outcomes of nuclear negotiations. This is because the causal factors behind a nuclear program are mostly constant during a negotiation but the outcomes of the negotiation vary: negotiations only succeed at some points in time but not at others.

In the end, nuclear negotiations represent a distinct class of cases, and therefore require an explanatory framework that is different from frameworks that examine the causes of proliferation. Prior studies of nuclear negotiations, such as those of US–Soviet arms control during the Cold War, do not provide appropriate analytical frameworks for examining contemporary nuclear negotiations.[3] This book develops such a framework to explain US nuclear negotiations with India.

A Summary of the Argument

US–India nuclear negotiations are best examined through a framework that links diplomacy with domestic politics. The main domestic factors influencing US–India negotiations were bureaucratic politics, legislative opposition, and mobilization by supporters and opponents. (As explained in Chapter 2, these factors shaped each state's 'win-set', which is the set of international arrangements that could win domestic approval in that state.) These factors prevented New Delhi from accepting arrangements with relatively higher non-proliferation provisions. They also affected Washington's position on arrangements with relatively lower non-proliferation provisions that New Delhi desired. Such a framework explains negotiating outcomes for the US–India nuclear agreement. It clarifies why several phases of negotiations were necessary to finalize the agreement and why, in each phase, both sides could only accept certain terms for nuclear cooperation.

In the first phase, completed in July 2005, the Bush administration announced the civilian nuclear initiative with India. At the time, because of bureaucratic resistance from its nuclear establishment, India's government only accepted an arrangement with relatively low non-proliferation provisions. Somewhat different bureaucratic considerations enabled the Bush administration to accommodate India: the senior-most US officials gave priority to strategic relations with India and were willing to accept New Delhi's position. Soon after this arrangement was announced, however, legislative opposition affected Washington's position: Congress sought more clarity on India's nuclear restraints.

Accordingly, in the second phase, from late 2005 to March 2006, the Bush administration and India's government negotiated restraints involving the separation of India's civilian and military nuclear facilities. Bureaucratic resistance then, again, affected India's position: India's nuclear establishment resisted placing key reactors under safeguards. As a result, New Delhi only accepted a civilian–military separation that had low-to-moderate non-proliferation provisions. While the US non-proliferation bureaucracy would not accept such an arrangement, regional and strategic affairs bureaucrats, as well as the senior-most US officials, accommodated the Indian position.

In the third phase, from March to December 2006, the Bush administration sought congressional approval for the civilian nuclear initiative. In March, the administration submitted a bill that had low non-proliferation conditions, but Congress rejected the proposal and drafted alternative legislation with moderate non-proliferation provisions. The president signed this bill, called the Hyde Act, in December 2006. This legislation, however, was not domestically acceptable in India.

New Delhi then sought to offset the Hyde Act when it negotiated a legally binding agreement required by Section 123 of the Atomic Energy Act. In the fourth phase, completed in July 2007, Washington and New Delhi negotiated a Section 123 Agreement having relatively low-to-moderate non-proliferation provisions.

Domestic mobilization considerably influenced the US and Indian positions during the third and fourth phases. In the US, non-proliferation groups mobilized and sought strong non-proliferation conditions in congressional legislation.[4] This influenced Congress to reject the Bush administration's March 2006 bill. On the other hand, strategic affairs experts, American business, and Indian Americans lobbied Congress to move ahead with the

Hyde Act. This counter-mobilization influenced Congress to pass legislation with moderate but not high non-proliferation provisions.

In India, the nuclear establishment, strategic affairs experts, and right-wing opposition parties, all opposed restrictive conditions in the nuclear agreement, while leftist parties objected to any strategic ties with the US. These factors caused New Delhi to oppose even the moderate non-proliferation provisions of the Hyde Act.

In the fifth phase, from August 2007 to July 2008, leftist parties warned that they would withdraw support for India's government – which would have led to the government's collapse – if it went ahead with the nuclear agreement. Thus, legislative opposition and the Indian government's political weakness prevented it from advancing the nuclear agreement until July 2008. India's government then obtained support from a regional political party to win a parliamentary vote of confidence. This increased the government's strength and enabled it to proceed with the nuclear agreement.

In the sixth phase, India negotiated a safeguards pact with the International Atomic Energy Agency (IAEA). Thereafter, in early September 2008, the NSG lifted nuclear trade restrictions on India.

In the seventh phase, just after the NSG decision, the Bush administration asked Congress to formally approve the Section 123 Agreement. In this instance, Democrats held a majority in both the House and the Senate, and the voting rules were tougher (approval required a two-thirds majority in the House and unanimous consent in the Senate); this stronger congressional position enabled it to press for stronger non-proliferation provisions in nuclear cooperation with India. However, the administration's efforts to address congressional concerns, mobilization by supporters, and an Indian letter-of-intent to purchase reactors potentially worth tens of billion dollars from US firms also influenced Congress; Congress therefore approved the Section 123 Agreement with moderate but not high non-proliferation provisions.

In summary, for each phase of the nuclear agreement, bureaucratic politics, legislative opposition, and domestic mobilization significantly influenced both the US and Indian negotiating positions. These factors required the US and Indian governments to proceed step-by-step, over seven phases, to advance the nuclear agreement. Moreover, in each phase, both sides had to compromise on the scope of nuclear cooperation to retain the agreement within their respective win-sets.[5]

The Outline of the Book

The following chapters explain US–India negotiations in detail. The next chapter discusses how domestic factors influence international negotiations and how they affected US nuclear talks with India. Subsequent chapters cover the seven aforementioned phases of the nuclear agreement. They examine the origins of the agreement from 1998 to July 2005 (Chapter 3); negotiations for India's nuclear separation plan in late 2005 and early 2006 (Chapter 4); a first round of congressional action in 2006 (Chapter 5); US–India talks on the Section 123 Agreement in 2007 (Chapter 6); Indian domestic politics that held up the nuclear agreement in 2007–08 (Chapter 7); talks with the IAEA (Chapter 8) and with the NSG (Chapter 9); and a second round of congressional action in 2008 (Chapter 10).

Chapters 11 and 12 extend the framework to additional cases. Chapter 11 explains why domestic politics did not hinder a US–India reprocessing pact, but why, by shaping India's nuclear liability bill, they prevented US firms from quickly realizing commercial rewards from the nuclear agreement. Chapter 12 reviews the US–India nuclear negotiations and explains how domestic dynamics influence US nuclear diplomacy with other countries. The appendix examines the military and energy aspects of India's nuclear program and non-proliferation issues in the nuclear agreement; these were intensely debated by supporters and opponents of the agreement.

Endnotes

1   The US Embassy, New Delhi, cable, 16 December 2005.
2   These differences overshadowed the convergence in US and Indian interests on some issues, such as their common democratic foundations, Washington's considerable developmental assistance to India, and its arms supplies to New Delhi during and after the 1962 Sino-Indian war. For historical overviews of US–India relations, see Gould and Ganguly (1992), Kux (1993), Limaye (1993), and McMahon (1994).
3   Numerous books examine arms control talks between the US and the Soviet Union. Many of these are historical and descriptive rather than analytical. Even those that are analytical are largely based on bargaining models and do not focus on domestic politics. And, while a very few political science studies of US–Soviet arms control do examine domestic politics, the domestic factors in such studies are only partially applicable to contemporary US nuclear dialogues.
4   These involved the termination of nuclear cooperation if India conducted a nuclear test; limiting fuel reserves for India's reactors; specifying the terms

for Indian reprocessing of spent fuel; banning reprocessing and enrichment technology transfer to India; and seeking India's alignment with US preferences on Iran.

5   On this point, in July 2005, Washington had committed to giving New Delhi 'full' nuclear cooperation, and it also affirmed that 'as a responsible state with advanced nuclear technology, India should acquire the same benefits and advantages as other such states'. Eventually, Washington placed small conditions on nuclear cooperation with India. New Delhi argued that these conditions gave it less than 'full' cooperation and that they accorded it fewer benefits than those given to the five NPT-defined nuclear weapons states. Subsequently, in 2010, New Delhi adopted liability laws that kept the US firms away from investing in India's nuclear sector.

CHAPTER TWO

Diplomacy and Domestic Politics

THE US–India nuclear agreement involved negotiations at both the international and domestic levels. It involved talks between US and Indian negotiators, between the Bush administration and Congress, and between India's government and other political parties. These negotiations may be best examined through the two-level framework, which specifies how bureaucratic factors, legislative politics, and domestic mobilization influence international negotiations. Such explanations offer advantages over alternative single-level and cross-level explanations.

Alternative Explanations

Explanations based on the international, domestic, and individual levels of analysis each offer important insights into the US–India nuclear agreement, but they also respectively omit key factors behind the agreement.

International-level explanations highlight how external factors and the structure of the international system influence national foreign policy initiatives. Such explanations note that, as the capabilities of their rivals increase, states will pursue alignments to restore power balances in the regional and international systems. Reflecting these themes, US policymakers made the case that, with an eye on a rising China, Washington 'should pay closer attention to India's role in the regional balance [in Asia]…India is an element in China's calculation, and it should be in America's, too' (Rice, 2000). Clearly, China was closing the power gap with the US: the US gross domestic product (GDP, measured by purchasing power parity) was six times larger than China's in 1990, but only four times larger by 1995, and 3.3 times larger by 2000, while the US composite national capability score was 1.3 times greater than China's in 1990, but only 1.15 times greater in 1995, and 1.13 times greater in 2000.[1] These power shifts would correctly explain the US strategic interest in nuclear accommodation with India to balance a rising China.[2] Still, power-based factors would predict that the US should have sought such accommodation in the mid-1990s, when China was narrowing the power gap with the US. Instead, during those years, Washington sought to cap rather than to accommodate New Delhi's nuclear program.

Domestic factors explain some of the stated discrepancy. Domestic explanations note that international agreements may be successfully completed when political parties that favour the agreement hold office. This reasoning would rightly suggest that a Republican administration, which prioritized balance of power over non-proliferation considerations, rather than a Democratic administration which strongly affirmed prevailing non-proliferation policies, would pursue a nuclear agreement with India. Still, even these explanations are incomplete because the Bush administration held office from 2001 onwards, but did not announce a nuclear agreement with India until 2005.

Individual factors can help explain this issue. At the individual level, changes in the State Department leadership resulted in changes in US nuclear policy towards India. Thus, Colin Powell, Secretary of State from 2001 to 2004, accepted the standard bureaucratic position of not bending long-standing non-proliferation policy to accommodate India, but Condoleezza Rice, Secretary of State from 2005 onwards, actively pressed for a new approach towards India.

In the end, a combination of international factors (related to changes in the balance of power), domestic factors (the different non-proliferation approaches taken by Democratic and Republican administrations), and individual factors (the different approaches taken by Secretary Rice and Secretary Powell) explain why the US finally announced a nuclear agreement with India in 2005 and not earlier. Yet, even this combination of three factors does not explain the fundamental puzzle behind the agreement. It does not explain why, despite all three factors being present from 2005 to 2008, the Bush administration could not complete the agreement in 2005, 2006, and 2007, and why it was able to complete the agreement, albeit with great difficulty, in

2008. Ultimately, domestic factors must be better linked with international ones to explain this puzzle.

One way to integrate domestic and international factors is the cross-level approach. Cross-level synthesis is a pragmatic way to explain political phenomena when the data fit with the right combination of theories (Moravcsik, 2003). For example, in a nuclear negotiation, a system-level factor may explain one piece of the negotiation, a domestic factor may explain a second piece, and an individual-level factor may explain a third piece. Still, such synthesis is largely case specific, because it does not clarify how the different factors may be combined to examine additional cases.

A similar shortcoming arises when numerous factors exist at any given level. For example, at the domestic level, scholars have identified several ways in which domestic factors influence international negotiations (Knopf, 1998). Domestic factors shape grand strategy. They are a constraint on cooperation but they may also channel state preferences towards cooperation. Further, bureaucracies, elites, and organized coalitions pursuing their self-interests can significantly influence state policy in favour of or against an international agreement. In addition, technical experts may recommend certain approaches towards an issue and national negotiators may adopt these in international negotiations. Finally, international norms influence state actors (such as the bureaucracy) and societal actors (such as interest groups) to advance particular policies in international agreements.

All these domestic factors explain aspects of the US–India nuclear agreement. The worldview of the Bush administration shaped US grand strategy towards accommodating India's nuclear program. Yet, legislative politics in both the US and India constrained the implementation of this grand strategy. Additional factors such as the preferences of governmental elites and non-governmental groups; the input of technical experts (who examined non-proliferation, security, economic, and energy issues); and transnational norms (for example, norms about maintaining the integrity of the non-proliferation regime and discourse about the environmental benefits of nuclear energy), all shaped policies on, and arguments for and against, the US–India nuclear agreement. In the end, all these domestic factors explain parts of the agreement. Yet, an ad hoc combination of these factors does not generate a framework that can be generalized to other cases.

In contrast, the two-level framework, where the state represents the nexus of the international and domestic levels of analysis, offers a less fragmented and more generalizable mid-range theoretical explanation for the US–India nuclear agreement.

The Two-level Framework

The two-level framework begins with the observation that international agreements involve bargaining at the international level (L1) between two national governments, as well as at the domestic level (L2) between each national government and domestic constituents whose support is required to approve an agreement (Evans et al., 1993; Putnam, 1988). Related to these observations is the 'win-set', which is the set of all international arrangements that can win domestic approval in a country. Thus, if both countries in a negotiation have large win-sets – that is, they have much room for negotiations – they are more likely to reach an agreement, while if they have little negotiating room, agreements become harder. It is then important to clarify the issues in the negotiation and the factors affecting each side's win-set.

In terms of the issues, US–India talks covered arrangements that could have had very high to very low non-proliferation provisions. Each country's win-set determines the provisions it can accept. As shown in Figure 2.1, if the US has a small win-set, extending from just point 0 to point 1, it would only be able to accept arrangement A1; however, if it has a large win-set, extending from point 0 to point 9, it could accept all arrangements, A1–A9.

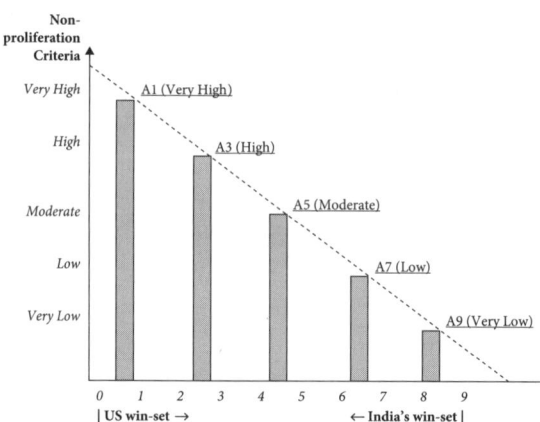

Figure 2.1 Arrangements A1–A9 and the Win-set

Notes: (a) A1: having very high non-proliferation criteria; A9: having very low non-proliferation criteria.

(b) The US win-set extends rightwards from point 0. Thus, a small US win-set spanning from point 0 to point 1 would only allow the US to accept arrangement A1, while a large win-set spanning from point 0 to point 9 would allow it to accept all arrangements, A1–A9. India's win-set extends leftwards from point 9, following the same logic.

India's win-set extended leftwards from point 9, following the same logic. On a related note, India's starting position was that, in July 2005, the US gave it the same rights as an NPT nuclear weapons state, and such states accept very low non-proliferation restraints. India could therefore easily accept similar arrangements, but found it harder to accept arrangements with higher non-proliferation provisions.

The L1 arrangement negotiated between Washington and New Delhi, or the equivalent L2 arrangement (that is, the domestic legislation required to implement an L1 arrangement), is thus the dependent variable in this study. It is operationalized according to the overall non-proliferation provisions in the arrangement, and has values ranging from A1 (an arrangement having very high non-proliferation provisions) to A9 (an arrangement having very low non-proliferation provisions). For example, assume that Washington and New Delhi are negotiating over the number of Indian reactors free of safeguards. Here, arrangement A1 is one where India keeps just 10 per cent of its reactors outside safeguards; India would keep a greater 20 per cent of its reactors outside safeguards in arrangement A2, 30 per cent in arrangement A3, 40 per cent in arrangement A4, 50 per cent in arrangement A5, 60 per cent in arrangement A6, 70 per cent in arrangement A7, 80 per cent in arrangement A8, and 90 per cent in arrangement A9. Thus, in Figure 2.1, a wide US win-set spanning from point 0 to point 9 would allow it to accept arrangement A9 where India kept 90 per cent of its reactors outside safeguards. Yet, a small US win-set spanning from point 0 to point 1 would only allow it to accept arrangement A1 where India kept 10 per cent of its reactors outside safeguards.

In practice, the US–India L1 arrangements covered not just a single issue (such as the number of reactors outside safeguards) but several issues. The overall non-proliferation provisions of these arrangements are therefore calculated by averaging the non-proliferation strength of each issue in the arrangement. This methodology is explained in subsequent chapters. To illustrate it with an example, the criteria for coding the July 2005 Joint Statement are shown in Table 3.3 (see Chapter 3). Based on these criteria, an A3-type Joint Statement would have relatively high non-proliferation provisions on all five issues in the statement (the issues of India's export controls, safeguards, testing obligations, fissile material obligations, and nuclear status); an A4-type Joint Statement would have relatively high provisions on half the issues and relatively moderate provisions on the remaining issues; and an A5-type Joint Statement would have relatively moderate non-proliferation provisions on all these issues.

In the end, the Joint Statement was an A7 arrangement with relatively low non-proliferation provisions; India's separation plan and the Section 123 Agreement were A6 arrangements with relatively low-to-moderate non-proliferation provisions; and the NSG exemption for India was an A5 arrangement with relatively moderate non-proliferation provisions. The main L2 arrangements – congressional legislation in 2006 and 2008 – were also A5 arrangements with relatively moderate non-proliferation provisions, while the legislative amendments that were rejected by Congress were A3 arrangements with relatively high non-proliferation provisions.

Domestic Factors influencing International Negotiations

In each phase of their negotiations, Washington and New Delhi could agree to only certain L1 arrangements because only these fell within both their win-sets. The factors that determine the size of the win-set are the independent variables in this study. These factors are bureaucratic politics, legislative opposition (which depends upon the political–institutional rules to approve an agreement, as well as political power considerations), domestic mobilization, and strategies and tactics used to shape win-sets.

Bureaucratic Politics

The preferences and relative power of bureaucratic actors influence the size of the win-set. Further, bureaucratic veto players, who wield power to block a policy, can substantially decrease the win-set (Hymans, 2011).

Within the US bureaucracy, non-proliferation specialists were concerned that the nuclear agreement with India would undermine long-standing American non-proliferation policies. Rather than taking sides with or against the Bush administration, these officials focused on limiting the damage to non-proliferation by upholding important non-proliferation positions in negotiations with India.[3] This would have decreased the US win-set, but strategic and regional affairs specialists had a more accommodative approach towards India, and they offset the non-proliferation position. Just as importantly, the most powerful bureaucratic actors – the president, secretary of state, national security advisor, and undersecretary of state for political affairs – made the final negotiating decisions. They were willing to make some nuclear concessions to advance strategic ties with India, and this expanded the US win-set, enabling it to accommodate L1 arrangements without strong non-proliferation provisions.

In India, the foreign ministry, formally known as the Ministry of External Affairs (MEA), has traditionally negotiated nuclear issues with the outside world (issues ranging from the test ban treaty to Tarapur fuel discussions with Washington), while India's nuclear establishment has historically been less involved in international negotiations. However, the nuclear establishment determines the technological contours of India's nuclear program and, along with the Prime Minister's Office (PMO), is the main actor shaping India's nuclear policy.[4] During negotiations for the US–India nuclear agreement, India's nuclear establishment acted as a veto player. The chairman of India's Atomic Energy Commission (AEC), who also serves as the secretary of the Department of Atomic Energy (DAE), often gave interviews spelling out DAE's red lines on the main issues. Such resistance from the nuclear establishment reduced India's win-set so that it could not accept L1 arrangements with high or even moderate-to-high non-proliferation provisions.

Political–Institutional Requirements

The political–institutional requirements for domestic approval of an agreement significantly influence the win-set. Typically, if an agreement does not require legislative approval, the win-set is larger; if it requires approval by 50 per cent of the legislature, the win-set decreases, because only certain L1 arrangements may receive favourable votes from half the legislature; if it requires approval by two-thirds of the legislature, the win-set further decreases.

In the US, the nuclear agreement had to be approved by criteria outlined in the Atomic Energy Act, which were further modified in talks between the Bush administration and Congress. Ultimately, the agreement required legislative approval in two steps. First, in 2006, it required approval by a majority in both the House and the Senate. Thereafter, in 2008, it required approval by two-thirds of the House and 60 per cent of the Senate, as well as the Senate's unanimous consent to this process. These requirements decreased the win-set, especially in 2008.

A related point is that, even when Congress must formally approve foreign policy initiatives, its actual approach varies between being disengaged, supportive, strategic, and competitive.[5] In general, presidents have the upper hand in foreign policy for a number of institutional, political, and historical reasons. For example, they can make a simple national security argument that, although the administration's policy has shortcomings, congressional rejection of the policy would harm American interests. Still, while a disengaged and deferential Congress would accept this argument, a competitive Congress would challenge it (Kelley, 2005; Lindsay, 2003).

Congress eventually adopted a competitive approach towards the nuclear agreement with India. Congressional staff, as well as key senators and representatives, did not unconditionally accept the Bush administration's stand that the agreement would strengthen national security; instead, they raised concerns that the agreement would weaken the non-proliferation regime. Congress therefore reviewed the agreement in great detail in 11 hearings and briefings (see Table 2.1). It heard testimony from 24 specialists: these included 12 non-proliferation experts, six South Asia regional experts, three strategic affairs experts, and one business, energy, and environmental expert each. While the regional and strategic affairs specialists favoured the agreement, thereby helping to increase the win-set, non-proliferation specialists raised concerns, decreasing the win-set. Thus, as shown in Table 2.2, a few key political–institutional factors decreased the US win-set so that L1 and L2 arrangements with relatively low non-proliferation provisions remained outside the win-set.

In India, political–institutional considerations should have increased the win-set, because, in its parliamentary system, the legislature did not have to approve foreign policy initiatives such as the nuclear agreement.[6] Moreover, the formation and execution of Indian foreign policy is traditionally dominated by a handful of elites – the prime minister, officials in the PMO, select cabinet ministers, and foreign affairs bureaucrats – with little input from the legislature (Miller, 2013; Narang and Staniland, 2012). Still, these considerations did not increase India's win-set because the executive's ability to implement policy was constrained by political power considerations.

Political Power Considerations

The distribution of power in the legislature determines whether the executive can gain legislative support for an international agreement, and this shapes the win-set on the agreement.

Table 2.1 Experts Testifying in Congressional Hearings

Hearing	Officials and Experts Testifying
2005	
26 July, SFRC	*South Asia expert*: Sumit Ganguly; *strategic affairs expert*: Randall Shriver; *economic affairs expert*: Mikkal Herberg
8 September, HIRC	*Administration officials*: Nicholas Burns, Robert Joseph
26 October, HIRC	*Nuclear affairs experts*: Robert Einhorn, Henry Sokolski, Leonard Spector, David Albright
2 November, SFRC	*Administration officials*: Nicholas Burns, Robert Joseph; *nuclear affairs experts*: Ron Lehman, Henry Sokolski, Michael Krepon
16 November, HIRC	*South Asia experts*: Ashley Tellis, Stephen Cohen, Francine Frankel, Satu Limaye
2006	
29 March, SFRC	*Administration officials*: Nicholas Burns, Robert Joseph
5 April, SFRC	*Administration official*: Condoleezza Rice
5 April, HIRC	*Administration official*: Condoleezza Rice
26 April, SFRC	*Nuclear affairs experts*: Robert Galluci, Ron Lehman, Robert Einhorn, Gary Milhollin; *South Asia experts*: Ashley Tellis, Stephen Cohen; *strategic affairs experts*: William Perry, Ashton Carter
11 May, HIRC	*Nuclear affairs experts*: Leonard Weiss, Daryl Kimball, Fred McGoldrick; *South Asia expert*: Ashley Tellis; *strategic affairs expert*: Richard Falkenrath
16 July, Senate Energy Committee	*Nuclear affairs expert*: Daniel Poneman; *environmental expert*: David Victor; *economic/energy affairs expert*: Michael Gadbaw
2008	
18 September, SFRC	*Administration officials*: William Burns, John Rood

Note: SFRC: Senate Foreign Relations Committee; HIRC: House International Relations Committee.
Source: Data compiled by author from House and Senate committee records.

First, legislative approval for a foreign policy initiative is more likely if the president's party has a majority in the legislature (this is shown as 'Political Power A' in Table 2.2). In 2005–06, Republicans held 53 per cent of the seats in the House and 55 per cent in the Senate; this increased the win-set and helped legislative approval of the nuclear agreement. In 2007–08, however,

Republicans held just 47 per cent of the seats in the House and 49 per cent in the Senate; this decreased the win-set and made legislative approval harder.

Second, the government must have the power to remain in office when its opponents disapprove of its foreign policy and seek to unseat the government (this is shown as 'Political Power B' in Table 2.2).[7] India's government did not have such power because the ruling UPA coalition held only 42 per cent of the

Table 2.2 Institutional and Political Factors and the Win-set

	Strength of Factor	*Notes on Factor*	*Impact on Win-set*
Political–institutional requirements for legislative approval of the nuclear agreement			
The US	Higher	• Two-step process; first step required 50% of the vote in both the House and Senate; second step required 67% of the vote in the House and unanimous consent in the Senate.	Decreases
		• Congress was not deferential; it held 11 hearings and closely scrutinized the issue.	
India	Not relevant	• No formal parliamentary approval required.	Increases
		• However, the prime minister made eight statements in the Parliament explaining the nuclear agreement and clarifying India's red-lines.	
Political Power A – Executive has the legislative votes to pass the nuclear agreement			
The US, 2005–06	Higher	• Republicans held a majority, with the distribution of power in the 100-member Senate and 435-member House as follows:	Increases
		Senate: Republican (55), Democrat (44)	
		House: Republican (232; 53%), Democrat (202; 47%)	
The US, 2007–08	Lower	• Republicans held a minority of seats:	Decreases
		Senate: Democrat (50), Republican (49)	
		House: Republican (202; 47%), Democrat (233; 53%)	
India	Not relevant	• Indian governments do not require legislative approval for international agreements.	Increases

	Strength of Factor	*Notes on Factor*	*Impact on Win-set*
Political Power B – Government has the strength to remain in office			
The US	Not relevant	• The Bush administration did not require legislative support to remain in office.	Increases
India	Lower	• India's government depended on leftist parties to remain in office, with the distribution of seats in a 542-member Parliament as follows:*	Decreases
		UPA coalition: about 225 (42%), including Congress Party with 145–153 seats (27–28%), RJD with 23 seats, DMK with 16 seats, NCP with 10 seats	
		Left: 59 (11%), including CPI(M) with 43 seats and CPI with 11 seats	
		NDA alliance: 181–189 (33–34%), including BJP with 130–138 seats (24–25%), Shiv Sena with 12 seats, BJD with 11 seats, Akali Dal with eight seats	
		Others: 82 (15%), including SP with 37 seats (7%), BSP with 19 seats (3.5%)	

Notes: (a) *The number of seats varied slightly between 2004 and 2008 because of by-elections and because some parties entered or left their respective coalitions.

(b) UPA: United Progressive Alliance; RJD: Rashtriya Janata Dal; DMK: Dravida Munnetra Kazhagam; NCP: Nationalist Congress Party; CPI(M): Communist Party of India (Marxist); CPI: Communist Party of India; BJP: Bharatiya Janata Party; BJD: Biju Janata Dal; SP: Samajwadi Party; and BSP: Bahujan Samaj Party.

seats in India's lower house of Parliament, and it relied on leftist parties, having 11 per cent of the seats, to remain in office. The government was also unable to secure support from the right. From 2005 to 2008, the right-wing BJP issued many statements to alert the government of its concerns. These clarified the BJP's technical objections to the nuclear agreement. They also highlighted its political concerns about preserving India's sovereignty and the integrity of its nuclear decision-making process.[8] For these reasons, the Indian government was in a politically weak position and this reduced its win-set so that it could not accept arrangements with relatively high non-proliferation provisions.

Domestic Mobilization

During the domestic approval process for an international agreement, mobilization by supporters helps increase the win-set by influencing a greater number of legislators to accept the agreement. Such mobilization also makes it politically easier for governments to pursue an agreement. Conversely, mobilization by opponents decreases the win-set. Mobilization generally involves interest groups, technical and strategic affairs experts, and the media.

Interest groups seek to affect policy in a number of ways (Baumgartner et al., 2009; Cigler and Loomis, 2011). They may use inside lobbying tactics, such as speaking with government officials, testifying in the legislature, and serving on public advisory boards. They may also use outside lobbying techniques, such as talking with and writing in the press, which then mobilizes the public to appeal to policymakers (Kollman, 1998). In the US, a coalition of advocacy groups, referred to as the 'India lobby', pressed Congress to accept the nuclear agreement, while arms control groups urged Congress to oppose it.

Technical and strategic affairs experts did not formally lobby but they still made influential arguments on the nuclear agreement. These professionals have recognized expertise and an authoritative claim to policy-relevant knowledge in their issue-domain. They provide technical information on an issue (for example, on the energy and non-proliferation costs and benefits of the nuclear agreement) and thereby shape debates and policies on the issue. In the US, a small number of non-proliferation and strategic affairs experts, many of whom were based at think tanks or university research centres, influenced the debate on the nuclear agreement. Similarly, in India, nuclear and strategic affairs experts offered both supporting and opposing views in the media, and these shaped India's win-set on the agreement.[9]

The Media

The media influence foreign policy in several ways: policy decisions are affected, in part, by how fully the media cooperate with the government and against its opponents; the media are important in agenda setting and framing and in giving more prominence to some issues or to some aspects of an issue; and policymakers may cite press commentary to bolster their case on an issue (Entman, 2004). These features were manifest in US and Indian media coverage of the nuclear agreement.

In the US, all leading dailies, except *The New York Times*, favoured the nuclear agreement (as shown in Table 2.3). Thus, *The New York Times* published 14 editorials and opinion-editorials against the agreement. Its global edition, the *International Herald Tribune*, published four

Table 2.3 US Media Positions on the Nuclear Agreement

	Oppose	*Neutral*	*Favour*	*Main Authors*
The New York Times				
Editorials	10			*Opposing*: Columnists Thomas
Opinion-editorial	4			Friedman, Bob Herbert; policymakers Edward Markey & Ellen Tauscher
Letters	2		4	
International Herald Tribune				
Opinion-editorial	9	1	4	*Opposing*: Policymakers/ex-policymakers Strobe Talbott, Edward Markey & Ellen
Letters	5		5	Tauscher, Jimmy Carter; analyst Sharon Squassoni
				Favouring: Columnists and experts Frank Ritch, David Victor; policymakers/ ex-policymakers Henry Kissinger, Karl Inderfurth & Bruce Reidel, Karl Inderfurth (letter), Ramesh Thakur (letter)
The Washington Post				
Editorials		3	4	*Opposing*: Policymakers/ex-policymakers Jimmy Carter, Lawrence Korb & Peter
Opinion-editorial	5		16	Ogden; Analysts Meera Kamdar, Deepti Choubey, Sharon Squassoni, Paul
Letters	5			Leventhal (letter), Daryl Kimball (letter)
				Favouring: Policymakers Condoleezza Rice, Nicholas Burns, Mohammed El Baradei; Columnists and analysts Selig Harrison, Jim Hoagland, Roger Cohen, Robert Kagan, Michael Levi & Ivo Daalder, Michael Levi & Charles Ferguson
The Washington Times				
Editorials		1	5	*Favouring*: Business voices Stanley Weiss, Ron Somers (letter)
Opinion-editorial			7	
Letters			1	
The Wall Street Journal				
Editorials			1	*Opposing*: Ex-policymaker Sam Nunn; analyst Henry Sokolski
Opinion-editorial	4		9	*Favouring*: Policymakers/ex-pol-icymakers William Cohen, John
Letters			3	Kerry, Karl Inderfurth (letter), Pete Domenici (letter); others Vinod Khosla, K. Subrahmanyam

Source: Data compiled by author

opinion-editorials supporting and nine opposing the agreement. In contrast, the nuclear agreement was largely endorsed by *The Washington Post* (which carried 20 supportive and five opposing pieces); *The Washington Times* (which had 12 pieces, all supporting the agreement); and *The Wall Street Journal* (which had 10 supportive and four opposing pieces).

In India, most major dailies favoured the nuclear agreement. A content analysis of over 200 editorials and opinion-editorials in six major papers shows that *The Times of India, The Indian Express,* and *Hindustan Times* carried many supportive and relatively few opposing views, while *The Telegraph* generally supported the agreement but also carried several opposing views. In contrast, *The Asian Age* was very strongly against the nuclear agreement, while the left-leaning newspaper, *The Hindu,* was substantially against the agreement though it still published some supporting views. Among other dailies and weeklies, *The Tribune, India Today,* and *Outlook India* were generally supportive, while the *Deccan Chronicle, Deccan Herald, The Pioneer,* and *Economic and Political Weekly* generally opposed the nuclear agreement.

The above-mentioned publications carried the writings of prominent experts. Thus, strategic affairs experts, K. Subrahmanyam (regarded as the doyen of India's strategic community) and C. Raja Mohan, strongly supported the nuclear agreement. A nuclear expert, former AEC Chairman M. R. Srinivasan, also favoured the agreement. Other supporters included retired foreign affairs officials such as K. Shankar Bajpai (former ambassador to Pakistan, China, and the US), Jagat Mehta (former foreign secretary), T. P. Sreenivasan (former representative to the IAEA), Arundhati Ghose (who had led India's opposition to the test ban treaty at the Conference on Disarmament), G. Parthasarathy (former high commissioner to Pakistan), and Ved Malik (former army chief). A number of foreign policy commentators also favoured the agreement, including Prem Shankar Jha (former editor of several leading dailies), Inder Malhotra (former editor of *The Times of India*), G. Balachandran (strategic affairs analyst), Raj Chengappa (science and technology writer), Manoj Joshi (security affairs analyst), and R. Rajaraman (professor emeritus of physics at Jawaharlal Nehru University). Finally, former President Abdul Kalam was an influential supporter.

Those expressing apprehensions about the nuclear agreement included strategic affairs analysts such as Bharat Karnad and Brahma Chellaney on the right, and Siddharth Varadarajan on the left (though Varadarajan adopted a conditionally supportive position in late 2007). They also included some senior nuclear scientists, particularly P. K. Iyengar and A. N. Prasad (both former AEC chairmen), as well as A. Gopalakrishnan (former chairman of India's Atomic Energy Regulatory Board).[10] Other opponents included ex-government officials such as V. P. Singh (former prime minister) and V. R. Krishna Iyer (former Supreme Court judge).

Analysing the Indian media, Sanjaya Baru notes that the critics were influential in the sense that they offered debating points for the opposition (Baru, 2009a). He adds that 'overwhelming media support for the civil nuclear agreement, with the exception of *The Hindu*…and *The Asian Age*…strengthened the Government's hand in politically defending its case at home, against political criticism from [the] Left and Right opposition' (Baru, 2009b; see also Mohan, 2009). He further notes that 'more than print, television played an extremely influential role in generating public support for the nuclear accord. No major TV news channel campaigned against the agreement, while many of them took a strong supportive stance' (Baru, 2009b).

In general, the Indian media supported the nuclear agreement because it was not leftist in orientation; it accepted the technical case for the nuclear agreement; its middle-class audiences accepted the strategic logic of advancing ties with the US to counter China and Pakistan; and the theme of a 'strategic partnership' resonated positively among Indian audiences, especially in the broadcast media.[11] This press convergence in favour of the nuclear agreement also hurt the BJP, especially amongst its traditional middle-class supporters, because the BJP then appeared to be siding with the left on the issue.

On a related note, since the main dailies favoured the nuclear agreement, the Indian government's media strategy did not excessively focus on these dailies.[12] Instead, while India's government briefed editors and senior correspondents from these outlets and from major television channels, it also reached out to its critics and accepted a regional diversity of views.[13] Further, India's government engaged the Urdu press, because it was concerned, from 2005 itself, that President Bush's unpopularity among Indian Muslims could hurt the Congress Party's electoral prospects in major states.

To summarize, media coverage significantly affected the US and Indian domestic debates, and their respective win-sets, on the nuclear agreement.

Societal Coalitions

The coalitions that mobilized for and against the nuclear agreement are summarized in Table 2.4. In relative terms, the US coalition supporting the nuclear agreement was the strongest; the US coalition opposing the agreement

Table 2.4 Societal Coalitions for and against the Nuclear Agreement

	Main Constituents	*(a)* *Societal* *Reach and* *Political* *and* *Financial* *Power* *(Relative* *Level)*	*(b)* *Coordination* *among* *Groups* *(Relative* *Level)*	*(a × b)* *Relative* *Impact on* *Win-Set*
US groups for	• Business • Indian Americans • Some strategic affairs experts and columnists • Others	High	High	High (increases)
US groups against	• Arms control groups	Low	High	Moderate (decreases)
Indian groups for	• Business • Many strategic affairs experts and columnists • Several ex-diplomats • Middle class	Moderate	Low-to-moderate	Moderate (increases)
Indian groups against	• Some senior ex-governmental nuclear scientists • Some strategic affairs experts and columnists • Some ex-policymakers • Anti-nuclear groups	Low-to-Moderate	Low	Low-to-moderate (decreases)

was moderately strong; Indian groups supporting the agreement were also moderately strong; and Indian groups opposing the agreement were low-to-moderate in strength.

The India Lobby

The US advocacy coalition for the nuclear agreement, also called the 'India lobby', had several components: Indian Americans, American business, strategic affairs experts, a formal 'Coalition' of these groups, the Indian government, Indian business, and additional constituents.

First, a number of Indian American groups lobbied for the nuclear agreement. These included the US–India Friendship Council (USIFC), the American Association of Physicians of Indian Origin (AAPIO), the Asian American Hotel Owners Association (AAHOA), and the US–India Political Action Committee (USINPAC). Second, US business lobbied for the nuclear agreement through the US–India Business Council (USIBC), the professional firms hired by USIBC, major American corporations partnering with USIBC, and the Contractors International Group on Nuclear Liability (CIGNL). Third, a number of strategic affairs experts, South Asia experts, columnists, and senior ex-policymakers supported the agreement. Fourth, USIBC and its lobbying firms actively recruited Indian Americans and strategic affairs experts to form a 'Coalition for the Partnership with India'. Fifth, India's government, through the Indian Embassy, hired two professional firms to lobby for the nuclear agreement. It had a $2.1 million contract, for the period September 2005–December 2008, with the Republican-leaning Barbour, Griffith, & Rogers (BGR). It also signed a $600,000 contract, for the period December 2005–December 2006, with the Democrat-leaning Venable LLP. Sixth, Indian business promoted the nuclear agreement through joint initiatives with USIBC.

Arms Control Groups

Arms control groups strongly opposed the nuclear agreement. They differed from the India lobby in important ways. First, they represented a much smaller section of US society. The few most prominent arms control groups had only a few hundred active members, while the India lobby could mobilize about two million Indian Americans as well as major US corporations. Second, arms control groups had little political power, in contrast to at least some voting power wielded by Indian Americans. Third, they had even less financial power, especially compared to the advocacy coalition that spent a few million dollars in lobbying (as shown in Table 2.5). In addition, because of their non-profit status, arms control groups could not directly lobby and make politically related appeals to lawmakers.

Table 2.5 Select Lobbying Activities in the US

Lobbying Firm	Fees/ Contributions	Period	Main Activities
Barbour, Griffith, & Rogers	$2,100,000	September 2005–October 2008	Over 500 meetings and communications (including 150 with officials from the executive branch and 360 with those from the legislature)
Venable	$600,000	December 2005– December 2006	Over 400 meetings and communications (including 50 with officials from the executive branch and 370 with those from the legislature)
Two firms hired by USIBC	$825,000	2006–08	Mobilizing Indian Americans, business, and strategic affairs experts to lobby Congress
Firms hired by CIGNL	~$400,000	September 2005–October 2008	Making the executive branch and Congress aware that India should adopt nuclear liability laws conforming with international standards
USINPAC	~$190,000	2005–08	• Contribution to candidates ($120,000 in 2006 election cycle and $70,000 in 2008 cycle) • Fundraisers generating additional financial contributions for members of Congress

Sources: Data compiled by author from the Department of Justice's Foreign Agents Registration Act website (www.fara.gov) and the Center for Responsive Politics (www.opensecrets.org).

Note: The lobbying firms focused mostly on the civilian nuclear agreement, but also spent some of their efforts on other issues in US–India relations.

The Supporters in India

In India, four societal constituencies supported the nuclear agreement: business; ex-governmental foreign policy officials; non-governmental experts (that is, strategic affairs analysts and foreign affairs columnists); and indirectly, a pro-US middle class. These constituencies occasionally interacted with each other. For example, representatives from each constituency participated in events sponsored by the other. However, they were not part of a structured coalition similar to the US 'Coalition for the Partnership with India'.

Indian business saw future commercial opportunities in an expanded nuclear energy sector. Further, it accepted the logic that environmentally friendly nuclear energy would help India's economic growth. For these reasons, it favoured the nuclear agreement, even though some Indian firms had reservations about nuclear energy because it competed with traditional energy sectors where they had greater stakes.

Indian business also partnered with American business. It undertook business-to-business interactions, where Indian business executives interacted with their counterparts from the US and from NSG countries to explain India's case for the nuclear agreement. It also undertook business-to-government interactions. Here, Indian executives informed India's opposition parties about the case for the nuclear agreement; they also explained to US congressmen that the agreement would benefit the Indian economy and would boost US–India relations.

Other pro-agreement constituencies – ex-governmental officials and non-governmental experts – voiced their opinions in the press, spoke at events organized by Indian business, and wrote the occasional letter to Members of Parliament.

Opposing Constituencies in India

Four constituencies mobilized against the nuclear agreement in India. One was a senior scientists group (a handful of scientists who formerly held senior positions in India's nuclear establishment). Describing their motivations and the process through which they mobilized, a senior scientist noted that 'a determined and experienced group of senior nuclear scientists who had spent most of their lives in building India's nuclear program' sought to preserve India's national interest on the nuclear agreement (Gopalakrishnan, 2007b). This group influenced India's opposition parties to raise objections to the nuclear agreement, and 'this eventually forced the prime minister to open a dialogue with the Senior Nuclear Scientists' Group and [to] give certain concrete assurances to the Parliament in August 2006'.

The three other opposing constituencies comprised strategic affairs experts, columnists, and anti-nuclear groups. However, they did not formally team with the nuclear scientists to form an organized coalition against the nuclear agreement. Instead, they acted as informal networks of individuals with concerns about the agreement.

Additional Factors Influencing the Win-set

Beyond the principal factors just discussed, additional factors that influence win-sets include the role of national leaders, domestic constraints, domestic negotiating strategies, and cross-country negotiating issues.

First, decisive interventions by national leaders can increase the win-set. Leaders intervene because of their investment in the issue: once leaders initiate, become publicly identified with, and politically invest in an agreement, they are reluctant to forgo this commitment if an agreement is not completed. Leaders may then accept negotiating concessions (thereby enlarging the win-set) to complete an agreement or they may spend political capital to press their political party and opposition parties to accept an agreement (thereby again enlarging the win-set). During negotiations for the nuclear agreement, President Bush and Prime Minister Singh both intervened at critical junctures to advance the agreement, and the president of India's Congress Party also took important decisions to press ahead with the agreement.

Second, domestic constraints affect win-sets and national positions on international negotiations. Domestic constraints that reduce win-sets can help an L1 negotiator extract concessions from their foreign counterparts (Iida, 1993; Mo, 1994). Also, by publicly promising an L2 constituent that they would not cross certain points in L1 negotiations, L1 negotiators can tie their hands on the issue (India's government adopted this strategy through statements in the Parliament that it would not compromise on certain issues). Still, a smaller win-set (that arises because of tying hands and domestic constraints) lowers the value of the agreement to the other side and may cause that side to prefer no agreement.

Third, L1 negotiators adopt various domestic strategies to increase their win-set. They may promise domestic opponents offsets from outside the L1 agreement or from the L1 bargain itself (Putnam, 1988). They can also shape formal and informal procedures for domestic approval; enforce party discipline; mobilize societal groups to support an agreement; and selectively disseminate information to make their case.

Fourth, L1 negotiators can expand the other side's win-set by meeting with that side's legislators and opposition parties, offering them incentives, linking extraneous issues to the L1 agreement, and appealing to opinion leaders.

The US and Indian governments adopted all these domestic and cross-country approaches to advance the nuclear agreement.

Aggregating the Factors

From 2005 to 2008, as the US and India negotiated their civilian nuclear agreement, the above-mentioned bureaucratic, legislative, and other factors influenced each side's win-set. The win-sets varied during these years because the factors also varied. Care should be taken in aggregating the factors because the model in this study is a heuristic framework rather than a precise mechanism for combining the factors. The factors can be combined through an in-depth examination of the case, which assesses the presence of and changes in factors in different time periods. Some standard counterfactual reasoning validates this analytical approach: if the factors that reduce the win-set (legislative constraints, bureaucratic resistance, and domestic mobilization) are initially absent, then the win-set is relatively large, and as the factors are added over time, the win-set decreases.

In July 2005, the US win-set was large because bureaucratic factors expanded the win-set (senior US officials were willing to accommodate India), while legislative factors and domestic mobilization did not reduce the win-set (they were absent, since Congress and domestic groups did not know about the nuclear agreement at the time). This is best illustrated in Figure 2.1: the win-set extended to point 7 in the figure.

During negotiations for India's separation plan and for the Section 123 Agreement, the US win-set slightly reduced, and extended to point 6 in Figure 2.1. This was because, on the one hand, bureaucratic factors still expanded the win-set (senior US officials were again willing to accommodate India), and mobilization by supporters also helped expand it. On the other hand, legislative factors reduced the win-set: Congress would not accept arrangements with weak non-proliferation provisions, and mobilization by opponents influenced Congress on this position. The win-set for congressional legislation in 2006 was about the same for similar reasons: mobilization by supporters helped expand the win-set, but legislative factors (that is, Congress was not deferential to the administration) and mobilization by opponents reduced the win-set. Finally, the win-set for congressional legislation in 2008 was even smaller (its outer boundary extended to point 5 in Figure 2.1) because political power considerations and political–institutional rules further reduced the win-set. At this time, Democrats held a majority in both the House and the Senate and the voting rules to pass legislation were much tougher.

India's win-set varied in a similar manner. Initially, when negotiating the July 2005 Joint Statement, India's win-set was small, extending from point 9 to point 6 in Figure 2.1. This was because bureaucratic resistance from India's nuclear establishment substantially reduced the win-set; legislative factors indirectly reduced it (India's government relied on the left to remain in office); and no countervailing factors helped expand the win-set (mobilization by supporters was absent). Thereafter, for much of the period from July 2005 to June 2008, the win-set was only slightly larger, extending from point 9 to point 5 in Figure 2.1. This was because, while the bureaucratic and legislative factors still reduced the win-set, the government's defence of its case and mobilization by supporters helped slightly expand it. After July 2008, once India's government won a vote of confidence in the Parliament and its political power increased, India's win-set expanded further, extending from point 9 to point 4 in Figure 2.1. It could then take the nuclear agreement to its completion.

Summing Up

This chapter has specified the main factors influencing the US and Indian win-sets on their nuclear agreement. It has also operationalized the variables in a reliable and valid manner (King et al., 1994). The dependent variable, the L1 arrangement, is operationalized on a scale of relatively very high to very low in terms of its non-proliferation provisions. The independent variables are also suitably operationalized. Thus, political power in the legislature is measured through the number of seats held by the ruling coalition and by opposition parties. Other factors are less precisely but still appropriately measured. For example, domestic mobilization is assessed in terms of the relative strengths of societal coalitions for and against the nuclear agreement. Overall, such methodological rigour not only makes for a stronger study but also makes the study replicable: researchers can draw upon the study's analytical framework to re-examine its findings based on new evidence; and also to examine additional cases that further test and refine its theoretical underpinnings.

Finally, to make the framework manageable, only the most relevant factors are considered. The framework is thereby not cluttered with excessive detail, and it serves as a useful building block for examining further cases. Thus, this study uses the most appropriate theoretical lens, that of two-level games, to explain the US–India nuclear agreement. It draws upon 40 interviews, dozens of government documents (mainly US Embassy cables), and other major primary and secondary sources. Clearly, each of these sources has limitations, but, taken together, they provide for the best possible scholarly analysis of the nuclear agreement. The following chapters discuss the diplomacy and domestic politics behind the nuclear agreement.

Endnotes

1   The composite index of national capabilities, drawn from the Correlates of War project, measures each state's share of the world's military, industrial, and demographic resources.

2   For an analysis of international factors behind the US–India nuclear agreement, see Pant (2011). For a related discussion on accommodating a rising India into the non-proliferation regime, see Paul and Shankar (2007).

3   Author interview L2, 15 September 2011. The traditional non-proliferation position was also somewhat diluted because key US officials representing non-proliferation interests, such as Robert Joseph and John Rood, were not part of the State Department's standard non-proliferation bureaucracy; instead, they came from different bureaucratic backgrounds such as the National Security Council and the Defense Department, and therefore had a mixed strategic and non-proliferation view of the nuclear agreement. Also, since many of the interviews were off-the-record, the interviewees are not named and are instead identified by a randomly assigned descriptor (for example, A1 and A2).

4   India's Department of Atomic Energy (DAE) falls under the PMO rather than under any government ministry, and the prime minister is therefore the government minister responsible for DAE. In turn, PMO personnel who handle nuclear affairs include: (a) Ministry of External Affairs (MEA) officials serving in the PMO; and (b) nuclear experts in the PMO such as the principal scientific advisor to the prime minister, who is often a former DAE secretary. See Abraham (1998) and Anderson (2010).

5   Typically, in response to the president's policy, Congress can be less active and comply (by being 'disengaged'); it can only selectively comply (by being 'strategic'); it can be active and comply (being 'supportive'); or it can be active and challenge (being 'competitive'). See Scott and Carter (2002).

6   For more on parliament's limitations in the area of foreign policy, see Martin (2000), Sartori (1997), and Weaver and Rockman (1993).

7   It should be clarified that, despite policy differences with the government, legislators rarely exercise the option of unseating a government: they are most

likely to do so if they are confident of replacing a government with one more to their liking, or if they expect to win any election after the government falls.

8   Author interview U4, 23 November 2011.

9   In India, strategic affairs elites include scientific–technical experts, former military officers, and civilians with expertise on military matters. They found a space to influence nuclear debates because of the absence of a governmental institutional mechanism for such debate; this void was only partly filled by India's National Security Advisory Board (Frey, 2006). On the challenges faced by elites in criticizing India's nuclear program, see Ramanna (2009).

10   The views of these scientists evolved, over time, 'from being cautiously supportive of nuclear cooperation with the United States and members of the Nuclear Suppliers Group if it ended up providing India access to advanced technology to getting progressively more disturbed as the [nuclear] negotiations proceeded'. See Iyengar et al. (2009).

11   Author interview C1, 12 July 2010.

12   Author interview D1, 25 November 2011.

13   The media from India's more economically developed states (those in south and west India and Punjab) largely supported the nuclear agreement, while those from north and east India, who were historically suspicious of international engagement, were more critical of the agreement.

CHAPTER THREE

Getting to July 2005

IN May 1998, India conducted a series of nuclear tests and declared itself to be a nuclear weapons state. Strongly condemning New Delhi's actions, President Clinton stated that 'I am deeply disturbed by the nuclear tests which India has conducted, and I do not believe it contributes to building a safer 21st century' (The White House, 1998). He added, 'our laws have very stringent provisions [requiring sanctions]…in response to nuclear tests by non-nuclear-weapon states and I intend to implement them fully.'[1] The Clinton administration went on to impose sanctions on India. Over the next seven years, the US not only lifted these sanctions but also acknowledged India's nuclear weapons status. In July 2005, it formally recognized India to be 'a responsible state with advanced nuclear technology' (The White House, 2005). Several US–India dialogues on easing sanctions, advancing high-technology cooperation, and developing a strategic partnership were behind the process of getting to July 2005.

An Overview of US–India Negotiations

From 1998 to 2005, Washington and New Delhi discussed a series of steps each side could take to remove nuclear irritants in their bilateral relations. New Delhi wanted Washington to act in six areas (these are shown in

Tables 3.1 and 3.2). The first two concerned: lifting economic, military, and technological sanctions imposed on India after its 1998 nuclear tests (areas 1A, 1B, and 1C, respectively); and giving India more substantial access to dual-use technology and civilian space cooperation (areas 2A and 2B, respectively). The others involved progressively increasing forms of civilian nuclear cooperation, such as permitting India to obtain balance-of-plant items for nuclear reactors (area 3A), have access to nuclear safety technology (area 3B), participate in international research efforts (area 3C), and obtain steam-cycle technology (area 3D). New Delhi also sought fuel for the Tarapur reactors (area 4), fuel for its many other reactors (area 5), and reactors from international suppliers (area 6).[2]

In return, Washington asked New Delhi to comply with five non-proliferation benchmarks. It wanted New Delhi to adopt stronger export controls (benchmark 1); separate its civilian and military reactors and safeguard the civilian reactors (benchmark 2); not conduct nuclear tests and join the test

Table 3.1 US and Indian Action on Non-proliferation Issues

Areas	*US Action: Removing Barriers versus India Concerning:*
1	1998 economic (1A), military (1B), and technology (1C) sanctions;
2	dual-use technology transfer (2A) and civilian space cooperation (2B);
3	nuclear cooperation on balance-of-plant items (3A), safety technology (3B), international research (3C), and steam-cycle technology (3D);
4	nuclear fuel for the Tarapur reactors;
5	nuclear fuel for many other Indian reactors; and
6	nuclear reactor imports.
Non-proliferation Benchmarks	**Indian Action on:**
1	stronger export controls;
2	separating civilian and military reactors;
3	nuclear test restraints;
4	missile restraints; and
5	fissile material production restraints

Note: The full-scope safeguards rule in US law and in the international non-proliferation regime bars civilian nuclear cooperation (areas 3–6) for countries outside the NPT.

Table 3.2 Overview of US and Indian Actions, 1998–2005

	US Action in Areas 1–6	India's Action on Non-proliferation Benchmarks 1–5
Clinton administration, 1998–2000	Partially eased sanctions in area 1A	• Limited action on benchmark 1 • Non-binding statement on benchmark 3
Bush administration's first term, 2001–04	2001: Lifted sanctions in area 1A, 1B, and much of 1C 2002–03: action on area 2A via a high-technology group 2004: action in areas 2B and 3A, and consideration of areas 3B and 3C (but not 3D), via the Next Steps in Strategic Partnership initiative	• More action on benchmark 1
July 2005 Joint Statement	Commitment to nuclear cooperation extending to areas 4, 5, and 6	• More substantial measures on benchmark 1 • Commitment to benchmark 2 • Reiterate stand on benchmark 3

ban treaty (benchmark 3); maintain missile restraints (benchmark 4); and restrain its fissile material production (benchmark 5).

Under the Clinton administration, New Delhi and Washington could only agree to some US concessions on area 1A in exchange for limited Indian action on non-proliferation benchmarks 1 and 3. In its first year in office, the Bush administration lifted the 1998 sanctions on India, thus accommodating India on almost all of area 1. Thereafter, from 2002 to 2004, it undertook a technology cooperation dialogue that covered much of area 2 and some of area 3, in exchange for more Indian progress on benchmark 1. Still, any arrangement covering all of area 3 and areas 4–6 fell outside the US win-set. Early in the Bush administration's second term, however, because of bureaucratic changes, the win-set widened. The Bush administration then offered India full civilian nuclear cooperation, all the way to area 6. In return, India took action on benchmarks 1 and 2 and reiterated its earlier commitment on benchmark 3.

The Clinton Administration's Nuclear Dialogue

The Clinton administration undertook a sustained nuclear dialogue with New Delhi after its 1998 nuclear tests. In the years before these tests, the administration had focused on 'nudging US–Indian relations forward', while still 'keeping the lid on the proliferation of nuclear [programs in South Asia]' (Talbott, 2004). It had also recognized that India's growing importance needed high-level attention. Accordingly, Secretary of State Madeleine Albright visited India in 1997, and President Clinton was scheduled to visit India in 1998, but this visit was postponed because of India's nuclear tests.

In response to these tests, which were followed by Pakistani nuclear tests, the Clinton administration imposed economic and military sanctions and tightened technology embargoes on both countries. Thus, it substantially curbed international economic aid to India, which fell from $3 billion to $4 billion annually in 1996 and 1997 to $1 billion annually in 1998 and 1999. It halted military cooperation programs such as arms sales, joint military exercises, and officer training initiatives (though India actually had little military cooperation with Washington at the time). And it restricted the transfer of high-technology items, such as engines for Indian light combat aircraft and helicopters, by placing 200 Indian nuclear and defence organizations on its Entity List.[3] These technology transfer restrictions of 1998 augmented technology control regimes that had emerged after India's 1974 nuclear test; those regimes denied dual-use technology to India because it remained outside the NPT.

Subsequently, Deputy Secretary of State Strobe Talbott and External Affairs Minister Jaswant Singh negotiated over arrangements whereby Washington would lift the 1998 sanctions in exchange for New Delhi's compliance with four non-proliferation benchmarks (Singh, 1998). Washington wanted New Delhi to strengthen its export controls (benchmark 1), adhere to the test ban treaty (benchmark 3), and demonstrate restraints in its missile program (benchmark 4) and fissile material production (benchmark 5). (Benchmark 2 was not part of the formal US–India dialogue at this time.)

By the time the Clinton administration left office, Washington and its allies had lifted some economic sanctions on India (that is, they partly eased sanctions in area 1A) but they did not lift military sanctions and technology restrictions. In return, India acted on benchmark 1 by somewhat strengthening its export controls.[4] Further, on benchmark 3, New Delhi declared a moratorium on nuclear testing, and, in a September 1998 speech at the

United Nations (UN), indicated that it could join the Comprehensive Nuclear Test Ban Treaty (CTBT) if other countries did the same. Eventually, however, international movement on the CTBT stalled, and New Delhi did not sign the treaty; nor did it accept restraints on benchmarks 4 and 5.

It is also worth clarifying that the US–India negotiations did not extend to easing the post-1974 technology control regimes versus India (that is, areas 2–6). India's government had called for lifting these regimes. For example, in November 1999, Indian officials had 'dusted off an old demand that India be given various rights and privileges available to signatories of the nuclear Nonproliferation Treaty even though India would remain a nonsignatory' (Talbott, 2004).[5] Indian policymakers sought the removal of technology barriers not just because they wanted to be recognized as a nuclear weapons state but also for energy and environmental reasons. The themes of energy security and of nuclear energy having positive environmental implications had then entered Indian policy discourse.[6] Thus, in 1999–2000, Indian policymakers were thinking about separating their civilian and military nuclear programs to avail of nuclear imports for India's energy sector.[7] Simply put, they were conceptualizing action on non-proliferation benchmark 2 in return for US action on areas 2–6, which was the eventual outcome in the July 2005 Joint Statement.

Still, the Clinton administration was not negotiating on benchmark 2, and it was not considering action on areas 2–6. On this point, Strobe Talbott affirmed that 'unless and until they [Pakistan and India] disavow nuclear weapons and accept safeguards on all their nuclear activities they will continue to forfeit the full recognition and benefits [that is, the lifting of the post-1974 technology control regimes] that accrue to members in good standing of the NPT' (Talbott, 1998). For this reason, when the Clinton administration left office, many of the post-1998 sanctions and the entire post-1974 technology control regime on India remained in place. These continuing sanctions did not prevent President Clinton from making a successful visit to India in March 2000, but they remained an irritant to more significant improvements in US–India relations.

The Bush Administration's First Term

The Bush administration entered office with the intention of substantially transforming US–India ties. Senior administration officials considered a partnership with a rising India to be a major US foreign policy objective. Illustrating these views, in a November 1999 speech ahead of his presidential campaign, George W. Bush noted, 'This coming century will see democratic India's arrival as a force in the world…we should work with the Indian government, ensuring it is a force for stability and security in Asia' (Bush, 1999). The administration's 2002 national security strategy similarly noted that 'the Administration sees India's potential to become one of the great democratic powers of the twenty-first century and has worked hard to transform our relationship accordingly' (The White House, 2002).

US policies towards India reflected the above-mentioned approach, and US–India strategic cooperation increased. For example, from 2002 onwards, the US and Indian militaries began conducting joint exercises, and India also began purchasing small quantities of American military equipment.

Despite these improvements in their bilateral ties, Washington and New Delhi could not develop a firmer strategic partnership. New Delhi still had differences with Washington over US engagement with Pakistan after 11 September 2001 and over the persistence of technology denial regimes against India. Indian officials regularly informed their American counterparts that the lifting of technology denial regimes was their 'litmus test' for transforming US–India relations (Juster, 2003). They noted that 'we have been saying very candidly that a trinity of issues – high technology commerce, civilian nuclear energy cooperation and collaboration in space – can take the Indo-US relationship to a qualitatively new level of partnership' (Mishra, 2003).

The Bush administration sought to address New Delhi's position in incremental steps. First, it removed the post-1998 sanctions, and this facilitated the increase in US–India military collaboration noted earlier; second, it initiated a high-technology dialogue with India; and third, it formalized the Next Steps in Strategic Partnership (NSSP) process.

Lifting Sanctions and Initiating Technology Cooperation

In its first months in office, the Bush administration sought to remove the 1998 sanctions against India but encountered bureaucratic resistance (Harrison, 2001; Limaye, 2002). Some senior officials such as National Security Advisor Condoleezza Rice and Deputy Secretary of Defense Paul Wolfowitz favoured ending the sanctions. However, key members of Congress as well as State Department officials such as Assistant Secretary of State for South Asia Christina Rocca and Deputy Secretary of State Richard Armitage preferred to lift sanctions incrementally and only after reciprocal steps from New Delhi. Still other officials such as Undersecretary of State for Arms Control John Bolton took an even firmer line on keeping the sanctions in place. Washington eventually lifted the 1998 sanctions on 22 September 2001, but only because they were simultaneously lifted on Pakistan, whose assistance Washington required for its military campaign in Afghanistan. Thus, by late 2001, the Bush administration had acted on almost all of area 1, but it did not go much beyond this area.[8]

In subsequent months, the US sought to advance technology cooperation with India through three bureaucratic initiatives. First, as a result of its dialogue with Indian officials, the US Embassy in India (headed by Ambassador Robert Blackwill who was advised by Ashley Tellis) urged greater technology cooperation with India.[9] Blackwill had a mandate from President Bush to transform US–India relations, and he sought to convince the US bureaucracy to remove obstacles to civilian nuclear, civilian space, and high-technology cooperation with India. In October 2001, Blackwill cabled the State Department on this issue. The State Department rejected the civilian nuclear aspect of these recommendations, but it included the civilian space and high-technology themes in a November 2001 Vision Statement between Prime Minister Vajpayee and President Bush.

Second, the Defense Department promoted the sale of high-technology military equipment to India. At the February 2001 Munich Security Conference, Defense Secretary Donald Rumsfeld offered India missile defence cooperation, though India's national security advisor noted that India was also interested in civilian nuclear and space cooperation.[10] Soon thereafter, the Defense Department went ahead with the sale of Firefinder radars to India: this was the first major US military sale to India in several years.

Third, technology cooperation was part of a broader dialogue between India's National Security Advisor, Brajesh Mishra, his US counterpart, Condoleezza Rice, and Rice's deputy, Stephen Hadley. In several meetings from 2001 to 2003, Mishra urged Rice and Hadley to ease restrictions on high-technology transfers to India, recognizing that this could eventually facilitate civilian nuclear cooperation.[11] The Rice–Mishra dialogue led to the creation of a High Technology Cooperation Group (HTCG). At a November 2002 meeting, Undersecretary of Commerce Kenneth Juster and Foreign Secretary Kanwal Sibal set up this group to implement the Vision Statement.

The HTCG's essential themes were outlined in a December 2002 paper that Washington handed to New Delhi (known as the Rice–Mishra paper): first, Washington acknowledged the importance New Delhi placed on high-technology cooperation; second, Washington would not undermine national and international non-proliferation laws and policies; third, India would adopt strong export controls and end-use assurances to participate in high-technology trade; and fourth, Washington accepted the possibility of limited civilian nuclear trade with India but linked this to stronger Indian export controls.

Overall, the HTCG lowered barriers to US–India technology trade: US dual-use technology exports to India rose from under $30 million in fiscal year 2002 to over $90 million during fiscal year 2004 (Department of Commerce, 2003). Still, it did not alter the US restrictions on civilian nuclear trade with India, and it did not extend technology cooperation much beyond area 2A.

New Delhi continued to seek such cooperation. India's national security advisor recognized that bureaucratic resistance had limited the scope of technology cooperation and he informed Secretary Rice and President Bush that further cooperation could be advanced through a top-down approach where the senior-most US officials pressed the issue.[12] During his May 2003 speech at the Council on Foreign Relations, Mishra noted that 'the road to free high technology commerce' was advancing well, but that 'we have to cover the same path for civilian nuclear cooperation' (Mishra, 2003). Sketching India's position that was eventually accommodated in July 2005, he stated that in return for civilian nuclear transfers from international suppliers, India would restrict its strategic nuclear program 'to the minimum levels required for our national security' and 'would put all nuclear projects of foreign collaboration under safeguards'. (Mishra had privately raised this issue earlier, in a 28 July 2002 meeting with Secretary of State Colin Powell when he suggested that India could initially safeguard a couple of reactors and then safeguard more reactors in return for civilian nuclear cooperation.[13])

Thereafter, in June and July 2003, New Delhi asked the Bush administration to adjust US dual-use licensing policies to facilitate greater technology cooperation. India's foreign secretary gave US officials a non-paper on ways to advance civilian nuclear, civilian space, and high-technology cooperation, and Washington added another item, missile defence, to the agenda. These four items became part of the NSSP initiative.

The NSSP Initiative

In 2003, recognizing the limitations of the HTCG, but drawing upon its themes, Bush administration officials conceptualized a 'glide path' for civilian nuclear and space cooperation with India. In a September 2003 visit to Delhi, Stephen Hadley discussed these issues and the first draft of NSSP with Indian officials. In December, an Indian delegation visited Washington for further talks. In January 2004, the two sides institutionalized the glide path by announcing NSSP. Its agenda, implementation, and progress are worth reviewing.

In terms of its agenda, US and Indian officials focused on high-technology, civilian space, and civilian nuclear issues because these mattered to India; because they conveyed the message to domestic audiences that both sides were building a strategic partnership based upon substantive issues; and because they affirmed that both states remained committed to civilian nuclear cooperation despite US legislative barriers and NSG restrictions.[14]

In terms of its implementation, NSSP required both states to take reciprocal steps in four phases (a preliminary phase and three additional phases) over five years.[15] The preliminary phase, in late 2003, focused on initiating NSSP. The first phase began in January 2004, with the announcement of NSSP, and was complete in September 2004. The second and third phases advanced faster than either side expected, so that, by early 2005, New Delhi pressed for moving beyond NSSP to full civilian nuclear cooperation.

In terms of its actual progress, NSSP's first phase concluded in September 2004 with a particular outcome. India acted on non-proliferation benchmark 1 by signing an end-use verification agreement with the US (under this agreement, it accepted a US export control attaché at the American Embassy in New Delhi). Reciprocally, the US modified its licensing policies covering areas 2B and 3A. First, it removed the Indian Space Research Organisation (ISRO) headquarters from its Entity List. Second, it eased licensing requirements for exporting low-level dual-use items to ISRO subordinates, though it would not ease restrictions on space rocket technology because this could be used in missiles. Third, it permitted transfers of dual-use items intended for the balance-of-plant portion of safeguarded Indian nuclear facilities. This action in area 3A would enable cooperation in areas 3B and 3C during NSSP's second phase.

In early November, Washington and New Delhi outlined the agenda for NSSP's second and third phases.[16] In the second phase, India would enhance its export control legislation and enforcement, particularly concerning intangible technology transfers, brokering, transit, re-export, and catch-all controls. It would also agree to adhere to the Missile Technology Control Regime (MTCR) and the NSG.[17] In the third phase, India would harmonize its national export control lists with those of the MTCR and NSG and then formally adhere to these regimes. (Here, it should be noted that UN Security Resolution 1540 of April 2004, which required all countries to adopt strong export controls, was an important accomplishment for the Bush administration, and many of India's NSSP commitments were also covered in Resolution 1540).

In return, Washington would act on NSSP's issue-areas. In the high-technology area, it agreed to remove licensing requirements for transferring dual-use technology to safeguarded facilities in India. On civilian space issues, it would initially explore joint US–India satellite ventures, after which, in NSSP's third phase, it expected to sign a Space Launch Agreement with India that was similar to US agreements with Russia and Ukraine. And, in the nuclear area, it agreed to discuss nuclear safety cooperation with India.

In summary, NSSP had some key themes. First, like the HTCG, it permitted high-technology cooperation with India under 'firewalls' that prevented the transfer of technology from the civilian to the military domain. Second, stronger Indian export controls on its industrial technology relevant to weapons of mass destruction (WMD) would strengthen the non-proliferation regime.

Third, NSSP permitted much more high-technology transfer to India than the HTCG.[18] However, technology cooperation in the nuclear area was still limited because Washington continued to uphold the full-scope safeguards rule of the non-proliferation regime. Thus, NSSP's first phase did allow civilian nuclear transfers to India, but only in area 3A. Thereafter, NSSP's second phase would extend civilian nuclear cooperation to area 3B (nuclear safety), and Washington also kept open the possibility of cooperation in area 3C (Indian participation in international nuclear research projects). Still, any nuclear safety and research cooperation was restricted to India's safeguarded reactors (at the time, India had accepted safeguards on just six of its 22 nuclear power reactors). And NSSP would not extend cooperation to all of area 3: in inter-agency discussions, the State Department's non-proliferation bureau rejected cooperation in area 3D, the steam cycle of nuclear reactors (Tellis, 2005).

Thus, NSSP's first phase, and plans for its second and third phases, extended technology cooperation with India to areas 2A, 2B, 3A, 3B, and 3C, but it did not cover area 3D, nor did it extend into areas 4–6: these areas remained outside the US win-set.

The US Win-set

The win-set in the Bush administration's first term, and in the HTCG and NSSP processes, was determined almost entirely by bureaucratic factors.

Washington would only offer New Delhi as much technology cooperation as would 'win' acceptance among the US bureaucracy, and this was limited for three main reasons.

First, the State Department leadership under Secretary of State Colin Powell only endorsed a limited approach to civilian nuclear cooperation, and it would not unravel the NPT regime for India. Illustrating this, administration officials repeatedly noted that 'we also have to protect certain red lines that we have with respect to proliferation' (Kessler and Slevin, 2003); they added that 'we need to advance our cooperation in high-technology trade, civilian space activities, and other areas in ways that do not undermine the general international framework on non-proliferation' (Juster, 2004).

Second, much of the US bureaucracy did not accept the strategic case for greater technology cooperation with India. While some senior administration officials were enthusiastic about the case, many other senior and mid-level officials in the State Department and the Department of Energy were skeptical, and personnel at the lower levels of government were even more skeptical: 'Consequently, many officials interpreted NSSP in highly restrictive ways because of their continuing discomfort with both India's nuclear program and the administration's "exceptionalist" strategies for dealing with it' (Tellis, 2005).

Illustrating this, the National Security Council (NSC) had created an inter-agency process to implement NSSP, but the working groups in this process could only agree to incremental steps on technology transfers to India.[19] Typically, officials from the Defense Department (for example, Undersecretary of Defense Doug Feith who chaired the US–India Defence Policy Group), some sections of the Commerce Department, and some from the State Department (its South Asia bureau and the policy planning staff) favoured greater technology cooperation with India. They were opposed by export control officials who objected to the rapid easing of US technology transfer restrictions; non-proliferation specialists in the State Department, including Undersecretary Bolton and the bureau of International Security and Arms Control, who opposed undermining US non-proliferation policy; and some regional affairs experts who were concerned about disrupting US ties with Pakistan.

Third, the regional political situation was not conducive to a civilian nuclear initiative with India. From late 2001 to mid-2002, Pakistan and India had mobilized a million troops on their border, and the Bush administration's main regional priority was to avert an India–Pakistan war.

For these reasons, the Bush administration did not offer substantial civilian nuclear cooperation to India during its first term. The administration also rejected New Delhi's attempts to get France and Russia to waive the NSG's full-scope safeguards rule for India. Still, in late 2004, India's new government, led by the Congress Party, continued its efforts to get technology transfer restrictions lifted. It raised the issue when Foreign Secretary Shyam Saran visited the US in mid-November 2004, just after the Bush administration was elected to a second term in office.

The Bush Administration's Second Term

In the first seven months of its second term, as part of a new foreign policy strategy towards South Asia, the Bush administration rapidly advanced a policy of full civilian nuclear cooperation (meaning cooperation all the way to area 6). First, in late 2004 and early 2005, senior US and Indian officials discussed moving beyond NSSP to full nuclear cooperation. And, in a March 2005 visit to India, Secretary Rice informed India's government that Washington's new foreign policy strategy would accommodate India on nuclear cooperation. Second, from April to June, the senior-most US officials informed their Indian counterparts about their intention to advance nuclear cooperation. Third, this push from the senior-most levels of government influenced US inter-agency debates on ending NSSP and commencing full nuclear cooperation. Fourth, Washington and New Delhi negotiated the terms for civilian nuclear cooperation and announced these in their 18 July Joint Statement.

The Strategic Vision behind Civilian Nuclear Cooperation

Washington's new foreign policy strategy for South Asia began with the same principle that was outlined during the Bush administration's first term: that deeper engagement with India would advance American strategic interests in the twenty-first century. Some administration officials viewed alignment with India as a way to counter a rising China. Others noted that Washington would have to work with New Delhi to address major international challenges such as terrorism, WMD proliferation, and the security of Indian Ocean sea lanes, and it therefore needed to develop stronger relations with India.[20]

Following from this principle, but extending it to include India's economic and military power (which was not covered in NSSP), the Bush administration now took the position that a stronger India could better advance US strategic objectives. It then made the argument that civilian nuclear cooperation would not only enhance India's economic power, but would simultaneously address several other issues.

First, diplomatically, a civilian nuclear agreement would remove long-standing irritants in US–India relations that arose because of India's status outside the NPT. Second, a civilian nuclear agreement would integrate India into the international non-proliferation regime. Third, the lifting of technology embargoes and improvements in bilateral relations would increase US defence technology transfers to India, thus boosting Indian military power. Fourth, civilian nuclear energy would assist India's economic development and increase its economic power. Fifth, on energy and environmental issues, India's increasing use of nuclear power would reduce competition in global energy markets and would help counter the challenge of global warming.

This new foreign policy strategy was clarified in a number of documents. One was a six-page memo that Secretary Rice dictated to State Department Counsellor, Philip Zelikow, and sent to President Bush, just after Rice's visit to India.[21] Rice's memo noted that the administration should change India's place in the international nuclear order and position India to become one of the US' closest international partners. Essentially, Washington sought to substantially improve ties with India at the early stages of its rise, to include India in the same inner circles of international politics as China, and to approach India in a way befitting of a major power. (Here, Washington observed that India had historically been distrustful of outside powers and this was reflected in India's autarkic economic policies until the early 1990s; it recognized that if India pursued similar approaches in the future, these would hurt US interests; for these reasons, it sought to facilitate India's rise in a positive manner.) It also drew an analogy to the way the US developed relationships with Western Europe and Japan after World War II: Washington pursued such relationships with the expectation that West European and Japanese democratic influences would spread to nearby regions, and it held similar expectations for ties with a democratic India.

Themes from this memo were outlined in a second document, a 25 March press briefing on the new US strategy for South Asia. Here, senior administration officials stated that the 'US goal is to help India become a major world power in the 21st century. We understand fully the implications, including military implications [via US arms sales], of that statement' (Department of State, 2005). They added that the US and India were developing a 'very robust strategic dialogue' that 'will include global issues, the kinds of issues you would discuss with a world power', and that this dialogue would include civilian nuclear energy.

A third document was a paper by Ashley Tellis, which built upon prior memos between Tellis and Zelikow; the paper was drafted by mid-May and publicly released on 14 July. It called for strengthening US–India relations and assisting the growth of Indian power through defence cooperation and via high-level strategic, energy, and economic dialogues. It placed the civilian nuclear issue within the energy framework, noting that the energy dialogue would enhance India's economic power and, 'most important of all, [would explore] ways of integrating India into the global nuclear regime so as to address [the area 5 and 6 issues of] New Delhi's desire for renewed access to safeguarded nuclear fuel and advanced nuclear reactors' (Tellis, 2005). Thus, it argued that nuclear cooperation was central to the broader US foreign policy strategy for India.

The above strategic vision influenced the Bush administration to change long-standing non-proliferation policies and proceed towards full civilian nuclear cooperation with India.

High-level Engagement up to March 2005

From late 2004 to March 2005, senior US and Indian officials discussed civilian nuclear cooperation during talks on transforming US–India relations.

First, Washington and New Delhi discussed the issue in a November 2004 meeting between India's foreign secretary and Condoleezza Rice (who had by then been nominated to be Secretary of State).[22] Washington sought a state visit by Prime Minister Manmohan Singh in 2005 and wanted to announce a US–India partnership during such a visit. New Delhi mentioned that the European Union (EU)–India partnership offered a template for the issues that could be covered in a US–India partnership. It noted that the EU–India partnership included an energy panel, under which the EU had agreed to discuss civilian nuclear issues. Secretary Rice observed that New Delhi and Washington could set up a similar energy panel.

New Delhi also noted that it planned to complete its NSSP obligations through a WMD export control bill, and it was therefore looking beyond NSSP to full nuclear cooperation. It made the case that to develop strategic ties with India, Washington would, in the long term, have to change its laws to allow civilian nuclear cooperation. It added that, in the short term,

Washington could begin this process by acting on area 4: Washington could allow fuel supplies for India's Tarapur reactors and permit India to repro-cess the spent fuel from these reactors that it had accumulated since its 1974 nuclear test.

Second, a small group of senior US officials more actively explored the issue of full civilian nuclear cooperation. In January 2005, Secretary Rice asked Assistant Secretary Rocca about the feasibility of congressional action to enable civilian nuclear trade with India. Soon thereafter, the administra-tion combined its planned announcement of F-16 aircraft sales to Pakistan with the issue of civilian nuclear cooperation for India. Secretary Rice wanted Deputy Secretary of State Robert Zoellick to find ways to inform New Delhi about the F-16 sales. Zoellick asked Counsellor Zelikow, rather than Assistant Secretary Rocca, to work on the issue. These State Department officials placed the F-16 issue within the new US strategy for South Asia, so that Washington would inform New Delhi of the F-16 sale to Pakistan and simultaneously offer it civilian nuclear cooperation.

Third, during a 15–16 March visit to India, Secretary Rice informed Indian officials about the new US strategy of assisting India become a major world power. Rice placed the F-16 issue within this strategy, noting that, like Pakistan, India could purchase advanced weapons from the US. More sig-nificantly, Rice noted that both sides could transform their relations through cooperation on civilian nuclear issues, and also informed Prime Minister Singh that President Bush had decided to advance the nuclear energy dia-logue (Kessler, 2007). Indian officials took the position that they would complete their NSSP obligations by passing WMD export control legislation within two months, and they asked Washington to move beyond NSSP to full civilian nuclear cooperation.

Fourth, in subsequent weeks, US and Indian officials made further men-tion of civilian nuclear cooperation. At a 21 March track-2 meeting in Jaipur, participants discussed a framework for nuclear cooperation.[23] At a 25 March briefing on their new strategy for South Asia, senior US officials stated that 'in parallel [with the US–India strategic and economic dialogues], there's an energy dialogue that would include civil nuclear and nuclear safety issues' (Department of State, 2005). Thus, Washington was augmenting, and laying the foundations to replace, the NSSP process with senior-level US–India dialogues on strategic, economic, and energy issues.

Fifth, and most significantly, upon her return from India, Secretary Rice sent a memo to President Bush outlining the rationale for civilian nuclear cooperation and for a strategic partnership with India. The president accepted this case. He had long wanted to 'intensify collaboration with India on the whole range of [security and economic] issues that currently confront the international community' and had accordingly taken 'a global approach to U.S.–Indian relations, consistent with the rise of India as a world power' (Blackwill, 2005). Further, it is likely that, in the prevailing 'war on terror', the president recognized the importance of new allies in South Asia; India then became the right ally at the right moment, especially because Washington's ties with its traditional European allies were strained by the war in Iraq (Warburg, 2012). The president then moved ahead with the nuclear initiative. On 25 March, he called and informed Prime Minister Singh of his intention to develop a strategic partnership with India that included civilian nuclear cooperation. He also informed the prime minister of the F-16 sales to Pakistan. India's foreign policy establishment was restrained in its response to the F-16 issue: it simply stated that the US 'intends to upgrade' the strategic partnership with India and that Washington 'is [also] considering offering civilian nuclear energy and nuclear safety cooperation with India' (Government of India, 2005).

High-level Engagement, April–June 2005

From April to June, the senior-most US and Indian officials discussed full civilian nuclear cooperation and Indian officials pressed their US counterparts to announce such cooperation during Prime Minister Singh's visit to Washington.

First, in an 8 April meeting with the US ambassador, External Affairs Minister Natwar Singh emphasized that New Delhi had two main priorities in any prime ministerial visit to the US: its place on the UN Security Council; and its access to US-origin nuclear power technology.[24]

Second, during his 12–14 April visit to the US, the external affairs minister discussed civilian nuclear issues with President Bush, Secretary Rice, and other US officials. The president informed the minister that Washington viewed India as a global power and that India and the US needed to work on energy issues 'which would include the area of civil nuclear cooperation' (Embassy of India, 2005). The president specifically mentioned nuclear reactors, implying that he was looking towards cooperation all the way to area 6 (Mohan, 2006a). Further, the Indian delegation accompanying the minister included representatives from India's nuclear and space programs, its foreign secretary, and the deputy chairman of India's planning commission, and these officials also discussed nuclear energy issues with their US counterparts.

Third, at an 18 April meeting with Assistant Secretary Rocca in Delhi, National Security Advisor M. K. Narayanan noted that India's government was seriously considering a prime ministerial visit to the US, but he urged Washington to place substantial deliverables, such as civilian nuclear cooperation, on the agenda.[25]

Fourth, at a 9 May event in Moscow, President Bush and Prime Minister Singh discussed India's energy needs and the president mentioned that the two countries should talk about civilian nuclear issues. Fifth, during a 16–19 May visit to Washington, Foreign Secretary Saran discussed civilian nuclear issues with Undersecretary Burns and Counsellor Zelikow as part of the agenda for Prime Minister Singh's visit to the US. Sixth, at a 31 May US–India energy dialogue meeting, participants discussed two aspects of nuclear cooperation: safety collaboration; and the role of nuclear power in the global energy future.

To summarize, just ahead of and after Secretary Rice's visit to India, the senior-most US policymakers overcame the fundamental – the conceptual – hurdle to the idea of full civilian nuclear cooperation with India; prior administrations had not been able to surmount this hurdle. Thereafter, they more seriously discussed full civilian nuclear cooperation. In these high-level discussions, they also pressed New Delhi to act on its export controls. Such high-level information exchanges sensitized India's government to the importance of quickly passing export control legislation.

In turn, Indian officials repeated the points they had made in prior years. They noted that India was a responsible nuclear state with a good export control record; that it should be able to import civilian nuclear technology to meet its energy needs; that on non-proliferation benchmark 1, it would further strengthen its export controls; and that on non-proliferation benchmark 2, it would place reactors availing of international cooperation under safeguards.[26] Also, having learned of a US timeline (noted subsequently) to announce some form of civilian nuclear cooperation during Prime Minister Singh's visit to the US, New Delhi asked Washington to settle at least the Tarapur issue during the visit.

Bureaucratic Debates on Nuclear Cooperation

By the spring of 2005, the senior-most US policymakers – President Bush and Secretary Rice – had decided to pursue full civilian nuclear cooperation with India. Counsellor Zelikow and National Security Advisor Stephen Hadley worked to implement this policy, while Undersecretary of State for Political Affairs Nicholas Burns engaged his Indian counterparts on the issue. (Burns was not involved in US–India discussions until Secretary Rice appointed him to lead these discussions after her visit to India. Rice informed Burns about her meetings with India's prime minister, the US grand strategy of building a defence and strategic relationship with India, and in this context, the importance of tackling the contentious nuclear issue. Burns then viewed the issue as a major challenge but also a major strategic move in US foreign policy.[27]) These officials, joined by a very few others, discussed various options for nuclear cooperation with India.

First, they debated two alternative timelines.[28] One was a fast-track approach where the Bush administration would announce a policy of full civilian nuclear cooperation during Prime Minister Singh's July 2005 visit to the US. The second was a slow-track approach where the administration would only announce a nuclear study group in July, and the study group would develop a nuclear cooperation policy by the time President Bush visited India in 2006. Secretary Rice and Counsellor Zelikow favoured the first approach, while the State Department's non-proliferation bureau urged caution and a more gradual approach, and the national security advisor initially sought a compromise between the two approaches but then came around to supporting the first approach. Eventually, in May, the Bush administration opted for the first approach: it sketched a timeline of announcing a policy of full civilian nuclear cooperation in July 2005, and then implementing the policy by 2006 when President Bush visited India. And it did not opt for a slow-track process because, once it was publicly known that a study group was discussing full nuclear cooperation with India, the expected strong opposition to such cooperation would have prevented the administration from going ahead with it.

Second, the administration debated executive and legislative options to facilitate varying degrees of civilian nuclear cooperation. The advocates for full nuclear cooperation recommended a mix of executive and legislative action. They favoured executive action in the short term, which would still require the acquiescence of the Nuclear Regulatory Commission (NRC) and Congress, as well as consultations with the NSG, to quickly facilitate cooperation in areas 3 and 4.[29] They also recognized the need for legislative action to fundamentally change US laws and extend nuclear cooperation with India all the way to areas 5 and 6. Still, they noted that this would take longer, because it would require 'working with Congress' and 'coordinating with the international community to develop the appropriate carve-outs to enable treatment of New Delhi as a legitimate exception to the existing rules' (Tellis, 2005).

The more traditional bureaucracy expressed concerns about the fast-track timeline and the administration's preferred executive and legislative options.[30] It was concerned that any fundamental changes in non-proliferation laws would undermine the non-proliferation regime and jeopardize US non-proliferation efforts versus North Korea and Iran. Further, in early 2005, a non-proliferation civil servant wrote a memo outlining the legal obstacles to nuclear cooperation with India and noting that Congress could pose problems if its prerogatives were not respected (Kessler, 2007). The traditional bureaucracy expressed these concerns in inter-agency meetings hosted by the NSC in May and June, where some non-proliferation specialists also supported the advocates' approach because they believed that it would not ultimately be feasible (Jaishankar, 2009).

Four further issues affected the debate between the advocates for full nuclear cooperation and the traditional bureaucracy. First, in terms of timing, Prime Minister Singh's visit to the US represented a major opportunity for the Bush administration to announce its new foreign policy strategy for India. Had it delayed, the administration would have had to wait until the 2006 presidential visit to India for another such high-profile opportunity.[31]

Second, the effort required for different approaches to civilian nuclear cooperation appeared to be similar. In early 2005, as US and Indian officials looked into accommodating India on fuel for the Tarapur reactors, they recognized that the Bush administration would have to undertake a substantial bureaucratic and legislative effort to facilitate even this small amount of nuclear cooperation. They observed that for a slightly greater effort, they could lift the more fundamental barriers to civilian nuclear cooperation with India and extend it all the way to areas 5 and 6.

Third, New Delhi took three actions in mid-2005 that helped the advocates' case in US bureaucratic debates. Most importantly, in early May, India adopted its WMD export control bill, which indicated that it was moving to complete its NSSP requirements. Further, on 28 June, India signed a defence framework agreement with the US, which illustrated that it could undertake substantial military and defence cooperation with Washington. Finally, although UN Security Council reforms were one of New Delhi's two major priorities for the prime minister's visit to the US, New Delhi did not press this issue when Washington would not act on it.

Fourth, the traditionalists and the advocates held different views on a strategic partnership with India. The traditional bureaucracy believed that India was not ready for a strategic partnership with the US and was, therefore, cautious about a fast-track approach to civilian nuclear cooperation. The advocates embraced the vision of India as an emerging strategic partner. Influenced by this strategic vision, President Bush, Secretary of State Rice, and a small group of advocates actively sought to change long-standing US non-proliferation policy to advance what they believed was a more important US foreign policy objective, that of strategic engagement with India.

To summarize, the above factors tilted bureaucratic debates in the spring of 2005, towards a policy of faster and fuller civilian nuclear cooperation with India. Washington was then willing to end NSSP and to simultaneously negotiate with New Delhi over the terms for civilian nuclear cooperation.

Ending NSSP

Washington and New Delhi completed NSSP in five steps in 2005. First, in early 2005, they continued to implement NSSP's second phase. On non-nuclear issues, Washington briefed New Delhi on the Patriot-2 missile defence system and the two sides discussed other defence technology transfers at a meeting of the HTCG defence industry group.[32] On nuclear issues, Indian officials pressed for access to nuclear safety equipment and for Indian participation in the international thermonuclear experimental reactor (ITER), especially because these initiatives could help convince skeptics in India's DAE about the benefits of NSSP.[33]

Washington then advanced the safety dialogue when NRC Commissioner, Jeffrey Merrifield, visited India on 11–12 February.[34] Merrifield focused on the US–India nuclear safety exchanges (area 3B), while Indian officials sought to expand the discussion. They suggested that, on area 3C, Washington and New Delhi could explore proliferation-resistant reactors, new reactor designs, and Indian participation in ITER. And, on area 5, they asked the US to not block other countries from providing fuel for India's reactors. Commissioner Merrifield acknowledged these points and upon returning to Washington, promoted the ideas of safety cooperation and a US–India energy dialogue.

Second, from March onwards, US and Indian officials discussed further bilateral initiatives on high-technology, space, and civilian nuclear issues.

These also came under the strategic, energy, and economic tracks that Secretary Rice had outlined during her March visit to India.[35]

Third, India's government overcame bureaucratic and legislative obstacles to complete its WMD export control bill in May, and it also took steps to enforce the bill. The bill advanced through India's inter-agency process in just four months for three main reasons. First, under the HTCG and NSSP processes, Indian officials became less suspicious about US intentions on export controls (Gahlaut, 2008). Second, the lead agency for the bill, the MEA, informed other government departments that the bill would expand rather than constrain their areas of responsibility.[36] Third, the PMO pressed for the quick completion of the bill.

India's government then presented the bill to India's cabinet on 5 May, after which the ministers of external affairs, defence, and parliamentary affairs met leftist parties, who allowed the bill's passage before the Parliament adjourned. Parliament then debated the bill on 12 May and approved it on 13 May.

Fourth, India's WMD legislation influenced US bureaucratic debates on NSSP. The advocates were then willing to announce the completion of NSSP during Prime Minister Singh's visit to the US.[37] On the other hand, the traditional bureaucracy argued that Washington had already done much to accommodate New Delhi on civilian nuclear cooperation and that, as per the step-by-step NSSP process, New Delhi had to take additional steps before Washington permitted more nuclear cooperation.[38] The traditionalists wanted New Delhi to fully adhere to the MTCR and NSG, to also adhere to the Australia Group and the Wassenaar Arrangement, and to accept the Proliferation Security Initiative (PSI).[39] Ultimately, the president and senior-most US officials overruled such a position because it would take too long to implement and would prevent them from announcing a civilian nuclear initiative during Prime Minister Singh's visit to the US. Washington then accepted that New Delhi could complete its NSSP obligations by simply agreeing to adhere to the MTCR and NSG.

Fifth, US and Indian officials worked on these issues to complete the NSSP process. Indian officials wanted to combine their NSSP second phase and third phase obligations by harmonizing their export control lists with the MTCR and NSG and adhering to these regimes in a single step; however, US officials noted that these were distinct processes with harmonization preceding adherence.[40] US officials also raised additional issues: they had technical questions about India's WMD export control bill; they wanted India's government to support PSI; and they gave India's government a non-paper mentioning 17 cases of suspected inwards and onwards proliferation by Indian entities.

Washington and New Delhi resolved their differences over these issues by mid-July. On 11 July, Undersecretary Robert Joseph provided the Indian ambassador with a paper on the final steps for completing NSSP. India responded on 14 July, stating that India's cabinet had approved the harmonization of India's export control lists with the MTCR and NSG, though India did not actually adhere to these regimes at this time. New Delhi also addressed the US concerns via two non-papers. One clarified issues in India's WMD bill and addressed US concerns about re-export, brokering, catch-all provisions, and intangible technology transfer. The second mentioned that India's government had undertaken some industry outreach and preventive enforcement efforts to augment its WMD export control bill.[41]

As a result of these steps by New Delhi, Washington agreed to end NSSP; the July 2005 Joint Statement formally noted that NSSP had ended and that the US would move on to full civilian nuclear cooperation with India.

Finalizing the Joint Statement

US officials began outlining the terms for US–India nuclear cooperation soon after Secretary Rice's visit to India, and they finalized these in negotiations with New Delhi in June and July.

Initially, three officials (two with non-proliferation and one with strategic affairs backgrounds) outlined the two basic issues for civilian nuclear cooperation. Their outline noted that India would: (a) adopt strong export controls; and (b) separate its civilian and nuclear facilities; they recognized that the details of this outline would only be formalized well after the Joint Statement was announced.[42] This opening draft was approved by senior US officials and discussed with New Delhi.

In June and July, Washington and New Delhi finalized the terms for civilian nuclear cooperation. On 24 June, Undersecretary Burns held several hours of talks with India's foreign secretary in Delhi. Alluding to the possibility of civilian nuclear cooperation, Burns expected the prime minister's US visit to be the most important one ever for the two countries.[43] On 6–8 July, Undersecretary Burns and Secretary Rice met India's foreign secretary on the sidelines of the G8 summit.

US and Indian officials undertook a final round of negotiations from 15 July to 18 July. Going into these talks, Indian officials were prepared for cooperation that did not extend all the way to areas 5 and 6. As a result, Indian officials heading to Washington on 14 July mainly sought an agreement on area 4, the Tarapur reactors.[44] And, if they were unable to achieve full nuclear cooperation, the Indian delegation was reconciled to coming back with just a working group on the issue.

Eventually, from July 15 to 17, Indian and US officials drafted a statement whereby the United States committed to full civilian nuclear cooperation in exchange for India's separating its civilian and military facilities. Secretary Rice then sought to complete an agreement on July 17 evening in a meeting with India's external affairs minister, who arrived in Washington a day ahead of the prime minister. Yet DAE officials, who had arrived in Washington on July 17 afternoon (on the same flight as the prime minister), had concerns with the draft. The DAE's historical mistrust of the United States and its concerns about technical issues held back the completion of negotiations until the next day (Mohan, 2006a).

The Indian side focused on issues such as India's status as a de facto nuclear weapons state; the reciprocity of obligations; Indian sovereignty in, and the voluntary nature of, separating its civilian and military facilities; a phased process for bringing civilian reactors under safeguards; and the kinds of safeguards, including whether they would be equivalent to those accepted by the five nuclear weapons states. Indian officials discussed these issues with their US counterparts, but, by July 17 night, both sides had not agreed to language on a phased timeline for identifying Indian civilian and military facilities, nor to the Indian position on the words 'voluntary' and 'reciprocal.' Indian officials then informed US officials that no agreement was possible because the US terms were politically too difficult for the Indian government—Indian officials were concerned that placing even civilian Indian-built reactors under safeguards would be criticized domestically as compromising India's sovereignty.[45]

On the morning of July 18, Secretary Rice persuaded Prime Minister Singh to let the talks continue (Rice, 2011). US and Indian officials eventually reached an agreement while Prime Minister Singh and President Bush were meeting. They finalized the last contentious word – the word 'voluntary' instead of 'voluntarily' (as discussed below) – during lunch, thereby completing the Joint Statement.

The July 2005 Joint Statement

The Joint Statement placed the issue of civilian nuclear cooperation squarely within the framework of broader US–India relations. In the statement, Washington and New Delhi affirmed 'their resolve to transform the relationship between their countries and establish a global partnership'. The two sides agreed to cooperate on economic issues, energy and environmental issues, democracy and development, non-proliferation and security, and high technology and space. They then outlined the terms for civilian nuclear cooperation.

The US committed to full civilian nuclear cooperation. Specifically, rather than taking just incremental steps from area 3A (where NSSP's first phase ended) to areas 3B and 3C (that was part of NSSP's second and third phases) to area 3D and area 4, the Bush administration agreed to achieve 'full nuclear cooperation' with India, which meant cooperation on the full spectrum of civilian nuclear areas extending to area 6. It also made specific commitments to provide 'fuel supplies for safeguarded nuclear reactors at Tarapur' (area 4) and to India's inclusion in international research efforts such as 'ITER, and the Generation IV International Forum' (area 3C).

India agreed to reciprocal steps on five main issues, which corresponded with four of the five non-proliferation benchmarks. First, on export controls (non-proliferation benchmark 1), New Delhi made two sets of commitments. One was to augment its May 2005 export control legislation by affirming its NSSP second phase and third phase obligations. New Delhi thus committed to 'harmonization [of its control lists] and adherence to Missile Technology Control Regime (MTCR) and Nuclear Suppliers Group (NSG) guidelines', though it did not actually adhere to these regimes at this time. A second commitment was to refrain from transferring enrichment technology to states that did not have such technology and to support international efforts to limit the spread of this technology.

Second, on civil–military separation (non-proliferation benchmark 2), India undertook to 'identifying and separating civilian and military nuclear facilities and programs in a phased manner'; 'to place voluntarily its civilian nuclear facilities under IAEA safeguards'; and to sign 'an Additional Protocol with respect to civilian nuclear facilities'. Still, many aspects of safeguards remained contentious.

One contested aspect was the word 'voluntarily'. Indian officials preferred the words 'voluntary safeguards', which were closer to the term 'voluntary offer safeguards agreements' that the IAEA adopts for the five NPT-defined nuclear weapons states. US officials were concerned that this Indian preference could enable India to initially designate facilities as civilian but then remove them from safeguards. The final wording was only settled at the 18 July lunch meeting between Secretary Rice and Prime Minister Singh, as mentioned earlier.

Another tough aspect was the nature of safeguards. Washington wanted New Delhi to accept standard IAEA safeguards and the IAEA's standard model Additional Protocol, while New Delhi would not accept these because they applied to non-nuclear weapon states. Washington raised these items early in the 15–18 July discussion, and Indian officials stated that they would walk away from the talks rather than accept such conditions. These safeguards issues were only resolved in the final hours of negotiations.

Third, on nuclear testing (non-proliferation benchmark 3), New Delhi resisted the US preferences to even mention the CTBT. Instead, it only committed to 'continuing India's unilateral moratorium on nuclear testing'. Fourth, on fissile material restraints (non-proliferation benchmark 5), New Delhi only accepted very low obligations of 'working with the United States for the conclusion of a multilateral Fissile Material Cut-Off Treaty (FMCT)'. Such obligations would not affect India's fissile material production for at least the next decade, because negotiations on an FMCT had not even begun in 2005.

US regional affairs specialists recognized that New Delhi would not accept fissile material restraints and informed senior US officials about keeping this issue outside the negotiations.[46] Still, US non-proliferation officials sought a process whereby, on benchmark 5, India would restrict itself to a minimum deterrent and produce under safeguards any fissile material for its nuclear power program (that is, for its breeder reactor and its three-phase program).[47] Relatedly, on benchmark 2, they preferred that India keep all its power reactors under safeguards and confine military plutonium production to its two unsafeguarded research reactors. This would ensure that 'firewalls' between India's civilian and military programs were in place, so that any assistance to civilian reactors would not result in the US even indirectly assisting India's military programs. Yet, during their 24 June meeting, Indian officials informed Undersecretary Burns that they would not accept outside influence on India's nuclear weapons program such as limits on using any particular reactors for fissile material production.

Fifth, on India's nuclear status, an early draft of the Joint Statement suggested that New Delhi could be acknowledged, and have the same rights and obligations, as a de facto nuclear weapons state. Still, after considering the legal implications of this term, Washington opted for an alternative term, which recognized India as a state with 'advanced nuclear technology'.

To summarize, the Joint Statement had relatively low non-proliferation provisions, as shown in Table 3.3. On a scale of A1 (representing very high non-proliferation provisions) to A9 (representing very low non-proliferation provisions), it was an A7 arrangement. While it had relatively moderate non-proliferation provisions on one issue (export controls), it had relatively low or very low provisions on the other issues (safeguards, testing, fissile materials, and India's nuclear status), and therefore had relatively low overall non-proliferation provisions. And, although US non-proliferation officials desired an A4, A5, or A6 Joint Statement with relatively moderate non-proliferation provisions, the Bush administration accepted an A7 statement when only this arrangement fell within India's win-set.

Table 3.3 Alternative Arrangements for the Joint Statement

Type	*Example*	*Issues and Non-proliferation Provisions*
A1	Very strong non-proliferation position	*Very high non-proliferation provisions on all issues*
A3	Strong non-proliferation position	*High non-proliferation provisions on all issues*
A4	Closer to NSSP provisions	*High non-proliferation provisions on about half and moderate provisions on the other half of the issues*
A5	Balance between the US strategic and non-proliferation perspectives	*Moderate non-proliferation provisions on almost all the issues*
A6	Closer to the US strategic perspective	*Moderate non-proliferation provisions on about half and low provisions on the other half of the issues*
A7	July 2005 Joint Statement	*Low or very low non-proliferation provisions on the majority of the issues*
		*India's export controls (moderate): WMD bill and adherence to NSG and MTCR

Type	Example	Issues and Non-proliferation Provisions
		**India's safeguards (low): IAEA safeguards but 'voluntarily' and in a 'phased' manner and with reciprocity
		***India's testing obligations (low): a 'moratorium on testing'
		****India's fissile material obligations (very low): only to support talks on FMCT
		*****India's nuclear status (low): a state with 'advanced nuclear technology' having the same rights as other such states
A7-typical	Typical arrangement with relatively low non-proliferation provisions	*Low non-proliferation provisions on all issues*
A9	Ideal position of India's nuclear establishment	*Very low non-proliferation provisions on all issues*

Notes: The non-proliferation provisions are coded from very high to very low as follows:

1. *India's export controls: India adopts the following: a strong WMD bill and adheres to five initiatives (the MTCR, NSG, PSI, Australia Group, and Wassenaar Arrangement), with strong consequences if it violates these commitments (very high); a strong WMD bill and adheres to five initiatives with some consequences if it violates these commitments (high); a moderate WMD bill and adheres to only two initiatives, the NSG and MTCR (moderate); a moderate WMD bill (low); no WMD bill (very low).

2. **India's safeguards: India accepts the following: standard IAEA safeguards and the model Additional Protocol (very high); standard IAEA safeguards but only limited commitment to Additional Protocol (high); IAEA safeguards 'voluntarily' but not in a phased manner (moderate); IAEA safeguards 'voluntarily' and in a 'phased' manner and with reciprocity (low); voluntary safeguards (very low).

3. ***India's testing obligations: India accepts the following: CTBT with very strong (very high) or strong (high) consequences for testing; test moratorium with some consequences for testing (moderate); a 'moratorium on testing' with no consequences for testing (low); no restrictions on testing (very low).

4. ****India's fissile material obligations: India agrees to the following: entirely end fissile material production (very high); halt unsafeguarded fissile material production with only the Dhruva research reactor outside safeguards (high); restrict itself to a minimum deterrent and place two-thirds of power reactors under safeguards (moderate); place 10 of 22 power reactors under safeguards and keep two research reactors and breeder reactor outside safeguards (low); no restrictions (very low).

5. *****India's nuclear status: India considered a non-nuclear weapons state (very high); no mention of India as a state with advanced nuclear technology, or specific mention that India's rights are not the same as those of a nuclear weapons state (high); India considered a state with 'advanced nuclear technology' but no mention of the same rights as other such states (moderate); India considered a state with 'advanced nuclear technology' having the same rights as other such states (low); India has rights similar to the NPT nuclear weapons states (very low).

The Win-set in 2005

Four factors enabled an A7 arrangement – where Washington extended nuclear cooperation to area 6 in exchange for relatively low non-proliferation provisions from India – to fall within the US win-set.

First, in terms of bureaucratic politics at the highest levels of government, the positions of key decision makers changed in 2005. From 2001 to 2004, the State Department leadership, headed by Secretary of State Colin Powell, would not overturn fundamental US non-proliferation rules to allow full nuclear cooperation with India. In 2005, however, the State Department's leadership under Secretary Rice actively sought full nuclear cooperation, and Rice also convinced President Bush to accept this position. This widened the US win-set so that it could allow for such a policy.

Second, four particular bureaucratic developments (concerning personnel shifts at the upper levels of the bureaucracy and the fact that potential opponents were not involved in decision making or were outnumbered) made it hard for opponents to block full nuclear cooperation and this expanded the win-set.

Specifically, at the upper levels of the bureaucracy, a potentially strong opponent, John Bolton, left his position as Undersecretary of State for Arms Control and International Security after he was nominated to become the permanent representative to the UN. And Bolton's successor, Robert Joseph, only took office on 1 June; by then, it was too late to alter the US position because talks with India had advanced considerably.

Further, at the mid-levels of government, the traditional foreign policy and non-proliferation bureaucracy had few opportunities to influence the quick policy shift towards full nuclear cooperation. This was because they were excluded from almost all discussion on the topic that took place in closed-group meetings. They were only involved in a few inter-agency meetings of the NSC in May and June. Even in these meetings, because India moved faster on its NSSP export control obligations than they expected, they had little time to develop a position on how far the US could accommodate India.[48]

In addition, some non-proliferation officials who were involved in the closed-group discussions were less concerned about how the nuclear initiative with India would affect the NPT and they, therefore, did not strongly resist the initiative. Instead, they looked at non-proliferation issues through the lens of US interests and therefore mainly sought to ensure that India adopted the strongest possible export controls.[49]

Finally, in most of the closed-group discussions, as well as during the final round of negotiations from 15 July to 18 July, non-proliferation representatives were outnumbered. Thus, Undersecretary Joseph was not present at the talks in July, though he was following the negotiations by phone. As a result, the NSC director for non-proliferation was the only official with a strong non-proliferation background on a US negotiating team that largely comprised advocates willing to accept limited non-proliferation restraints from India.

Third, legislative politics did not constrain the Bush administration and this widened the US win-set. To begin with, the Joint Statement was just a framework document that did not require congressional approval. Moreover, the administration did not inform Congress about the Joint Statement before it was announced, and therefore Congress did not know about it. It did not approach Congress because of concerns about press leaks and because talks with India moved very quickly: administration officials noted, 'We also did not believe, frankly, for a long time before the [Indian prime minister's July 2005] visit that it would be possible to reach this agreement.'[50]

Fourth, in early and mid-2005, there was little domestic mobilization against full nuclear cooperation with India because, like Congress, non-proliferation interest groups did know about – and therefore did not mobilize against – such a policy. This absence of mobilization widened the US win-set.

In the end, the above-mentioned factors, combined with the high-level push to finalize the civilian nuclear initiative during Prime Minister Singh's visit to the US, resulted in non-proliferation interests being marginalized in the US position, and this widened the US win-set. In contrast, if the traditional bureaucracy and Congress had been more involved in early and mid-2005, the US win-set would likely have been smaller, and Washington would then have only accepted an A5 or A6 arrangement.

Somewhat similar bureaucratic and legislative issues affected India's win-set, but they reduced rather than widened the win-set. First, bureaucratic politics decreased India's win-set. India's negotiating team included DAE officials who opposed arrangements having moderate or high non-proliferation provisions such as fissile material restraints and the IAEA's model Additional Protocol.

Second, legislative politics restricted the Indian government's policy autonomy and reduced its win-set. Strictly speaking, the Joint Statement did not require parliamentary approval. However, India's government relied on the left to remain in office. In June and July 2005, differences between India's government and the left were widening over economic policies, and the left also strongly opposed the 28 June US–India defence agreement, arguing that it exceeded the terms of the UPA–Left common minimum program. Accordingly, before leaving for Washington, India's prime minister assured the left that he would not make major changes in policy towards the US.

Third, domestic mobilization reduced India's win-set. In particular, commentators in the Indian press opposed the 28 June defence agreement. As a result of such press commentary, the Indian government had to ensure that it would not be seen as making excessive concessions to the US.

To summarize, bureaucratic factors, legislative considerations, and domestic mobilization all narrowed India's win-set and New Delhi could not accept a Joint Statement that contained anything more than relatively low non-proliferation criteria.

Implementing the Joint Statement

The Joint Statement had relatively low non-proliferation provisions, which were just enough to fall within India's win-set while also remaining within the US win-set. In subsequent months, as the Bush administration sought congressional approval to implement the Joint Statement, Congress raised many issues that had been left out of the Statement.

Congress sought details about the separation of India's civilian and military facilities, a firmer Indian commitment to its moratorium on testing, clarifications on safeguards in perpetuity, and restrictions on sensitive enrichment and reprocessing technology transfer to India. Washington and New Delhi negotiated over these issues in subsequent arrangements. Thus, from 2006 to 2008, the Joint Statement that had relatively low non-proliferation provisions was converted into arrangements with low-to-moderate or moderate non-proliferation provisions, enabling these to fall within the US win-set. At the same time, the Joint Statement was the starting and ending point for all future negotiations. It had fixed some basic terms that the US bureaucracy, Congress, and the NSG could not renegotiate, and all subsequent US–India talks crafted documents that preserved the terms of the Joint Statement.

Endnotes

1   The Clinton administration referred to India as a 'non-nuclear weapon state', which is a term used in the NPT for all states other than the five recognized by the treaty as having nuclear weapons. The same term is used in the Atomic Energy Act and in other US legislative and policy documents.

2 In substantive terms, progress in area 3 would not make large short-term contributions to India's power sector. These could only occur with cooperation in area 4 (the Tarapur reactors generated 320 megawatt [MW] of electricity), area 5 (India's 18 other power reactors could generate some 4,000 MW of electricity), and area 6 (where India sought to import several 1,000 MW reactors). See the Appendix for details on these reactors.

3 Such high-technology exports to India were worth $43 million in 1995–96, $149 million in 1996–97, and $150 million in 1997–98, but fell considerably in 1998–99.

4 In 1999, India's government constituted a Small Group on Strategic Export Controls; and in 2000, it developed a more comprehensive list of Special Chemicals, Organisms, Materials, Equipment and Technology (SCOMET) whose export would be controlled.

5 For a related discussion, see *Hindustan Times* (1998).

6 These themes were outlined in early 2000 in *Hydrocarbon Vision 2025*, a report of an inter-ministerial energy group set up by the PMO.

7 Echoing this view in 1999, Jaswant Singh noted: 'What is needed is for the political–military leadership of the country to separate the two strands: the entirely military from the purely peaceful…it is precisely on account of such [civilian–military] ambiguity that the country's energy security has also suffered' (Singh, 1999).

8 In October 2001, Washington acted on area 1C by reducing the number of Indian companies on the Entity List from 159 to 16; it lifted sanctions on most of the remaining 16 entities in 2004–05.

9 Author interview V1, 7 September 2011; see also Blackwill (2005) and Tellis (2006a).

10 Author interview N2, 1 November 2011; see also Rumsfeld (2011).

11 Author interview O3, 25 November 2011.

12 Ibid.

13 Ibid.; for related press reports, see Chengappa (2007); Shishir Gupta (2008). For reports on the issue in early 2004, when India was considering a civilian–military separation and accepting some form of the Additional Protocol in return for acknowledgement of its nuclear status, see Bagchi (2004).

14 Author interview J1, 12 October 2011.

15 Author interview Y1, 2 November 2011.

16 The US Embassy, New Delhi, cables, 3 November and 5 November 2004; see also Varadarajan (2004).

17 The MTCR and NSG are groups of states that have developed guidelines and restrictions for the transfer of technology relevant to missiles and nuclear weapons programs, respectively. In their industrial exports and technology transfers, members of these regimes undertake to ensure that the transfer would not contribute to the proliferation of missiles and nuclear weapons. The NSG was established in 1975 and the MTCR was formed in 1987.

18 Illustrating this, between October 2004 and January 2005 (which was just after NSSP's first phase came into effect), the US approved 185 licences for technology transfers to India and denied only 22.

19   Author interview J1, 12 October 2011; author interview U3, 11 October 2011.
20   Reflecting the balance of power perspective, US officials noted that 'there is a tre-
       mendous strategic upside to our growing engagement with India', and that such
       engagement held 'real promise for the global balance of power' (Burns, 2007b).
       Reflecting broader US interests, Condoleezza Rice noted that Washington pur-
       sued the nuclear agreement to 'unlock a wide range of possible areas of coopera-
       tion with a country that was an emerging power in Asia' (Rice, 2011).
21   Author interview with officials familiar with the memo; author interview B1,
       26 September 2011.
22   Author interview with officials familiar with the discussions; author interview
       U1, 26 November 2011.
23   This was the annual meeting sponsored by the Confederation of Indian Industry
       (CII) and the Aspen Strategy Group. Author interview R1, 12 August 2010.
24   The US Embassy, New Delhi, cable, 8 April 2005.
25   The US Embassy, New Delhi, cable, 19 April 2005.
26   It is worth clarifying that, during Nuclear Regulatory Commission (NRC)
       Commissioner Jeffrey Merrifield's February 2005 visit to India, Indian officials
       were willing to place nuclear power plants availing of fuel imports under site-
       specific safeguards, but they noted that, as per its existing policy, New Delhi
       would not place Indian-built power plants under safeguards. This suggests that
       India's bureaucracy was still reluctant to safeguard Indian-built power plants
       that did not use imported fuel. The US Embassy, New Delhi, cable, 17 February
       2005.
27   Author interview D4, 25 October 2011.
28   Author interview B1, 26 September 2011.
29   These points were made in a hearing, 'The United States and South Asia', Hearing
       before the Subcommittee on Asia and the Pacific of the House Committee on
       International Relations, 14 June 2005.
30   The 'traditional' bureaucracy comprised some 10–20 mostly mid-level officials
       who handled routine South Asia policy or nuclear cooperation policy at the
       State Department, the Department of Energy, and other government depart-
       ments and agencies.
31   Author interview B1, 26 September 2011; author interview L2, 15 September
       2011.
32   The US Embassy, New Delhi, cable, 8 March 2005.
33   The US Embassy, New Delhi, cables, 4 January, 20 January, 24 February, and
       11 March 2005.
34   The US Embassy, New Delhi, cables, 17 February 2005.
35   The US Embassy, New Delhi, cable, 30 March 2005.
36   The US embassy, New Delhi, cables, 5 May and 18 May 2005. These factors
       reduced bureaucratic resistance to the WMD export control legislation, though
       some agencies remained concerned about items such as catch-all controls. As a

result, advancing the bill through the Indian bureaucracy was still difficult: in the words of a senior Indian civil servant, it was 'my most difficult exercise in 35 years'. The US Embassy, New Delhi, cable, 14 May 2005.

37   Author interview Y1, 2 November 2011.

38   Author interview U2, 13 September 2011.

39   Author interview U3, 11 October 2011.

40   The US Embassy, New Delhi, cable, 29 June 2005.

41   For example, India's Directorate General for Foreign Trade (DGFT), which issues licences for SCOMET list items, held outreach meetings with Indian industry exporters. Other government departments such as the Department of Chemicals conducted similar meetings, often teaming with industry associations. In addition, India's Central Board of Excise and Customs formed a core group to train other government agencies on SCOMET enforcement. The US Embassy, New Delhi, cable, 14 July 2005.

42   Author interview T1, 25 October 2011.

43   The US Embassy, New Delhi, cable, 1 July 2005.

44   The prime minister had informed the left that he would discuss fuel for the Tarapur reactors but did not mention other areas of nuclear cooperation (Mohan, 2006a).

45   The Indian press echoed these views, noting that 'The Indian atomic establishment is wary of safeguards except at any new facility that is created with outside equipment or help' and that 'the suggestion made in some quarters about separating civilian and military facilities for safeguards purposes is not feasible' (Varadarajan, 2005).

46   Author interview U3, 11 October 2011.

47   Thus, in response to the question, 'Did the United States originally seek to have India end its fissile material production for weapons?', Robert Joseph noted, 'We did. India was not willing to do that.' Moreover, at a spring 2005 meeting between the British, French, and the US national security advisors, when Washington mentioned its civilian nuclear initiative with India, the United Kingdom (UK) accepted that nuclear cooperation would not be conditioned on Indian fissile material restraints. See Boese (2006).

48   Author interview U2, 13 September 2011.

49   Author interview L2, 15 September 2011.

50   This point was made in a statement by Undersecretary Burns at the House International Relations Committee, 8 September 2005; and in author interview D3, 9 July 2010.

CHAPTER FOUR

Separating India's Nuclear Facilities

I N December 2005, the Indian press carried the headline, 'N-Separation Plan Ready' (Bagchi, 2005). It noted that 'India has readied its plan to separate civilian nuclear facilities from the military' and that 'over the past few weeks, there has been hectic activity in the Indian nuclear establishment and the external affairs ministry to put the separation list together' (ibid.). New Delhi expected Washington to accept this separation list, but Washington rejected it, and US and Indian negotiators were unable to resolve their differences over the list for the next two months. Ultimately, the list was only finalized on 2 March 2006, during President Bush's visit to India. Washington and New Delhi then agreed to a separation plan with relatively low-to-moderate non-proliferation provisions.

Domestic politics significantly influenced the process of separating India's civilian and military nuclear facilities. On the US side, Congress, influenced by non-proliferation groups, made it clear that it would not accept a separation plan with relatively low non-proliferation provisions. Accordingly, US negotiators worked hard to increase the non-proliferation credentials of the plan and they regularly informed their Indian counterparts about this congressional concern.[1] In India, however, bureaucratic resistance from the nuclear establishment caused it to keep key reactors outside safeguards. Legislative opposition from India's political left and right, along with domestic mobilization, further affected India's position. This prevented India's government from accepting a separation plan with even moderate non-proliferation provisions.

US–India Negotiations

The US and India initially discussed the separation plan in September 2005, and then held more detailed talks on 21–22 October in Delhi, 21–22 December in Washington, 19–21 January in Delhi, and 23–24 February in Delhi. They discussed five main issues: the number of India's power reactors that would be placed on the civilian list and under safeguards; the status of India's breeder reactor; the permanent nature of safeguards and their links with fuel supply assurances; India's Cirus reactor; and India's nuclear facilities beyond its reactors. The first three issues were extremely difficult to negotiate, while the other two were less contentious.

In early September 2005, Washington and New Delhi set up a joint working group, headed by Undersecretary Nicholas Burns and Foreign Secretary Shyam Saran, to discuss the separation plan. At the time, US non-proliferation officials had sketched an outline where any reactor providing power to India's electricity grid would be classified as a civilian facility and, according to the contamination principle, all upstream and downstream facilities linked to that reactor would also be considered as civilian facilities. Thus, they categorized almost all of India's reactors and related facilities as civilian, and the US provided India's government with a non-paper outlining this position.[2] India's government rejected it on the grounds that, as per the July 2005 Joint Statement, India, rather than the US, would determine the separation plan.

US–India talks on 21–22 October focused on a timeline for the separation plan.[3] New Delhi stated that its export control commitments in the Joint Statement were sufficient for Congress to approve nuclear cooperation with India and, after such congressional approval, it would proceed with the phased separation of its military and civilian facilities. US officials stressed that New Delhi should first present a credible separation plan, which would then allow Congress to authorize nuclear cooperation with India. They noted that the Bush administration did not seek expedited congressional action by attaching civilian nuclear legislation as a rider to a larger unrelated bill. Instead, it opted for congressional hearings and a broad debate to increase congressional support for the nuclear agreement. It expected India's separation plan to be finalized by late 2005, which would then 'allow us to refer legislation to Congress by early 2006', so that such legislation could be approved ahead of President Bush's visit to India.[4] However, negotiations for India's separation plan took longer than the Bush administration expected.

In their 21–22 December talks, Washington and New Delhi discussed India's draft separation plan. New Delhi intended to send two messages to Washington via this plan: that its list of civilian nuclear facilities was long enough to satisfy the more realistic sections of the non-proliferation community; and that this would enable the Bush administration to proceed with congressional action. India's government had undertaken much internal discussion in shaping this plan and had taken positions opposed by the Indian nuclear establishment.[5] Still, India kept a majority of its power reactors outside the civilian list. Washington then believed that New Delhi had taken an extreme position and that it had not fully debated its stand internally, particularly because it did not satisfactorily explain why it kept so many reactors outside the civilian list.[6] Washington then rejected India's proposal for being neither credible nor defensible on non-proliferation grounds.

US–India talks on 19–21 January 2006 failed to advance the separation plan. By early February, New Delhi had also hardened its position on the breeder reactor, as discussed later. US officials then held the view that India needed to do much more to make its separation plan defensible to both the administration and to Congress. Consequently, they did not expect the separation plan to be finalized before the president visited India.[7] However, because of the importance of this visit, the administration was willing to send Undersecretary Burns to India if he could finalize the separation plan. Further, the president desired more certainty about the outcome of his India visit, and Undersecretary Burns' talks would enable the administration to determine whether it could announce a breakthrough on civilian nuclear cooperation or whether it should focus on other issues during the presidential visit.

India's government then provided Washington with proposals for moving forward.[8] Washington responded to these during Undersecretary Burns' 23–24 February talks in India. Still, the two sides did not reach an agreement. US officials noted that 'both of us want to complete these negotiations but there are still some differences between us and those need to be worked out' (rediff.com, 2006). Similarly, alluding to unresolved issues, Prime Minister

Singh noted in his 27 February statement to the Parliament that 'negotiations are currently at a delicate stage...we are not underestimating the difficulties that exist in these negotiations'.

US officials then suggested a compromise that they assumed New Delhi would accept, but when they arrived in India on 1 March, the US ambassador informed them that New Delhi had rejected the compromise.[9] US negotiators accordingly informed the president that no agreement appeared possible, but the president asked the negotiators to work out a solution, and the US and Indian national security advisors then brokered a further compromise. Thus, National Security Advisor Hadley, along with Undersecretary Burns, discussed the outstanding issues with their Indian counterparts until past midnight on 1 March. Hadley then suggested a solution to the contentious fuel supply issue. The two sides met again on the morning of 2 March to finalize this item. They thereby completed a separation plan covering the five main negotiating issues.[10]

Power Reactors

In its September 2005 non-paper, Washington had placed almost all of India's 22 power reactors (that is, 16 Indian-built reactors that were outside safeguards and six imported reactors that were under safeguards, as shown in the Appendix) on the civilian list. Indian officials suspected that Washington wanted 16–18 power reactors on the civilian list, though Washington simply suggested that New Delhi place 'a majority' of its reactors on that list (Kessler, 2007).

In its December 2005 draft plan, New Delhi offered to place just 10 reactors under safeguards, but Washington rejected this position. New Delhi then offered to safeguard 12 and, by late February, 14 of its power reactors, a number previously considered by the BJP government.[11] Washington then accepted this position that placed two-thirds of India's existing reactors, as well as all of its future civilian reactors, under safeguards.[12]

The Cirus Reactor

India's nuclear establishment had used plutonium from the Canadian-supplied Cirus reactor for its 1974 nuclear test. The Cirus reactor was then kept outside safeguards and, by the mid-2000s, had produced plutonium sufficient for 25–30 nuclear weapons (which was an estimated 25–30 per cent of India's weapons-grade plutonium at the time). India's December 2005 draft separation plan excluded the Cirus reactor from the civilian list.

In January 2006, US and Indian negotiators considered three options for the Cirus reactor. First, New Delhi could keep this reactor outside safeguards if Canada agreed to this position. Second, India could place the Cirus reactor under safeguards, but would keep outside safeguards the weapons-grade plutonium previously produced by Cirus. Third, Washington proposed that New Delhi could make a positive non-proliferation gesture by shutting down Cirus and, in return, India would retain the plutonium produced by Cirus. In February, both sides agreed to this option and New Delhi committed to shutting down Cirus by 2010.

The Breeder Reactor

India's breeder reactor represented the second stage of its three-stage nuclear power program. India had begun constructing a 500 MW breeder reactor in 2004 and after this was completed, it planned to build four additional such reactors by 2020–25. Since the breeder reactors were intended for India's electricity grid, they were, in this sense, civilian reactors. Further, each breeder could, under certain conditions, produce weapons-grade plutonium sufficient for 20–30 nuclear weapons annually (this issue is discussed in the Appendix). US negotiators wanted these reactors to be placed under safeguards.

India's December 2005 draft separation plan kept the breeder reactor outside safeguards. During the 21–22 January 2006 talks, Washington formally asked New Delhi to safeguard the breeder (Varadarajan, 2006a). Washington would not accept New Delhi's position that the breeder was a research and development program. It argued that there was nothing distinctive about fast breeder technology and that Japan had placed its Joyo experimental breeder reactor and Monju prototype breeder reactor under safeguards using non-sensitive advanced verification systems.

New Delhi responded that the Joint Statement placed it on par with 'countries with advanced nuclear technology, such as the United States', and therefore India could not be compared with Japan; that the breeder reactor was less important for Japan's nuclear energy mix than it was for India's; and that inspections would hinder ongoing research on the breeder.

US and Indian negotiators then considered a compromise. Ahead of their 23–24 February talks, they discussed keeping the breeder reactor outside safeguards for about seven years. Washington noted that New Delhi could work on the breeder unhindered by inspections for that long because the reactor was expected to become operational around 2010 and it would not produce fissile material requiring inspections for a further two years.[13] In the 23–24 February talks, Washington again pressed the issue and pointed out that if India kept the breeder outside safeguards, then its nuclear scientists would find it difficult to participate in the Global Nuclear Energy Partnership program.[14]

India's nuclear establishment, however, strongly opposed safeguarding the breeder, and India's government eventually accommodated its position. New Delhi still made one concession to Washington: it agreed to safeguard its future civilian breeder reactors, though the decision to categorize these as civilian remained India's alone. In his 2 March press conference, Undersecretary Burns noted the importance of this Indian commitment: he called attention to 'a comprehensive agreement that would place the breeder reactors in the future – future civilian breeder reactors – under safeguards'.[15]

Safeguards and Fuel Supply Assurances

The July 2005 Joint Statement had not specified whether safeguards on India's civilian nuclear facilities would be permanent. New Delhi initially sought non-permanent safeguards that were similar to those for the nuclear weapons states. Reflecting this position, DAE Secretary Anil Kakodkar noted that 'nuclear weapon states do place their civilian facilities under the Voluntary Safeguards Agreement of the IAEA. We will do the same' (Subramanian, 2005b). This, however, would enable India to import fuel or technology for a facility and subsequently withdraw the facility from safeguards. US negotiators therefore wanted India to accept standard IAEA safeguards that would apply in perpetuity.

Indian officials then sought to resolve the safeguards issue by linking it with fuel supplies. India made this linkage for two reasons. First, it could not accept safeguards on its reactors if fuel supplies to these reactors were interrupted. Second, it sought to prevent a repeat of the Tarapur experience and to ensure that future operations of its reactors would not be disrupted by fuel supply suspensions. New Delhi outlined this position in December 2005, stating that if there was a guaranteed lifetime supply of fuel for its reactors, India could accept permanent safeguards.[16] Yet, the US did not traditionally provide lifetime fuel assurances to other countries and US officials argued that India could always find fuel suppliers on the international market.[17]

The safeguards issue remained unresolved in January and February 2006. Reflecting its importance to the US, President Bush mentioned it in his 22 February speech at the Asia Society, stating that 'India first needs to bring its civilian energy programs under the same international safeguards that govern nuclear power programs in other countries' (Asia Society, 2006). Secretary Rice similarly stated, on 28 February, that 'the one thing that is absolutely necessary is that any agreement would assure that once India has decided to put reactors...[under] safeguards, that it remains permanently under safeguards' (The White House, 2006a). On the other side, Prime Minister Singh announced in the Parliament that India sought guarantees on uninterrupted fuel supplies. In the end, while US officials were unwilling to concede ground on fuel supplies, President Bush accepted New Delhi's position. In eight hours of talks on 1 and 2 March, the US and Indian national security advisors reached a settlement on the issue.

Under a compromise, Washington offered fuel supply assurances for India's safeguarded reactors through three mechanisms: a bilateral Section 123 Agreement; a three-party agreement between the IAEA, India, and the US; and via a group of friendly supplier countries such as Russia, France, and the UK, who would supply fuel to India in case of any dispute in the other two mechanisms. If none of these mechanisms worked, the separation plan also provided for 'corrective measures that India may take to ensure uninterrupted operation of its civilian nuclear reactors in the event of disruption of foreign fuel supplies'.[18]

In return, India accepted that 'In light of the above understandings with the United States [on fuel supply assurances]', it would negotiate a safeguards agreement 'to guard against withdrawal of safeguarded nuclear material from civilian use at any time [that is, it would accept fallback safeguards]', and in addition, 'India will place its civilian nuclear facilities under India-specific safeguards in perpetuity'. Significantly, while New Delhi committed to safeguards in perpetuity, it insisted on, and Washington accepted, the term 'India-specific'. This meant that India's safeguards would be slightly different from standard IAEA safeguards because they accommodated India's specific position that permanent safeguards would be linked with fuel supply assurances.

Other Nuclear Facilities

India operated several nuclear facilities beyond its reactors. It had an enrichment plant at Mysore, three reprocessing facilities, and other upstream and downstream facilities. Washington's September 2005 non-paper counted many of these as civilian and when India's December 2005 draft separation plan placed these outside the civilian list, Washington pressed New Delhi to keep them under safeguards.

The US and India eventually reached a compromise on the issue. New Delhi kept its enrichment plant outside safeguards. It also kept its reprocessing plants at BARC and Kalpakkam outside safeguards. However, as per the existing practice, it placed the Tarapur reprocessing plant under safeguards when it operated in the campaign mode (that is, when it reprocessed materials derived from imported fuel). In addition, India safeguarded a few upstream facilities (three of its seven heavy water production plants as well as the Nuclear Fuel Complex at Hyderabad) and some downstream facilities (the spent-fuel storage pools that were located away from the Tarapur and Rajasthan reactors). It also declared nine research facilities as civilian but irrelevant to safeguards.

Finally, Washington sought to limit the transfer of personnel between India's civilian and military programs. New Delhi argued that this was not practical and could not be monitored in a way acceptable to its scientists, and Washington then acquiesced to New Delhi's position.

In summary, India's eventual separation plan had relatively low-to-moderate non-proliferation provisions: it represented an A6 arrangement shown in Table 4.1 and Figure 2.1. It had relatively moderate non-proliferation provisions on two issues (the number of power reactors under safeguards and the Cirus reactor), low-to-moderate non-proliferation provisions on one issue (permanent safeguards linked with fuel supply assurances), and low non-proliferation provisions on two issues (the breeder reactor and safeguards for other nuclear facilities). Such a separation plan was the only arrangement that stayed within both the US and Indian win-sets, which were shaped by domestic politics.

Table 4.1 Alternative Arrangements for India's Separation Plan

Type	Example	Issues and Non-proliferation Provisions
A1	Very strong non-proliferation position	*Very high non-proliferation provisions on all issues*
A3	Strong non-proliferation position raised in congressional hearings	*High non-proliferation provisions on all issues*
A4	Closer to the US September 2005 non-paper	*High non-proliferation provisions on about half and moderate provisions on the other half of the issues*

(Continues)

Table 4.1 Alternative Arrangements for India's Separation Plan (*Continued*)

Type	Example	Issues and Non-proliferation Provisions
A5	Balance between the US non-proliferation and strategic perspectives	*Moderate non-proliferation provisions on all issues*
A6	March 2006 separation plan	*Moderate non-proliferation provisions on about half and low provisions on the other half of the issues*
		*Safeguards for 14 power reactors (moderate)
		**Cirus shut down (moderate)
		***Breeder outside, but future breeders under, safeguards (low)
		****Permanent IAEA safeguards but India-specific (moderate)
		*****Significant fuel supply assurances and corrective measures (low)
		******21–40% of other facilities under safeguards (low).
A7	Closer to India's December 2005 and January 2006 draft plans	*Low non-proliferation provisions on the issues*
A9	Ideal position of India's nuclear establishment	*Very low non-proliferation provisions on all issues*

Notes: The non-proliferation provisions are coded from very high to very low as follows:

1. *Number of power reactors under safeguards: 22 (very high); 18–20 (high); 14 (moderate); 10 (low); six (that is, only the imported) (very low).

2. **Cirus reactor: shut down and all (very high) or most of (high) its previously produced fissile material sequestered; shut down (moderate); operating but under partial safeguards (low); no constraints (very low).

3. ***Breeder reactor: All breeders under safeguards and research and development information disclosed (very high); existing and future breeders under safeguards (high); existing breeder outside safeguards for only 6 years (moderate); existing breeder outside, but future breeders under, safeguards (low); no constraints (very low).

4. ****Safeguards: Permanent standard IAEA safeguards and the Additional Protocol (very high); permanent standard IAEA safeguards (high); permanent IAEA safeguards but India-specific (moderate); permanent safeguards but conditional (low); voluntary safeguards (very low).

5. *****Fuel Supply Assurances: In the event of an Indian nuclear test, immediate termination of fuel supplies (very high); no fuel supply assurances and no corrective measures (high); fuel supply assurances but no corrective measures (moderate); significant fuel assurances and corrective measures (low); extensive fuel supply assurances and strong corrective measures (very low).

6. ******Percentage of other facilities under safeguards: over 80% (very high); 61–80% (high); 41–60% (moderate); 21–40% (low); less than 20% (very low).

US Domestic Politics

Bureaucratic factors, legislative politics, and domestic mobilization influenced the US position on India's separation plan. First, in internal bureaucratic debates, the senior-most policymakers were willing to make non-proliferation concessions to advance talks with India, thereby enlarging the win-set. Second, Congress would not approve a separation plan with relatively low non-proliferation provisions, thus reducing the win-set. Third, substantial mobilization by non-proliferation groups heightened congressional awareness of the non-proliferation issues, thereby further reducing the win-set. At the same time, mobilization by advocates reinforced the administration's broader strategic case for the civilian nuclear agreement, enlarging the win-set. This enabled the Bush administration to accept an Indian separation plan that had low-to-moderate rather than moderate or high non-proliferation provisions.

Bureaucratic Factors

Bureaucratic factors affected Washington's position on the separation plan in two ways. First, non-proliferation specialists were adequately represented in the US negotiating team.[19] This enabled them to influence the US position on power reactors and safeguards. Thus, they influenced early discussions on India's power reactors. When the Joint Statement was announced in July 2005, these specialists noted that it was a significant opportunity to thoroughly separate India's civilian and military nuclear programs. By September 2005, they drafted a non-paper that categorized all of India's electricity-producing reactors and related upstream and downstream facilities as civilian. Accordingly, in December, when New Delhi submitted a plan that placed the majority of its facilities outside the civilian list, the US, influenced by this non-proliferation position, rejected it.

In addition, non-proliferation specialists urged that India adopt standard IAEA safeguards that applied in perpetuity. The Bush administration accepted this point: it took a decision, at a deputy committees meeting in February 2006, to focus not on the number of Indian reactors under safeguards but on requiring safeguards in perpetuity, and Washington strongly pressed this issue with New Delhi.

Second, non-proliferation officials were not well represented in senior-level decisions on the separation plan (the highest-ranking non-proliferation official, the undersecretary for arms control and international security, did not participate in these decisions, nor in the negotiations for the separation plan). And, in such decisions, the senior-most foreign policy officials were willing to make three non-proliferation concessions to finalize the separation plan.

First, non-proliferation specialists were concerned about India's fissile material production, but regional and strategic affairs experts argued that New Delhi itself was unclear about its fissile material limits (even though this went against the notion that as NSSP and the US strategic dialogue with India advanced, India would become clearer about its nuclear program).[20] In early 2006, senior US officials then overruled the non-proliferation position of asking New Delhi to place almost all its reactors under safeguards. Undersecretary Burns took the view that this position, and the related idea that India would greatly expand its nuclear stockpile if it retained many reactors outside safeguards, was misplaced (Kessler, 2007, pp. 62–63). Washington thus accepted that about one-third of India's power reactors, as well as its breeder reactor, would remain outside safeguards.

Second, non-proliferation specialists had misgivings about civilian technical knowledge leaking through to India's weapons program, especially because this could result in the US breaching its NPT Article I obligations.[21] They, therefore, sought a physical separation of India's military and civilian programs as well as a separation of Indian personnel having responsibilities for each of these programs. Yet, because of time pressures to finalize a separation plan, senior US officials opted to override these technocratic doubts.

Third, in February 2006, the US negotiating team felt that New Delhi's positions would not enable them to complete a separation plan before the president's visit to India. Still, the president would not give up, and Undersecretary Burns then visited India to advance the talks. Even so, Undersecretary Burns could not broker a compromise and, on 1 and 2 March, the president asked US negotiators to finalize the outstanding issues; the national security advisor then worked with the negotiators to settle these issues.

Overall, the involvement of the president and the senior-most US officials, who gave priority to strategic considerations over non-proliferation concerns, and therefore opted to settle the separation plan so that it would not remain an irritant in future dialogues with India, tilted the bureaucratic balance of power in favour of strategic interests. This kept an Indian separation plan having relatively low-to-moderate non-proliferation provisions within the US win-set. Yet, because of congressional activism, the win-set would not accept a separation plan with relatively low non-proliferation provisions.

Congressional Initiatives

Congress shaped the win-set on the separation plan in five ways. First, Congress resisted the Bush administration's push for quick legislative approval of the civilian nuclear agreement. In the fall of 2005, the administration discussed with influential members of Congress, often individually, where it could best begin congressional action. The senior-most administration officials engaged Congress: Secretary Rice briefed the House and Senate leadership, while Undersecretaries Burns and Joseph testified before the HIRC on 8 September and the SFRC on 2 November. The administration also extensively briefed House and Senate staff.

The administration made a strong strategic, economic, and environmental case for the nuclear agreement. Still, members of Congress expressed concerns about the administration's position. Their overall concern was that Congress was not informed about the Joint Statement ahead of its July 2005 announcement. They added that, even in subsequent months, 'the Congress as a whole have received little, if any, information from the Administration regarding either the details of its ongoing discussions with the Indian Government [on the separation plan], or the legislation it plans to introduce'.[22] As a result, in October, the Republican chairman and senior Democrats on both the Senate and House foreign affairs committees urged Secretary Rice 'to begin substantive discussions with our respective committees as soon as possible' (Brinkley, 2005). In short, Congress would not consider legislation on the nuclear agreement without knowing the details of India's separation plan.

Second, congressional hearings from 8 September to 16 November influenced the separation plan both directly and indirectly.[23] Most directly, congressmen and experts raised technical concerns about the separation plan. They focused on the Cirus reactor, the permanent nature of safeguards, and the status of India's enrichment and reprocessing facilities. Illustrating this, Leonard Spector called for restrictions on the Cirus reactor: 'I would urge the Committee to demand that India's past violations of international nuclear transfer agreements [that occurred when it used plutonium from the Cirus for its 1974 nuclear test] be rectified before the United States will consider renewed nuclear trade, by requiring that India declare Cirus to be a civilian facility and place that reactor, and the plutonium it has produced, under IAEA safeguards.'[24]

Further, calling attention to the importance of permanent safeguards, Robert Einhorn noted that 'consistent with existing U.S. law, such [civilian nuclear] exports should only be permitted to facilities that are under safeguards in perpetuity'.[25] Thus, Congress directly indicated that it would oppose a separation plan which did not cover at least some of these issues.

Non-proliferation experts and congressmen also raised issues outside the separation plan, such as bans on sensitive technology transfers and India's export controls. These made it clear that Congress had broader non-proliferation concerns about the nuclear agreement and therefore indirectly suggested that Congress would oppose a separation plan with weak non-proliferation provisions.

Finally, congressmen and experts discussed the overall costs and benefits of the nuclear agreement. Some experts questioned the Bush administration's argument that the agreement had non-proliferation and economic benefits. Others noted that the nuclear agreement could be improved if India pledged to halt fissile material production. However, regional affairs experts such as Francine Frankel and Ashley Tellis opposed any fissile material freeze because it would trigger substantial opposition in India and derail the nuclear agreement. Also, some experts noted that the nuclear agreement could offer significant strategic benefits: Ashley Tellis mentioned that New Delhi had supported 10 US foreign policy initiatives in the early 2000s and that this illustrated how the US could benefit from a strategic partnership with India.[26] Taking a middle ground, most congressmen and experts took the view that the overall gains from the nuclear agreement and the partnership with India would be modest rather than huge, but that these initiatives were still worth pursuing.[27]

Third, Congress augmented its hearings with some very detailed questions. On 2 November 2005, Senator Richard Lugar submitted 82 questions to the State Department, which released its replies on 17 January 2006. These questions built upon non-proliferation issues raised in congressional hearings. They covered issues in the separation plan (such as the Cirus reactor, India's enrichment facility, and the need for permanent safeguards) as well as issues for subsequent congressional legislation (such as India's relations with Iran, its export control record, its approach to the PSI, and NSG issues).

Fourth, Congress highlighted non-proliferation concerns in a concurrent resolution. On 15 December 2005, Representatives Edward Markey and Fred Upton introduced a bipartisan resolution, House Concurrent Resolution 318, opposing nuclear cooperation with India. The resolution noted that Congress supported strengthened ties with India but still had non-proliferation concerns.

Fifth, congressmen publicly and privately informed India's government about their positions on the nuclear agreement. For example, during his January 2006 visit to India, Senator John Kerry declared his overall support for the nuclear agreement but still sought more details on India's separation plan. He highlighted the importance of India placing a majority of its reactors under safeguards, accepting permanent safeguards, and clarifying its fissile material requirements.[28]

Overall, congressional activism reduced the US win-set, but not excessively. Congress clearly signalled that any separation plan with relatively low non-proliferation provisions would remain outside the win-set. Yet, it also accepted the strategic case for the nuclear agreement and was therefore likely to accept a separation plan with moderate non-proliferation provisions. Domestic mobilization by non-proliferation groups and by an advocacy coalition influenced this congressional position.

Non-proliferation Groups

A well-established non-proliferation lobby mobilized quickly and strongly against the nuclear agreement with India. It made its case in three ways.

First, as noted earlier, non-proliferation experts testified in Congress. Second, non-proliferation groups submitted two sets of questions to Congress (these augmented the 2 November questions submitted by Senator Lugar to the administration). On 18 November 2005, 18 experts sent over 50 questions to Congress.[29] They covered the main issues in India's separation plan, such as the status of the Cirus reactor and the need for permanent safeguards. Here, they observed that 'if other safeguards are contemplated that are not permanent, how would they prevent the diversion of civilian materials or technologies to weapon use once the putative U.S.–India agreement expires or is otherwise terminated'.

Representative Edward Markey incorporated these questions in a 30 November letter to the administration. As mentioned earlier, the State Department responded to these and other questions (that were submitted by Senator Lugar) on 17 January 2006, but its responses did not satisfy the non-proliferation lobby. Accordingly, on 14 February, six non-proliferation experts sent a second set of clarifying remarks and policy suggestions to Congress.[30]

This second set of remarks again raised issues in India's separation plan: the need for India to accept permanent safeguards; shut down the Cirus reactor; and safeguard its existing spent fuel, its breeder reactor, and its enrichment plant. They added that without these provisions, 'the separation plan would allow civilian nuclear power-related facilities to be used to support weapons production and would not be credible from a non-proliferation standpoint'.

Third, non-proliferation groups undertook broader outreach efforts. Illustrating this, the Arms Control Association held press briefings on 16 September 2005 and 15 February 2006, and it published a number of pieces in *Arms Control Today*. The Stimson Center published issue briefs on 31 August, 23 January, and 21 February. A Carnegie Endowment expert outlined 'faulty promises' in the nuclear agreement in a separate issue brief (Perkovich, 2005). And, in a 3 November interview with the Council on Foreign Relations, a non-proliferation expert, Larry Scheinman, noted the non-proliferation drawbacks of the nuclear agreement (Council on Foreign Relations, 2005). Further, in a 15 February letter, nine arms control groups urged members of the House to co-sponsor Concurrent Resolution 318. Finally, a 27 February letter from the National Resource Defense Council (NRDC) to Representative Markey pointed out concerns about nuclear cooperation with India.[31]

To summarize, non-proliferation groups drew attention to the need for strong non-proliferation provisions in India's separation plan.

The Advocacy Coalition

An advocacy coalition for the nuclear agreement with India countered the non-proliferation lobby, but only to a small extent, because this coalition had not fully formed in late 2005 and early 2006. At this time, two main groups – USINPAC and the firms hired by the Indian Embassy – lobbied for the nuclear agreement.

USINPAC organized a November 2005 discussion on the nuclear agreement. India's ambassador and several members of Congress attended this discussion. It also pressed for including pro-India voices in congressional hearings.

The lobbying firms hired by the Indian Embassy reached out to both the executive branch and the legislature.[32] Thus, Barbour, Griffith, & Rogers was involved in about 35 meetings and communications with officials from the executive branch and 70 meetings and communications with congressional staff and members of Congress. Venable's meetings focused on the legislature: just three involved officials from the executive branch and about 70 involved the legislature.

Overall, the advocacy coalition reinforced the Bush administration's argument that strategic ties with India were important enough to allow some non-proliferation concessions in the separation plan.

The Press

In 2005 and early 2006, six major US dailies published about 30 pieces on the nuclear agreement with India. About two-thirds of these endorsed the agreement, but most did so with caution and were sensitive to non-proliferation concerns. Specifically, *The Washington Times* and *The Wall Street Journal* largely supported the agreement; *Los Angeles Times* and *The Washington Post* carried pieces both for and against the agreement; and *The New York Times* and *International Herald Tribune* were strongly against the agreement.

Reflecting critical views, *The New York Times* expressed serious concern that 'Washington wants to allow India an end run around the [NPT] treaty's basic bargain' (*The New York Times*, 2005). And, ahead of President Bush's visit to India, it noted that: 'it's a pity that this trip, which should focus American attention on such a rich array of issues, now revolves largely around whether India and America will manage to conclude a nuclear deal that shouldn't have been initiated to begin with' (*The New York Times*, 2006a).

The Washington Post and other papers were generally balanced in their views. The *Post's* neutral-toned editorial noted, on 20 July 2005, that 'The [strategic] gains from this shift [in US policy] could be considerable, but so too could the [non-proliferation] risks' (*The Washington Post*, 2005). On 26 February 2006, it argued that the details of India's separation plan would ultimately determine whether the civilian nuclear agreement had net benefits: 'The Bush administration needs to tell its friends in India that the details of the deal matter – to America's security and India's' (*The Washington Post*, 2006).

To summarize, the media, foreign policy experts, and Congress, all gave reasonably equal consideration to strategic and non-proliferation issues as they debated the nuclear agreement and the separation plan. This helped keep the US win-set wide enough to accommodate an Indian separation plan that did not include strong non-proliferation provisions. Still, the separation plan had to include at least some moderate non-proliferation provisions: a plan with mostly low non-proliferation provisions would have fallen outside the win-set.

India's Domestic Politics

Several domestic factors influenced India's win-set on the nuclear separation plan. First, bureaucratic resistance from India's nuclear establishment reduced the win-set so that any separation plan that safeguarded a large number of reactors remained outside the win-set. Second, opposition from India's leftist and right-wing political parties to the overall nuclear agreement reduced the win-set. Third, the left's strong objections to another issue – the Indian government's aligning with the Bush administration against Iran at the IAEA – further reduced India's win-set. Still, some other factors balanced the opposition. Here, the Indian government's defence of the nuclear agreement, and mobilization by supporters, made the agreement more acceptable within the Congress Party and among its allies in the UPA coalition. These factors helped expand the win-set so that a separation plan with relatively low-to-moderate non-proliferation provisions remained within the win-set.

Bureaucratic Resistance

India's nuclear establishment recognized some positive aspects of the Joint Statement soon after it was announced. For example, it recognized that imported reactors would contribute to India's energy requirements and that imported uranium fuel was cheaper and superior in quality to Indian-supplied uranium.[33] India's government also reached out to the nuclear establishment: in the fall of 2005, it hosted a dinner for senior nuclear scientists. Still, as negotiations on the separation plan advanced, India's nuclear scientists expressed their concerns about the plan in governmental working groups and in the press.

India's government set up two working groups, concerned with strategic and nuclear issues, to outline its nuclear separation plan. The bureaucratic debate within these groups centered around two competing views.[34] India's MEA and the PMO held the political–strategic view that, by implementing the nuclear agreement, India would become recognized as a nuclear weapons state and could then undertake substantial nuclear energy cooperation with the international community. This approach implied making reasonable non-proliferation concessions, such as placing many reactors on the civilian list.

The other view, taken by India's DAE, focused on nuclear-related objectives. The DAE viewed the nuclear agreement largely as a means to obtain reactors and reactor fuel from international suppliers. This view implied placing very few reactors – only those that India could not fuel with its limited uranium capabilities – on the civilian list. It influenced DAE to raise three concerns with India's separation plan.

First, DAE objected to placing the breeder reactor under safeguards. In a 12 August 2005 interview, the DAE secretary noted that 'Any research and development program, we are not going to put under safeguards...The PFBR [breeder] will not come [under safeguards]. The PFBR is a proto-type. Why should it go under safeguards?' (Subramanian, 2005b). In late January 2006, when US negotiators pressed the issue, India's foreign ministry appeared willing to safeguard the breeder (Varadarajan, 2006b, 2007a). The DAE officials then sought to convince the Indian government to protect the research and development integrity of the breeder and they noted the problems of conducting breeder research under international safeguards. However, India's government hesitated to accept the DAE position, and several articles in the Indian press criticized DAE for its stand. In response, in a 6 February interview, the DAE secretary stated that placing the breeder on the civilian list 'will not be in our strategic interest'; he added that this position was based 'both, from the point of view of maintaining long-term energy security and for maintaining the minimum credible deterrent' (Bagla, 2006).

Thereafter, the DAE secretary met India's prime minister; India's government asked the cabinet secretary to consult India's scientists and diplomats; and the DAE secretary met the cabinet secretary (Bagchi, 2006; Gupta and Samanta, 2006; Laxman, 2006). Since the breeder reactor was expected to be operational around 2010, DAE wanted to keep the breeder outside safeguards for a few years beyond 2010. Thus, after internal talks involving India's prime minister, national security advisor, cabinet secretary, DAE representatives, foreign secretary, and ambassador to the US, India's government discussed with Washington ways to keep the breeder reactor outside safeguards for some years after 2010. US and Indian negotiators worked this theme into India's separation plan: India kept its existing breeder reactor outside safeguards but it accepted that future breeder reactors (essentially those that were constructed after 2010) could be placed under safeguards.

Second, DAE sought to keep many power reactors outside safeguards, especially because these would supply plutonium to the breeder that was outside safeguards. This influenced India's December 2005 position of keeping 12 of its 22 power reactors outside safeguards. When Washington pressed New Delhi to place more reactors under safeguards, DAE still insisted on keeping a substantial eight power reactors outside safeguards.

Third, DAE influenced New Delhi's position on permanent safeguards. Given their international orientation, India's MEA and the PMO better understood Washington's stand on India's accepting internationally applicable IAEA safeguards. On the other hand, DAE pressed for exceptions to standard international safeguards and sought India-specific safeguards.[35]

To summarize, resistance from DAE reduced India's win-set so that it could not accept safeguards on the breeder reactor and on eight power reactors, and it could only accommodate India-specific safeguards that were linked to fuel supply assurances.

Political Opposition

India's leftist and right-wing parties opposed the Joint Statement soon after it was announced and they also raised concerns about the separation plan. On the other hand, the Indian government defended the nuclear agreement and secured the support of the Congress Party, thereby balancing the opposition. Three aspects of this domestic political debate should be noted.

First, the BJP criticized the terms of the Joint Statement. In mid-July 2005, just before Prime Minister Singh's departure for Washington, India's government had informed BJP leaders Jaswant Singh, L. K. Advani, and Atal Behari Vajpayee about the US–India negotiations. Still, when they reviewed the Joint Statement, senior BJP leaders opposed it: they initially raised concerns about technical and strategic nuclear issues, and eventually also raised questions about energy issues and the political process.

On nuclear issues, BJP leaders privately expressed concern about any restraints on India's fissile material production and about the Indian government's stand of supporting a FMCT.[36] Publicly, in a 20 July statement, they raised concerns about the costs of civil–military separation, its impact on India's nuclear deterrent, international inspections, their impact on India's nuclear research, and the question of India's nuclear status. Thus, they noted that 'first and the foremost…separating the civilian [nuclear facilities] from the military would be very difficult, if not impossible. The costs involved will also be prohibitive. It will also deny us any flexibility in determining the size of our nuclear deterrent.'[37] They added that India accepting safeguards under an Additional Protocol 'is also fraught with dangers…since it will have to allow international inspectors free access to our nuclear facilities anywhere anytime'. They further noted that 'The Bush administration may have recognized India "as a responsible state with advanced nuclear technology," but it is far from recognizing India as a legitimate and responsible nuclear weapons state'.

In subsequent weeks, the BJP continued to raise these themes; it cited additional points from the press debate (noted later); and it argued that the nuclear agreement would not enhance India's energy security (Sinha, 2005). Finally, just ahead of President Bush's visit to India, the BJP welcomed the visit but raised concerns about the political process by questioning the lack of transparency on the separation plan and on the entire nuclear agreement.

To summarize, India's government had assumed that the BJP would endorse the Joint Statement because it represented a continuation of the BJP's policies from 2001 to 2004. It was surprised by the BJP's opposition, and India's prime minister therefore asked former Prime Minister Atal Behari Vajpayee, through an emissary, why the BJP was jeopardizing the nuclear agreement (Chengappa, 2007). Yet, the BJP maintained its opposition to the agreement.

Second, the left strongly criticized the nuclear agreement. It raised questions about nuclear issues such as restraints on India's research and development (these were different from the BJP's concerns about restraints on India's military nuclear program), energy issues, political process issues, and foreign policy issues concerning the government's aligning with the US against Iran (these were different from the BJP's foreign policy concerns about India's nuclear status).

Thus, on the political process, the left noted that 'the first and central point which needs to be made is the manner [and lack of transparency] in which such a vital issue has been decided with the United States by the UPA government'.[38] And, on research and development, it noted that in any separation plan, 'restrictions will be imposed which are going to hamper the pursuit of an independent nuclear technology policy for peaceful purposes' (*People's Democracy*, 2005a). Further, on energy issues, it asked, 'Has there been any financial accounting, and is nuclear energy the most viable form of energy?' (*People's Democracy*, 2005b). In the end, given these concerns, and the possibility of the left withdrawing support for the government, India's government could not ignore the left's position as it proceeded with the separation plan.[39]

Third, countering the left and the right, India's government defended the nuclear agreement both within the Congress Party and in India's strategic community.

India's prime minister and external affairs minister worked to secure the Congress Party's support for the agreement (Khare, 2005). In late July and early August 2005, a senior government minister informed the Congress

Party president about his reservations with the nuclear agreement. India's external affairs minister then met the minister, who went on to express support for the prime minister. Also, at a Congress Working Committee meeting on 29 July, the prime minister faced tough questions from senior party members, but these same members defended the nuclear agreement in the Parliament. Further, the Congress Party president endorsed the nuclear agreement at a 21 February 2006 meeting of the Congress Parliamentary Party (*The Times of India*, 2006a).

India's government also defended the nuclear agreement in the Parliament. It highlighted energy issues, strategic nuclear issues, and foreign policy issues. Thus, in his 29 July 2005 statement to the Parliament, India's prime minister outlined the basic energy reasons for the nuclear agreement; he clarified that India's strategic weapons program and its nuclear research would not be affected by the agreement; and he noted that, on foreign policy issues, India was being recognized internationally as a responsible nuclear power. In a second statement to the Parliament on 27 February 2006, the prime minister repeated these points and addressed domestic concerns about the separation plan. He affirmed that 'in the Joint Statement, the United States implicitly acknowledged the existence of our nuclear weapons program', and that, under the separation plan, India's three-stage nuclear research program would be unaffected and the breeder reactor would remain outside safeguards.

In addition, India's government publicized the benefits of the nuclear agreement among India's strategic community. In August 2005, the PMO asked an advisory task force, chaired by K. Subrahmanyam, to look into this issue. And, in a 24 October speech at India's major think tank, the Institute for Defence Studies and Analyses, India's foreign secretary defended the nuclear agreement and rejected arguments that India had conceded ground to the US.[40]

To summarize, India's government defended the nuclear agreement and countered opposition from the left and the right. Each side drew upon a very extensive debate in the Indian press.

Domestic Mobilization

Commentators, analysts, scientific experts, and strategic affairs experts extensively discussed three issues in the Indian press. First, in July and August 2005, the press debated the overall costs and benefits of the Joint Statement. Advocates emphasized its foreign policy importance for US–India relations: 'Its significance lies in converting a decades-old intractable issue [that of India's nuclear program] into an area of productive cooperation' (Ravi, 2005). The press also noted the energy benefits of importing reactors and uranium fuel (Ramachandran, 2005; Subramanian, 2005a). Still, opponents questioned India's foreign policy tilt towards the US; they highlighted the perceived unequal nature of the Joint Statement; and they drew attention to the limited role of nuclear power in India's energy sector.[41]

Second, as the US Congress held hearings from September to November, the Indian press argued that US policy statements differed from those made by Indian officials (Bhushan, 2005; Zuberi, 2005). They noted that 'the fact of the matter is that the US has shifted the goal-post [on the terms of the Joint Statement] even further than it was on July 18, 2005. The bar today is much higher' (*Hindustan Times*, 2006).

Third, the press thoroughly discussed India's separation plan. Here, while critics noted the difficulties of any civilian–military separation, prominent experts countered these 'objections to separating civil and military nuclear facilities'; they noted that 'the proposal to divide reactors into two categories – civil and military – was originally made by the [BJP-led] NDA government as it negotiated...the Next Steps in Strategic Partnership with the US' (Subrahmanyam, 2005c).

Analysts also examined the number of reactors India could place under safeguards and whether it could safeguard the breeder reactor. On the number of reactors, some noted that India had enough fissile material for a minimum deterrent and could therefore place almost all its power reactors under safeguards (Rajaraman, 2005; Subrahmanyam, 2005b). Others noted that the overall benefits of the nuclear agreement were sufficient for India to place more reactors under safeguards (*The Times of India*, 2006b). Opposing such views, however, some analysts argued for keeping enough reactors outside the civilian list to ensure the supply of tritium (Karnad, 2005).

On the breeder reactor, some analysts did not object to placing this under safeguards because, although 'there are understandable concerns of intellectual property and trade secrets...it is not the US that will conduct the safeguarding but the IAEA' (Rajaraman, 2006). Others pointed out that, because the breeders would not contribute significantly to India's energy sector for two decades, they could be kept under safeguards (Mohan, 2006b).

Opposing these perspectives, a senior scientist provided detailed technical reasons for keeping key facilities off the civilian list: he noted that eight power reactors were necessary to supply plutonium for the breeder, and a few heavy water plants were needed for these power reactors, and therefore all these facilities should be kept outside safeguards (Gopalakrishnan, 2006a, 2006b). Others offered strategic reasons for keeping key reactors outside safeguards. Here, ex-Prime Minister V. P. Singh noted, 'The strategic interest of the nation lies in the government respecting the concerns of nuclear scientists and in keeping the fast breeder reactors from the purview of the Indo-US nuclear deal' (Singh, 2006). He added that 'If this deal is going to compromise our technological self-reliance and security interests as is being witnessed, it should be straightaway scrapped'.

To summarize, an extensive press debate, both directly and indirectly, influenced India's win-set on the separation plan. The points raised by advocates strengthened the Indian government's case, and thereby helped enlarge India's win-set so that it could accept a separation plan with low-to-moderate non-proliferation provisions. On the other hand, criticism in the press reinforced the bureaucratic and political opposition to many aspects of the separation plan and this reduced India's win-set so that key nuclear facilities remained outside the win-set.

One additional issue affected India's position on the separation plan: its IAEA votes against Iran in September 2005 and February 2006.

The Iran Issue

In mid-2005, the Bush administration urged India's government to vote against Iran at the IAEA. Undersecretary Burns discussed this issue with Indian officials three times in late August and early September. Congressmen also raised the issue in hearings, noting that New Delhi must be seen as 'supporting our efforts to refer Iran's 18 years of violations of the NPT to the UN Security Council. Anything less than full support will imperil the expansion of U.S. nuclear and security cooperation with New Delhi.'[42] Most significantly, President Bush and Secretary Rice took up the issue in their mid-September meetings with India's prime minister, on the sidelines of the UN General Assembly sessions.[43] New Delhi then joined the Western states in voting against Iran, while China, Russia, and many non-aligned countries abstained.[44] Despite significant domestic mobilization against this vote, India's government again voted against Iran at the IAEA meeting on 4 February 2006. At the time, Russia and China declared that they would vote against Iran, and this made it politically less difficult for India's government to also do so.

The Indian press extensively debated the Iran issue. Some analysts supported the Indian government's position, making the case that 'Iran carried on for well over a decade with its clandestine [nuclear] activity', and that Pakistan was linked with this activity, referring to Pakistani scientist A. Q. Khan's nuclear technology transfers to Iran (Subrahmanyam, 2005a).[45] The BJP also highlighted this Pakistani aspect and came out against Iran's nuclear program. However, others criticized the Indian government's position, and they also objected to US congressional remarks that India should vote against Iran on the grounds that these represented external interference in Indian foreign policy. For similar reasons, the Indian press strongly criticized a 25 January 2006 remark by the US ambassador, where he observed that Congress would oppose the nuclear agreement if India did not vote against Iran.

Such domestic mobilization, along with opposition from the left, affected India's position on the separation plan. India's prime minister, defence minister, and foreign secretary had briefed the left, on 28 September 2005, about why they voted against Iran. Still, the left charged that the government's alignment with the US 'violated the [UPA–Left] Common Minimum Program's [understanding about India's] pursuit of an independent foreign policy' (rediff.com, 2005). It also asked the government to not vote against Iran at the next IAEA meeting.[46] Further, the left asked for the recall of the US ambassador after his 25 January 2006 remarks. This very strong opposition from the left placed India's government on the defensive and reduced its win-set. Simply put, by early 2006, India's government did not have the political capital to simultaneously counter the left on the issue of Iran and the nuclear scientists on the issue of keeping many reactors outside safeguards. It eventually went ahead with the IAEA vote against Iran, but it gave in to the scientists by keeping key reactors outside safeguards.

Summing Up

From mid-2005 to early 2006, the US and India sought to advance their strategic partnership and implement the Joint Statement in a number of ways. They discussed issues ranging from agriculture to health to democracy promotion to energy, but they concentrated on advancing the civilian nuclear initiative.[47] To increase congressional support for this initiative, the Bush administration asked New Delhi to take three actions. First, it asked New Delhi to act on relatively low-profile supply-side initiatives such as the

PSI and export controls. Second, it urged New Delhi to vote against Iran at the IAEA. Third, and most fundamentally, it asked New Delhi to outline a credible separation plan, and this issue dominated US–India diplomacy in late 2005 and early 2006.

Domestic political factors shaped the US and Indian win-sets on the separation plan. They somewhat reduced the US win-set so that it excluded a separation plan with low non-proliferation provisions, and they substantially reduced India's win-set so that it excluded a separation plan with even moderate non-proliferation provisions. In the end, both sides compromised on a separation plan with low-to-moderate non-proliferation provisions.

Endnotes

1   Author interview U2, 13 September 2011.
2   Author interview F1, 2 September 2011.
3   The US Embassy, New Delhi, cable, 24 October 2005.
4   This point was made in a statement by Undersecretary Burns at the SFRC, 2 November 2005.
5   The US Embassy, New Delhi, cable, 16 December 2005.
6   Author interview T1, 25 October 2011.
7   Author interview I2, 16 September 2011; author interview U2, 13 September 2011.
8   The US Embassy, New Delhi, cable, 15 February 2006.
9   Author interview D4, 25 October 2011; author interview F1, 2 September 2011; author interview J1, 12 October 2011.
10 Some general underlying principles affected negotiations on these issues. Washington sought firewalls between India's civilian reactors (that is, those connected to its electric power grid) and its military reactors. New Delhi, however, argued that power reactors could be excluded from safeguards if: (a) the safeguards process affected India's strategic programs and 'would impact adversely on India's national security'; (b) safeguards affected research and development programs and were 'prejudicial to the three-stage nuclear program'; and (c) the facilities were 'located in a larger hub of strategic significance'. These two hubs were the Bhabha Atomic Research Centre (BARC), which housed the Cirus and Dhruva reactors and a reprocessing plant, and the Kalpakkam hub that included two power reactors, India's breeder reactor, and a reprocessing plant. These hubs were kept outside safeguards.
11 For a discussion on the BJP government considering safeguards for 70 per cent of India's facilities, see *The Indian Express* (2007c).
12 On a related issue, Washington sought to cap the number of Indian reactors on the military list. New Delhi rejected this approach and retained the right to build new reactors and not classify them as civilian; and the separation plan then noted that for all 'Future Reactors...the Government of India retains

the sole right to determine such reactors as civilian'. Author interview U1, 26 November 2011.

13   Eventually, these projected timelines were delayed and the breeder reactor was subsequently expected to be completed in 2014.

14   The US Embassy, New Delhi, cable, 24 February 2006.

15   These points were made in a press conference, 'Press Briefing by Under Secretary of State for Political Affairs Nick Burns', 2 March 2006, New Delhi, India.

16   The US Embassy, New Delhi, cable, 16 December 2005. Ahead of the December 2005 talks, Indian officials had anticipated disagreements with the US on the questions of non-voluntary safeguards and the perpetual nature of safeguards.

17   Author interview T1, 25 October 2011.

18   See the text of the Indian Separation Plan, 2 March 2006.

19   Non-proliferation interests were represented by the Department of Energy's National Nuclear Security Administration (NNSA) and legal sections, by arms control specialists in the State Department's T-bureau, and by NSC non-proliferation officials, while strategic and regional affairs interests were equally well represented by the State Department's South Asia bureau and by the US Embassy in Delhi.

20   Author interview U3, 11 October 2011.

21   Ibid.

22   This point was made in a statement by Chairman Hyde at the HIRC hearing, 26 October 2005.

23   As noted in Table 2.1, Congress heard testimony from six non-proliferation experts, six regional experts, and one strategic affairs expert at these hearings. Further, congressmen consulted experts outside the hearings. For example, Senator Lugar asked his policy advisory group, co-chaired by Ashton Carter, to assess congressional options that would advance US interests, while Senator Kerry consulted experts such as Robert Einhorn and Joseph Nye.

24   This point was noted in a statement by Leonard Spector at the HIRC, 26 October 2005.

25   This point was noted in a statement at the HIRC, 26 October 2005.

26   Tellis mentioned India's endorsement of the Bush administration's new strategic framework; support for the US initiative to remove the Director General of the Organization for the Prohibition of Chemical Weapons; offering of Indian military bases for the war in Afghanistan; seriously considering sending (though ultimately not sending) an Indian Army division to Iraq; not opposing the US decision to withdraw from the Anti-Ballistic Missile (ABM) Treaty; signing the June 2005 defence agreement with the US; and supporting the US against Iran at the IAEA. See the statement by Ashley Tellis at the HIRC, 26 November 2005.

27   Reflecting this position, Ashton Carter stated that 'when viewed as a nuclear-only deal, it is a bad deal for the United States...But it seems clear that President Bush did not view the India deal through a nuclear-only lens, and neither should we.' See the statement by Ashton Carter at the SFRC, 2 November 2005.

28   Senator Kerry asked Indian officials how large a nuclear deterrent India needed and whether these needs could be satisfied by having fissile material enriched

under IAEA supervision, such as through a partial sequester or an escrow of military nuclear material. Indian officials responded that as India's nuclear power base increased, the percentage of military reactors outside safeguards would decrease, and that, once the FMCT was adopted, the fissile material issue would become irrelevant. The US Embassy, New Delhi, cable, 14 January 2006.

29 For these questions, see a 'Joint Letter from Arms Control and Nonproliferation Experts to Members of Congress: Issues and Questions on July 18 Proposal for Nuclear Cooperation with India', Arms Control Association, Washington, DC, 18 November 2005.

30 For these questions, see 'Clarifying the Record on the July 18 Proposal for Nuclear Cooperation with India', 14 February 2006.

31 For details of the letter, see a press release, 'Coalition Forms to Block President's Granting India a "Dangerous Nuke Loophole"', 27 February 2006.

32 Information compiled by author from database hosted by the Department of Justice under the Foreign Agents Registration Act (FARA).

33 These points were made by the DAE secretary at an Energy Coordination Committee meeting on 6 August (see *Hindustan Times*, 7 August 2005). Beyond these points, Indian nuclear officials acknowledged that India could maximize its energy output by importing reactors and uranium fuel, and that it could benefit from a nuclear safety dialogue, but some officials noted that a joint working group would have to convince Indian skeptics that the benefits from the Joint Statement were greater than the costs. The US Embassy, New Delhi, cable, 22 July 2005.

34 The working groups were staffed by officials from DAE, the MEA, the PMO (which was represented by the NSC secretariat and the principal scientific advisor), the armed forces, and the Defence Research and Development Organisation (DRDO). For the competing views in these groups, see Mohan (2006a).

35 Author interview T1, 25 October 2011.

36 The US Embassy, New Delhi, cable, 26 July 2005.

37 These points were made in a 'Statement by Shri Atal Bihari Vajpayee on the Joint Statement Signed by PM Manmohan Singh and President Bush', 20 July 2005.

38 These points were made in a press statement by the Politburo of the Communist Party of India (Marxist), 21 July 2005.

39 In an interview, left leader Prakash Karat noted that the left 'seriously considered whether to continue the support and the government was told about it'. However, Congress Party officials noted that the CPI(M) politburo had only discussed whether to continue support for India's government, and it had informed the Congress Party of these discussions, but the politburo did not actually call for withdrawing support for the government. See *The Times of India* (2006f).

40 The US Embassy, New Delhi, cable, 24 October 2005.

41 Here, Indian critics also voiced their concerns in the international press; see, for example, pieces by Brahma Chellaney in the *International Herald Tribune* (8 August 2005 and 27 December 2005).

42 These points were made in a statement by Representative Lantos at the HIRC, 8 September 2005.

43 In initial discussions with the US ambassador, Indian officials appeared reluctant to acknowledge US concerns about Iran. The ambassador therefore urged Secretary Rice, in her meetings with India's prime minister and external affairs minister, to 'sketch the real challenges we face in implementing legislative actions [in Congress]' and 'to challenge India to take equally difficult steps on relations with Tehran and separation of India's civil and military nuclear [facilities]'. The US Embassy, New Delhi, cable, 13 September 2005.

44 After Prime Minister Singh's meetings with President Bush, India's external affairs minister, foreign secretary, and ambassador to the US discussed the Iran issue with US officials as well as with India's government. Within the Indian bureaucracy, officials working on the Middle East in the MEA recommended that New Delhi abstain rather than vote against Iran. Further, sections of the Congress Party were concerned about alienating Muslim voters. Still, the external affairs minister convinced his cabinet colleagues to support a vote against Iran.

45 For the broader Indian debate, see a report by the Observer Research Foundation (2005).

46 These points were made in a statement by the left at the UPA–Left coordination committee meeting, 27 October 2005.

47 The US Embassy, New Delhi, cable, 25 January 2006.

CHAPTER FIVE

Persuading Congress

In March 2006, soon after India announced its nuclear separation plan, the Bush administration submitted to Congress a bill that would authorize nuclear cooperation with India. Members of Congress expressed strong reservations about this bill, noting that it was 'so poorly drafted as to cast doubt on the administration's seriousness of purpose'.[1] Congress therefore did not act on the bill, and instead crafted bills with more substantive non-proliferation provisions. The HIRC and the SFRC voted on their respective bills on 27 and 29 June. The House then passed its bill on 26 July, and the Senate followed on 16 November. The House and Senate bills were combined into a conference bill, called the Hyde Act, that Congress approved on 8 and 9 December. President Bush signed the Hyde Act on 18 December.

Persuading Congress was harder than the Bush administration expected for three reasons. First, on political–institutional grounds, Congress had to approve nuclear cooperation with India, but it would not do so until it thoroughly debated and held hearings on the issue. Second, in terms of political power considerations, although Republicans held a majority in Congress, the Bush administration could not convince the House and Senate foreign policy leadership to advance its preferred legislation. Third, mobilization by non-proliferation groups influenced key members of Congress to oppose the administration's original bill. For these reasons, Congress did not accept the March 2006 bill with relatively low non-proliferation provisions.

On the other hand, some countervailing factors also swayed Congress. First, the Bush administration's substantial outreach effort convinced most representatives and senators to support the overall nuclear initiative with India. Second, mobilization by an advocacy coalition reinforced the administration's efforts. For these reasons, Congress approved legislation having moderate but not the strongest non-proliferation provisions.

Finally, India's government influenced the congressional position. Responding to significant domestic mobilization against the House and Senate bills, Prime Minister Manmohan Singh spelled out India's red lines in a 17 August speech to the Parliament. India's government repeatedly informed the Bush administration (which, in turn, informed Congress) that it could not accept legislation having strong non-proliferation provisions. This persuaded Congress to keep 'killer amendments' outside the legislation.

The Legislative Evolution of the Hyde Act

The March 2006 Bill

In late 2005 and early 2006, the Bush administration considered three approaches to advancing nuclear cooperation with India.[2] It initially looked into an executive-level approach that did not involve Congress. However, it rejected this because it recognized that nuclear cooperation was ultimately covered by an existing law (the Atomic Energy Act) and it would have to eventually engage Congress to change this law. It then examined a legislative approach of quickly obtaining a sense of Congress resolution favouring nuclear cooperation with India, but waiting until late 2006 to introduce a bill that amended the Atomic Energy Act. Still, because of the uncertainties involved in deferring the issue to late 2006, the administration rejected this approach and opted for a third approach. This involved advancing nuclear cooperation through a short but specific piece of legislation. The administration then submitted such a bill to Congress in March 2006 (the bill drew upon a draft outlined by NSC staff during the administration's first term).

The administration's short 500-word bill (introduced as House Resolution [HR] 4974 in the House and S 2429 in the Senate) stated that the president could exempt India from Sections 123(a), 128, and 129 of the Atomic Energy Act, and thereby facilitate civilian nuclear cooperation with India, by making a relevant determination.[3] The seven conditions for this determination, drawn from the July 2005 Joint Statement, were:

1. India had a credible plan to separate its civilian and military nuclear facilities;
2. an IAEA safeguards agreement for the civilian facilities had entered into force;
3. India and the IAEA were making progress on an Additional Protocol;
4. India was working with the US towards an FMCT;
5. India was supporting international efforts to prevent the spread of enrichment and reprocessing (ENR) technology;
6. India was adopting strong export controls; and
7. the NSG approved nuclear cooperation with India.

Further, the bill noted that nuclear cooperation would cease 'if the President determines that India has detonated a nuclear explosive device after the date of enactment of this Act'.

The Bush administration's bill entailed a one-step congressional approval process. Once Congress approved the bill, the formal US–India Section 123 Agreement that outlined the terms for nuclear cooperation, and which the Bush administration had yet to negotiate, would become effective without a second congressional vote. It would go into effect automatically unless Congress passed a resolution of disapproval, but the president could veto such disapproval and Congress could only override the veto with a two-thirds vote that would be difficult to attain.

From the One-step to the Two-step Process

Members of Congress raised objections to the Bush administration's one-step bill almost immediately after it was submitted to Congress. In May, Representative Tom Lantos suggested a compromise two-step process. In the first step, Congress would vote on legislation supporting the principle of nuclear cooperation with India. In the second step, after the administration addressed non-proliferation concerns in an eventual Section 123 Agreement with India, Congress would vote again to approve that agreement. However, the vote would take a fast-track approach, similar to that used in trade pacts, where Congress could not introduce amendments.

The administration initially opposed the two-step process. It assumed that it had enough votes to advance its preferred one-step bill, partly because lobbying for the bill had gained momentum and because, by mid-May, the number of co-sponsors for the bill had equalled that for House Conference Resolution 318 (the resolution introduced by opponents of the nuclear agreement). Outlining the administration's position, Philip Zelikow noted on 11 May that 'quite a few Senators and Congressmen in both parties…support the deal [with India]', and that therefore, 'right now, our view is to handle this differently [from Representative Lantos]'.[4] He added that 'the objectives that Congressman Lantos is seeking we think can be attained [with the one-step legislation]'.

In the end, however, the Bush administration acquiesced to the two-step process for four reasons. First, despite much lobbying, the administration's bill did not attract a huge number of co-sponsors. In the Senate, S 2429 had just 10 co-sponsors and all were Republicans. In the House, HR 4974 obtained 41 co-sponsors, but this number was inflated by a large number of co-sponsors (16) from Texas.[5]

Second, congressional staff informed the administration that advancing the one-step proposal largely through Republican votes would alienate Democrats, who could then successfully filibuster the legislation or impede it in the future. This was because Democrats who voted against the one-step legislation would be obliged to disapprove the Section 123 Agreement when this was submitted to Congress; thus, if Democrats gained a majority after mid-term elections, Congress could end up rejecting the Section 123 Agreement.

Third, while a one-step process was risky, a two-step bill was viable for two reasons. First, as it engaged Congress, the administration recognized that congressmen supported the idea of nuclear cooperation with India but sought more details in the legislation, and therefore legislation having such details would be approved. Second, if the administration attained a strong favourable vote in the first step, it was very likely to again prevail in the second-step vote.

Fourth, Democrats and Republicans were both willing to work with the administration. Senator Joseph Biden, the ranking Democrat in the SFRC, asked his staff to adopt a bipartisan approach that would be durable and would not be overturned after mid-term elections. Senator Richard Lugar, the SFRC Chair, also favoured a bipartisan approach.

The two-step process commenced in late June, when Representative Henry Hyde (the HIRC Chair) and Representative Lantos (ranking Democrat on the HIRC) introduced a bill in the House and Senator Lugar introduced a different bill in the Senate. Congressional staff drafted these bills and introduced subsequent amendments based upon three considerations. First, they recognized the overall parameters of the Joint Statement. Second, they still sought stronger non-proliferation provisions in the bills. Third, they sought to ensure that the administration and India's government would not undermine congressional intent on key issues (they therefore sought an NSG decision 'by consensus' so that the administration would not overturn the NSG's standard consensus mechanism; and they sought specific actions in the event of an Indian nuclear test to prevent the administration from overriding the Atomic Energy Act on this item).

Thus, the House and Senate bills sought to address non-proliferation concerns on 10 main issues. First, they sought to ensure that foreign-supplied uranium fuel would not enable India to increase its military fissile material production (issue 1). Relatedly, they wanted India to place all its electricity-producing reactors under safeguards or, going further, place all its reactors under safeguards and entirely halt military fissile material production (these were much stronger versions of issue 1). Second, they aimed to deter an Indian nuclear test by terminating nuclear cooperation if India conducted a nuclear test, preventing the US government and other countries from undermining sanctions on India in the event of a test, and clarifying that nuclear fuel assurances were not intended to help India overcome such sanctions (issue 2). Further, the bills sought to strengthen IAEA safeguards (issue 3); prohibit sensitive ENR technology transfer to India (issue 4); condition nuclear cooperation to India's support for US efforts against Iran (issue 5); condition cooperation to India's export controls (issue 6); uphold the standard procedures of the NSG (issue 7); address spent-fuel issues (issue 8); address other issues such as cooperative threat reduction and end-use monitoring (issue 9); and adopt stronger non-proliferation measures (issue 10). Ultimately, Congress accepted some amendments on these issues but rejected others that were perceived to be 'deal-killers' (Kimball, 2007).

The House

On 26 June, Representatives Hyde and Lantos introduced HR 5682 in the House. On 27 June, the HIRC voted 37–5 to approve it with amendments. On 25 July, the House Rules Committee permitted additional amendments to the bill and, on 26 July, the House accepted some of these amendments and adopted the bill by a vote of 359–68.

HR 5682 was considerably stronger than the March 2006 legislation. This approximately 4,000-word bill had short sections on the sense of Congress

(Section 2) and statements of policy (Section 3) and a 3,000-word section on the president's waiver authority and congressional approval (Section 4).

The sense of Congress section stated that civilian nuclear cooperation with a non-NPT country (rather than with India alone) 'may be in the interest of the United States' if that country demonstrated responsible nuclear behaviour; had a democratic government; adopted strong export controls; and if nuclear cooperation would 'induce the country to give greater political and material support to' US non-proliferation objectives such as 'dissuading, isolating, and if necessary, sanctioning and containing' states seeking nuclear weapons (this was a reference to Iran). It added that 'India meets the criteria' just mentioned.

The statement of policy section covered additional issues. For example, on nuclear testing, it noted that NSG members should terminate nuclear transfers to a recipient if it conducted nuclear tests. And, on export controls, it stated that it was US policy to secure India's participation in the PSI as well as India's 'harmonization [of its export control lists] and adherence to [the] Missile Technology Control Regime, the Nuclear Suppliers Group, the Australia Group, Wassennaar guidelines, and United Nations Security Council Resolution 1540'. (The references to PSI, the Australia Group, and the Wassennaar Arrangement were significant because the Bush administration had not required New Delhi to join these in mid-2005 as a requirement for ending the NSSP initiative.)

Section 4(a) then allowed civilian nuclear cooperation with India by relaxing Sections 123(a), 128, and 129 of the Atomic Energy Act. Section 4(b), the 'Determination by the President', contained the seven items from the March 2006 bill, noting that a presidential determination on these would enable nuclear cooperation with India. It also augmented the March 2006 bill. For example, in response to concerns about 'India-specific' safeguards in India's separation plan, the House bill required safeguards 'in perpetuity in accordance with IAEA standards, principles, and practices (including IAEA Board of Governors Document GOV/1621 (1973))'.[6] On export controls, it specified that New Delhi should not just adopt but also enact and enforce export control laws. Section 4(d) then stated that nuclear cooperation could be terminated 'if India makes any materially significant transfer' of nuclear and missile technology, but with some presidential discretion. And, on NSG approval, the House bill (as well as the Senate bill) noted that any NSG decision on nuclear cooperation with India should be 'by consensus' and that such cooperation should not violate NSG guidelines.

On 27 June, the HIRC strengthened HR 5682 by adopting six of 12 suggested amendments (Squassoni, 2006). These covered issue 1 (by seeking reports that foreign-supplied uranium was not enabling India to increase its military fissile material production); issue 7 (by specifying that the NSG consensus decision should not permit India to bypass the NSG and undertake nuclear commerce with any non-NSG state or other state that did not have full-scope safeguards); issue 8 (by requiring a policy statement and reports on spent-fuel disposal); and issue 9 (by seeking reports on new Indian nuclear facilities). The HIRC also rejected amendments that covered issue 1, stronger versions of issue 1, issue 8, and issue 10.

On 25 July, the House Rules Committee allowed six further amendments but rejected three covering stronger versions of issue 1, issue 10, and issue 5. The issue 5 amendment, introduced by Representatives Markey and Upton, sought a presidential determination on India's actions versus Iran.

On 26 July, the House formally considered six amendments. It passed three by a voice vote, covering sense of Congress items and issue 1 (by asking for reports assessing the relative level of India's fissile material production compared with the previous year). However, it rejected two amendments and a motion. First, on issue 1, it rejected an amendment introduced by Representative Brad Sherman by a vote of 155–268. This amendment required the president to annually certify that, during the preceding year, India had not increased the amount of domestic uranium used in its military program. Second, on a stronger version of issue 1, it rejected an amendment introduced by Representative Howard Berman by a vote of 184–241. This amendment sought to prevent nuclear fuel exports to India until it ceased production of unsafeguarded fissile material. Third, on issue 5, it rejected a motion introduced by Representative Markey by a vote of 192–235. This motion sought to refer the bill back to the House, with an amendment requiring the president to certify that India was actively participating in US efforts against Iran's nuclear program.

To summarize, the House accepted amendments with relatively low and moderate non-proliferation provisions, but rejected those with relatively high non-proliferation provisions.

The Senate

In late June 2006, Senators Lugar and Biden introduced S 3709 in the Senate. On 29 June, the SFRC approved the bill by a vote of 16–2, with amendments.

In July, however, Senator John Ensign put a hold on the bill because of language in Title II (that was not related to nuclear cooperation with India but covered the US' own actions on the IAEA's Additional Protocol). The Senate then adjourned from 3 August to early September and in mid-September, when Senator Ensign removed his hold, Democrats and Republicans could not agree on procedural issues. The Senate therefore did not act on the bill before it recessed on 29 September. It eventually passed the bill on 16 November, during a lame-duck session after congressional elections, by a vote of 85–12.

The approximately 3,000-word Senate bill, and amendments to the bill, contained stronger non-proliferation provisions than the House bill. In particular, it prohibited ENR technology transfers to India with minor exceptions, such as for a multinational project; it sought to better deter an Indian nuclear test; it required the creation of an end-use system that included fallback safeguards; and it sought to ensure US compliance with its NPT obligations.

On 29 June, the SFRC approved S 3709 with two amendments. One, on issue 1, noted that nuclear fuel exports to India should not contribute to increases in India's military fissile material production. The other, on issue 2, introduced by Senator Barack Obama, stated in the sense of Congress section that 'the United States should not seek to facilitate or encourage the continuation of nuclear exports to India by any other party if such exports are terminated under United States law' (such termination would occur if India conducted a nuclear test).

In November, the Senate considered 10 additional amendments and passed five by a voice vote or through unanimous consent. One was a manager's amendment. Two others dealt with issue 1 (seeking reports and analyses of Indian uranium production) and issue 9 (seeking a cooperative threat reduction program involving US and Indian scientists). A fourth, on issue 2, introduced by Senator Obama, aimed to prevent the US government from helping India override sanctions in the event of a nuclear test. It stated that 'It is the policy of the United States that any nuclear power reactor fuel reserve provided to the Government of India for use in safeguarded civilian nuclear facilities should be commensurate with reasonable reactor operating requirements.' A fifth, on issue 5, introduced by Senator Tom Harkin, required the president to determine that 'India is fully and actively participating in United States and international efforts to dissuade, sanction, and contain Iran for its nuclear program consistent with United Nations Security Council resolutions'. This language was different from that in the House amendments introduced by Representative Edward Markey, because it sought Indian action on Iran as per UN Security Council resolutions rather than according to US policy.

The SFRC also rejected five amendments that covered issue 1, stronger versions of issue 1, issue 5, issue 10, and a combination of the stronger version of issue 1 and issue 10.

On issue 1, Senator Russ Feingold introduced an amendment that sought 'determinations by the President that United States nuclear cooperation with India does nothing to assist, encourage, or induce India to manufacture or acquire nuclear weapons or other nuclear explosive devices'.[7] The Senate defeated this amendment by a vote of 25–71.

On the stronger version of issue 1, Senator Jeff Bingaman introduced an amendment that conditioned nuclear cooperation to a presidential determination that 'both India and the United States are taking specific steps to conclude a multilateral treaty on the cessation of the production of fissile materials' and that 'India has stopped producing fissile materials for weapons pursuant to a unilateral moratorium or multilateral agreement'.[8] The Senate defeated this by a vote of 26–74.

On issue 5, Senator Barbara Boxer introduced an amendment that sought 'a certification that India has agreed to suspend military-to-military cooperation with Iran, including training exercises, until such time as Iran is no longer designated as a state sponsor of terrorism'.[9] However, other senators opposed this amendment. For example, Senator Lugar defended India's limited engagement with Iran, stating that 'On a number of occasions the Indian–Iranian military relationship has been greatly exaggerated'.[10] Further, Senator Biden noted that 'this is the hardest piece to swallow... it is not reasonable to assume that India and Iran would not want to have a military relationship where they shared information and/or concerns relative to Pakistan'.[11] The Senate defeated this amendment by a vote of 38–59.

On issue 10, Senator Byron Dorgan introduced an amendment proposing that it was the policy of the US 'to continue to support implementation of United Nations Security Council Resolution 1172 (1998)', a resolution that had condemned India's nuclear tests and required India to adopt several non-proliferation benchmarks.[12] The Senate defeated this by a vote of 27–71.

Finally, Senator Dorgan introduced an amendment that combined stronger versions of issue 1 and issue 10. It required the president to determine that India had placed all its electricity-producing reactors under safeguards. It also required that, like the NPT-defined nuclear weapon states, India join a legally binding nuclear test moratorium, reduce its nuclear weapons stockpile, and agree to nuclear disarmament. It was similar to Representative Barbara Lee's amendment that was rejected by the House Rules Committee. The Senate defeated this by a voice vote.

The Conference Bill

In early December, the House and Senate bills were reconciled into a conference bill. House and Senate staffers combined these in just one day.[13] They worked overnight via e-mail to merge the bills, and then met the next morning to fine-tune the legislation, while administration officials such as Assistant Secretary Stephen Rademaker provided substantive inputs on some issues. On 8 December, the House approved the bill 330–59 and on 9 December, the Senate gave its unanimous consent to the bill.

The 4,200-word conference bill was drafted by beginning with the House bill and adding relevant portions of the Senate bill. It merged the House and Senate bills' statements of policy and sense of Congress sections, and it reconciled differences between the bills on the issues of Iran, ENR technology transfer, and India's export controls. Overall, because it combined the House bill (having relatively low-to-moderate non-proliferation provisions) and the Senate bill (having relatively moderate non-proliferation provisions), it was stronger than both these bills, as shown in Table 5.1. It had relatively moderate non-proliferation provisions overall, with relatively moderate-to-high provisions on five issues, moderate provisions on two issues, and low-to-moderate, low, and very low provisions on three issues.

Table 5.1 Alternative Arrangements for Congressional Legislation

Type	Example	Issues and Non-proliferation Provisions
A1	Even Stronger Hyde Act	*Relatively very high non-proliferation provisions*
		*A4 arrangement
		+ almost all the rejected amendments to HR 5682 and S 3709
A3	Stronger Hyde Act	*Relatively high non-proliferation provisions*
		*A4 arrangement
		+ some of the rejected amendments to HR 5682 and S 3709, so that nuclear cooperation is conditional upon India's signing the CTBT and halting fissile material production

(Continues)

Table 5.1 Alternative Arrangements for Congressional Legislation (*Continued*)

Type	Example	Issues and Non-proliferation Provisions
A4	Enhanced Hyde Act	*Relatively moderate-to-high non-proliferation provisions* *Combination of HR 5682 and S 3709 to include their original strong language regarding India's actions on Iran and India's export controls
A5 (tougher version)	Hyde Act	*Relatively moderate non-proliferation provisions* *Combination of HR 5682 and S 3709, but diluting their original strong language regarding India's actions on Iran and India's export controls
A5 (moderate version)	Senate bill S 3709	*Relatively moderate non-proliferation provisions, but slightly lesser than the Hyde Act* *Two-step process *Adds to and strengthens the House bill on key issues[a]
A6	House bill HR 5682	*Relatively low-to-moderate non-proliferation provisions* *Two-step process * Adds to the March 2006 bill on several issues[b]
A7	March 2006 bill (HR 4974/S 2429)	*Relatively low non-proliferation provisions* *One-step process *Low non-proliferation provisions on the issues
A9	Ideal bill sought by India	*Relatively very low non-proliferation provisions* *Very low non-proliferation provisions on the issues

Notes:

[a] S 3709 added to and strengthened the House bill on issue 2 (via two Obama amendments to deter Indian nuclear testing); issue 4 (through bans on ENR technology transfers); issue 5 (by conditioning cooperation to Indian action on Iran); and issue 9 (with cooperative threat reduction and end-use monitoring programs).

[b] HR 5682 added to the March 2006 bill on issue 1 (by requiring reports on Indian fissile material); issue 2 (by discouraging NSG countries from nuclear cooperation with India if it conducted nuclear tests); issue 3 (by requiring IAEA safeguards in perpetuity as per IAEA document GOV/1621); issue 5 (via a statement of policy on India's actions toward Iran); issue 6 (by linking nuclear cooperation to India's export controls); issue 7 (by requiring an NSG decision by consensus); issue 8 (through reports on India's spent-fuel disposal); and issue 9 (through reports on new Indian nuclear facilities).

On issue 1 (India's fissile material production), it had relatively low non-proliferation provisions. Yet, these were slightly enhanced by the four accepted amendments to the House and Senate bills that sought reports on India's uranium use and fissile material production.

On issue 2 (deterring an Indian nuclear test), it had relatively moderate-to-high non-proliferation provisions. It retained the language on terminating nuclear cooperation if India tested a nuclear device, and it retained, in its statement of policy section, the amendments introduced by Senator Obama that sought to prevent the US and other countries from assisting India in overriding sanctions.

On issue 3 (safeguards), it had relatively moderate-to-high non-proliferation provisions because it combined the enhanced moderate provisions of both the House and Senate bills. It retained language from the House bill requiring safeguards in perpetuity as per IAEA document GOV/1621 and it retained language from the Senate bill on fallback safeguards.

On issue 4 (ENR technology transfers), it had relatively moderate provisions. It retained language from the Senate bill that banned the US from transferring such technology to India, and which also mentioned, in its statement of policy, that the US would work with the NSG to further restrict such transfers.

On issue 5 (Iran), it had relatively moderate-to-high non-proliferation provisions which somewhat diluted the relatively high provisions of the Senate bill (New Delhi had opposed those provisions). Specifically, the conferees changed the Senate bill's amendment introduced by Senator Harkin – which required a presidential determination that India was acting as per UN Security Council resolutions on Iran – to a reporting requirement. However, it retained other language on Iran from the sense of Congress and statement of policy sections of the House bill.

On issue 6 (export controls), it had relatively moderate-to-high non-proliferation provisions that somewhat addressed New Delhi's concerns about the slightly stronger language in the House bill. Specifically, the House bill had language on terminating nuclear cooperation 'if India makes' a materially significant transfer of nuclear or ballistic missile technology. The conferees modified this to give New Delhi and the president some flexibility. Here, they added an exception if the transfer: (a) 'was made without the knowledge of the Government of India'; (b) 'the Government of India did not own, control, or direct the Indian person that made the transfer'; and (c) 'the President certifies to the appropriate congressional committees that the Government of India has taken or is taking appropriate judicial or other enforcement actions against the Indian person with respect to such transfer'.

On issue 7 (NSG issues), it had relatively moderate provisions. It retained the language from the House bill and excluded the moderate-to-high provisions from the Senate bill that had sought to prevent Indian nuclear cooperation with non-NSG countries.

On issue 8 (spent-fuel issues), it had relatively low-to-moderate provisions. It retained the House bill's language seeking reports on Indian spent fuel.

On issue 9 (other issues), it had relatively moderate-to-high provisions. It combined the Senate bill's relatively moderate provisions for a cooperative threat reduction program and an end-use program and the House bill's amendment that sought reporting on new Indian nuclear facilities.

Finally, on issue 10, it had relatively very low non-proliferation provisions: a bill with moderate and strong provisions would have contained the amendments on this issue that were rejected by the House and Senate.

Overall, the Hyde Act had relatively moderate non-proliferation provisions and represented an A5 arrangement shown in Table 5.1.

The Win-set and the Signing Statement

Congress' win-set on legislation authorizing nuclear cooperation with India is best understood by referring to Figure 2.1 (Chapter 2): the win-set began just after point 3 and extended to point 6 in this figure. The Bush administration initially assumed that, because Republicans held a majority in Congress, the win-set extended to point 7 so that it could accept an A7 arrangement (that is, the March 2006 bill with relatively low non-proliferation provisions). Yet, influenced by non-proliferation concerns, Congress reduced the win-set to point 6. The A6 arrangement of the House bill, the A5 arrangement of the Senate bill, and the A5 arrangement of the Hyde Act, all remained within the congressional win-set. At the same time, the administration and the India lobby successfully pushed the inner boundary of the win-set outward, from point 0 to point 3. Thus, any strong A2 and A3 bills (that contained the rejected amendments) remained outside the US win-set. An A4 arrangement that fully combined the House and Senate bills still remained within the win-set, but the administration persuaded Congress to dilute this into an A5 arrangement to accommodate India. New Delhi, however, sought even more assurances and the president accommodated it through a signing statement.

The president's 18 December 2006 signing statement declared that the administration would consider two sections of the Hyde Act as advisory rather than binding. These were Section 103, the statements of policy section containing items of concern to India, and Section 104(d)(2), which had a statement of policy that nuclear transfers to India be consistent with

NSG guidelines (the administration objected to this on the grounds that it delegated power to an international body, that is, the NSG).

Analyzing the Votes

An analysis of votes in the House and Senate, shown in Tables 5.2 and 5.3, reveals five main themes. First, among all representatives and senators, large majorities favoured the final bills, but smaller majorities voted against the amendments. In short, while most representatives and senators favoured the nuclear agreement with India, a substantial number were still sensitive to non-proliferation concerns and sought to incorporate these in amendments.

Second, many Democrats took a free vote on the amendments to affirm their non-proliferation credentials. The majority of Democrats voted for the amendments to the House and Senate bills (that is, they took a more pro-non-proliferation and less pro-India approach). As shown in Table 5.2, 66 per cent, 74 per cent, and 85 per cent of the Democrats voted for the three main amendments to the 26 July House bill. Also, as shown in Table 5.3, 58 per cent, 58 per cent, 56 per cent, and 64 per cent voted for the four main amendments to the 16 November Senate bill.

Third, Republicans voted almost entirely in favour of the administration's preferences (only 11 per cent, 16 per cent, and 10 per cent voted for the three House amendments and 0 per cent, 0 per cent, 0 per cent, and 16 per cent voted for the four Senate amendments).

Table 5.2 House Votes, July 2006

	Yes/ No	Sherman Amendment	Berman Amendment	Markey Motion	HR 5682
Democrats	Y	130	146	170	140
	N	67	52	29	59
	% Y	66	74	85	70
Republicans	Y	25	37	22	219
	N	201	189	206	9
	% Y	11	16	10	96
Total	Y	155	183	192	359
	N	268	241	235	68
	% Y	37	43	45	84

Source: Data compiled by author from congressional voting records.

Table 5.3 Senate Votes, November 2006

	Yes/ No	Bingaman Amendment	Dorgan Amendment	Feingold Amendment	Boxer Amendment	HR 5682/S 3709
Democrats	Y	26	27	25	29	32
	N	19	18	19	15	12
	%Y	58	58	56	64	71
Republicans	Y	0	0	0	9	53
	N	54	53	52	44	0
	%Y	0	0	0	16	96
Total	Y	26	27	25	38	85
	N	73	71	71	59	12
	%Y	26	28	26	39	88

Source: Data compiled by author from congressional voting records.

Fourth, the issue of Iran resonated strongly with both Republicans and Democrats. Thus, a substantial 45 per cent of the House, and an overwhelming 85 per cent of the Democrats, voted for the Markey motion on this issue; had some 22 per cent of the Republicans, that is, slightly more than the 16 per cent that had supported Berman amendment, also voted for the Markey motion, it would have passed. (In the end, Republicans sided with the administration and only 10 per cent voted for the motion.) In the Senate, an equally substantial 39 per cent of the senators (including 64 per cent of the Democrats and 16 per cent of the Republicans) voted for the Boxer amendment on the Iran issue.

Fifth, while interest group lobbying, Indian American voting power, and Indian American financial contributions influenced members of Congress to advance the legislative process when it was stalling, these mechanisms of influence do not correlate well with the actual votes of most congressmen. Thus, congressmen who were subject to these mechanisms did not have a more pro-India vote than congressmen who were not subject to these mechanisms.[14]

US Domestic Politics

A number of factors influenced the US win-set on legislation authorizing nuclear cooperation with India. The arguments made by opponents and supporters in congressional hearings reduced and expanded the win-set, respectively; mobilization by the non-proliferation lobby reduced the win-set, while mobilization by the advocacy coalition and supportive pieces in the press expanded it; and most fundamentally, the administration's substantial engagement of Congress expanded the win-set. Thus, lobbying by the administration and by supporters enabled the Hyde Act to fall within the win-set and ensured that killer amendments remained outside the win-set.

Congressional Hearings

From March to July 2006, Congress held five hearings on the nuclear agreement. Senior administration officials, along with eight non-proliferation experts, two regional affairs experts, three strategic affairs experts, one business expert, and one environmental expert testified at these hearings.[15] The administration outlined the benefits of the nuclear agreement and defended its preferred one-step legislation. Some experts endorsed the administration's position, but many congressmen and experts raised three sets of concerns.

First, congressmen expressed major concerns about the lack of consultation with Congress, about the one-step process, and about India's separation plan. Reflecting these concerns, at the 26 April SFRC hearing, Senator Lugar noted that the administration had not explained several items in India's separation plan, including the terms 'India-specific safeguards', India's 'corrective measures', the US 'assurances regarding fuel supply', and 'a strategic reserve of nuclear fuel'.[16] He added that Congress would have to clarify these and close any loopholes through appropriate legislation.

Second, congressmen and experts highlighted non-proliferation weaknesses with the March 2006 legislation, covering issues 1–10 outlined previously. The following examples illustrate the debate on these issues.

On issue 1, concerning foreign-supplied fuel enabling India to expand its military fissile material production, experts noted: 'Congress should also consider requiring the President [to] certify annually that no form of civil nuclear assistance from the United States to India is being used directly or in any other way to assist India's nuclear weapons program. If such assistance were to occur, it would constitute a violation of one of our own key Nuclear Non-Proliferation Treaty obligations.'[17]

To take another example, on issue 2, that of dissuading an Indian nuclear test, Robert Einhorn noted that Congress should probe, 'whether an Indian nuclear test explosion – or some other Indian actions – would trigger the termination of U.S. nuclear cooperation. A related question is whether the U.S. would be committed to assist India in obtaining reactor fuel from third parties if U.S. fuel supplies had to be cut off.'[18]

Experts also raised additional non-proliferation issues such as India's actions on Iran, bans on ENR technology transfers, and loopholes in the March 2006 legislation on waiving Section 129 of the Atomic Energy Act.

Third, Congress debated the overall costs and benefits of the nuclear agreement. On non-proliferation issues, experts questioned the administration's argument about the non-proliferation benefits. For example, Robert Gallucci noted, 'There is no reason why we should attach any positive value to India's willingness to submit a few additional nuclear facilities of its choosing to international safeguards, so long as other fissile material producing facilities are free from safeguards.' He added that 'the other elements of the deal that are supposed to contribute to its nonproliferation value were in place before the deal was struck'.[19]

On the energy and environmental benefits of the nuclear agreement (these are discussed in the Appendix), experts had mixed views. In statements at the SFRC on 26 April, Gary Milhollin noted, 'The administration also argues that India has a great need for nuclear power to meet its electricity demand. This too is far-fetched.'[20] Ashton Carter similarly noted that 'the arithmetic does not support the case that nuclear power will add up to make the critical difference for India, though it can and should play a role'. On the other hand, supporting the environmental case, David Victor noted, 'Put very simply, this deal makes it possible to save something on the order of 100 million tons of carbon dioxide per year by the year 2020'. Similarly, William Perry endorsed the environmental and energy argument: 'The importance of nuclear power to India and to the global environment were convincingly outlined by Dr. David Victor in his opinion-editorial piece in the *International Herald Tribune* on 17 March. I associate myself with Dr. Victor's views on this subject.'

The administration and experts also called attention to economic benefits. Here, Secretary Rice stated that the nuclear initiative could create 3,000–5,000 new direct jobs, and about 10,000 to 15,000 indirect jobs, for US nuclear vendors (these numbers were derived from a report by a nuclear industry expert). And Michael Gadbaw noted that 'U.S. nuclear suppliers can thrive in the Indian market'.[21]

Overall, many experts endorsed the nuclear agreement despite its proliferation risks. For example, Stephen Cohen noted, 'On balance, the initiative should be welcomed. I have argued in print for a non-proliferation half-way house since 1990 – an admittedly imperfect response to an imperfect situation, but far better than the status quo.'[22] Richard Falkenrath and Ashton Carter both noted that congressional rejection of the nuclear agreement would hurt ties with India. And Ron Lehman stated: 'I urge that no "killer" conditions be placed on this bold initiative, but Congress should, periodically in the years ahead, review the Indo-U.S. strategic partnership and its vital nonproliferation element.'[23]

To summarize, while opponents raised significant non-proliferation concerns, supporters highlighted the strategic desirability of the nuclear agreement.

Non-proliferation Groups

Non-proliferation experts made extensive efforts to strengthen non-proliferation provisions in congressional legislation. They directly conveyed their concerns to a few representatives and senators such as Senator Obama, though they could not meet a large number of congressmen because of resource limitations; further, they could not make politically related appeals to members of Congress because of their status as non-profit groups.[24] They also undertook broader outreach initiatives.

The most active group, the Arms Control Association (ACA), highlighted non-proliferation concerns in many ways. In March 2006, it created a resource website providing information on the nuclear agreement for both specialists and a wider audience. On 10 March, it released a paper that countered the administration's 9 March fact sheet on the nuclear agreement. And it held press briefings on 20 June, ahead of the House and Senate mark up of legislation, and on 14 November, ahead of the Senate vote. ACA also served as a point of contact for letters written by experts. On 24 July, 12 non-proliferation experts released 'An Open Letter to Mohammed El Baradei'; this responded to IAEA Director General El Baradei's 14 June opinion-editorial in *The Washington Post*. On 12 September, 16 non-proliferation experts sent a letter to senators urging strong non-proliferation measures in Senate legislation.

Other groups added to the debate. The Stimson Center released 10 issue briefs between March and December 2006, outlining major non-proliferation concerns with the nuclear agreement. Experts at the Carnegie Endowment also critiqued the agreement. The Institute for Science and International Security (ISIS) issued a report on 24 July showing that Pakistan was expanding its plutonium-production capabilities, and thereby drew attention to a potential nuclear arms race in South Asia. The Federation of American Scientists, on 14 June, released a letter signed by 37 Nobel laureates opposing the nuclear agreement. The Nonproliferation Policy Education Center commissioned pieces and hosted workshops on various aspects of the nuclear agreement. And the International Panel on Fissile Materials argued that the nuclear agreement would contribute to the expansion of fissile material production in South Asia.

In the end, non-proliferation groups increased congressional awareness of not just the main nuclear-related issues but also the issue of Iran, which resonated with both Democrats and Republicans. Yet, stronger provisions on these issues were eventually removed from the Hyde Act because Congress conceded ground to the advocacy coalition.

The Advocacy Coalition

A large 'India lobby' of advocates countered the arguments of non-proliferation groups and pressed Congress to advance the nuclear agreement. The lobby had five main components and each undertook a range of activities.

First, the Coalition for the Partnership with India lobbied for the nuclear agreement.[25] It comprised USIBC and American business; Indian American groups such as USIFC; and strategic affairs experts. Its primary message was that the nuclear agreement's non-proliferation drawbacks would be offset by its non-proliferation benefits; that the strategic, economic, and environmental benefits were significant; and that these benefits would be lost if Congress rejected the nuclear agreement. The Coalition held dozens of meetings to individually convey this message to key lawmakers. In each meeting, it was represented by a business leader, a prominent Indian American, and a foreign affairs expert. It also organized letters written by strategic affairs experts and by the chief executives of major US firms. Further, Bush administration officials regularly met with the Coalition and informed it of the administration's position.

Second, numerous Indian American groups lobbied Congress. For example, USINPAC hosted events with Undersecretary Nicholas Burns, key members of Congress, and the Indian American community on 10 April and 21 June; it also held a lobbying day on Capitol Hill and met with the congressional leadership on 18 May. Other Indian American groups and the broader Indian American community also mobilized to advance the nuclear agreement. Partly directed by the Coalition for the Partnership with India, but also working independently, Indian Americans lobbied representatives and senators from their home districts.

Third, American business pursued several lobbying initiatives both within and outside the broader Coalition for the Partnership with India. Thus, executives from the nuclear, defence, and telecommunications sectors met legislators to make the economic argument for the nuclear agreement. And a USIBC gala event on 22 June included a keynote address by Vice President Cheney and a speech by Senator Biden. Here, Biden publicly endorsed the nuclear agreement, and this influenced several Democrats in the Senate to also support the agreement.

Fourth, strategic affairs experts, many of whom were recruited by the Coalition for the Partnership with India, endorsed the nuclear agreement. One set of experts included analysts and former government officials. For example, in a 10 March letter, 23 scholars, diplomats, and former US government officials endorsed the nuclear agreement. Another expert, Ashley Tellis, authored a publication countering the non-proliferation argument that India would greatly expand its fissile material production (Tellis, 2006b). Further, on 7 June, a Council on Foreign Relations report advocated a two-step process that balanced non-proliferation concerns with the strategic case for the nuclear agreement (Ferguson and Levi, 2006).

Another set of experts were prominent former secretaries of defence or state: William Perry, William Cohen, and Henry Kissinger. They supported the nuclear agreement in the press and in congressional testimony.

A further set of experts had non-proliferation credentials. These included Ashton Carter, John Ritch, and most significantly, IAEA Director Mohammed El Baradei. El Baradei had supported the nuclear agreement soon after it was announced in July 2005, and he again endorsed it on 14 June 2006 in *The Washington Post*.

Fifth, the Indian Embassy and its lobbying firms – BGR and Venable – made their case to Congress. Thus, India's ambassador met with dozens of senators and representatives to explain the merits of the nuclear agreement. Further, BGR undertook more than 240 activities and communications between March and December 2006, including about 60 involving executive branch officials and 180 involving those from the legislature.[26] In March, it held meetings with administration officials Nicholas Burns and Philip

Zelikow, Representatives Steny Hoyer (the House Minority Whip) and Ileana Ros-Lehtinen (HIRC member), and Senators Lamar Alexander and Mel Martinez (who were important members of the Republican leadership). In April, it met Senators Lincoln Chafee and Chuck Hagel (who were influential in the Republican leadership). And, in May, it met Representatives Howard Berman, Dan Burton, Henry Hyde, Ileana Ros-Lehtinen, Ed Royce, and Joe Wilson (all of whom held key positions in the House or were past leaders of the India Caucus), as well as Senators John Kyle and John McCain (who were influential in the Republican leadership). In addition, Venable undertook over 350 activities and communications, including 50 with executive branch officials and 300 with those from the legislature.

The Press

The American press largely supported the nuclear agreement. From March to December 2006, six major dailies published 38 pieces (10 editorials and 28 opinion-editorials) on the agreement, of which 25 favoured the agreement, 10 opposed it, and three were neutral. All major dailies, except for *The New York Times*, supported the agreement.

The New York Times carried two editorials and three opinion-editorials (one by Tom Friedman and two by Bob Herbert) against the agreement. One editorial drew attention to Senator Lugar's remarks ('The central question, Mr. Lugar says, is, "How important is India?"') and declared, 'We beg to differ. The central question is not the importance of India, but rather the importance of deterring a global nuclear arms race' (*The New York Times*, 2006b). And Tom Friedman echoed this point, stating that 'we should not go ahead with this deal until India is ready to halt its production of weapons-grade material' (Friedman, 2006).

Other dailies strongly endorsed the nuclear agreement. For example, *The Washington Post* had one editorial and nine opinion-editorials favouring, and just one opinion-editorial against, the agreement. Secretary of State Condoleezza Rice, IAEA Director General Mohammed El-Baradei, and columnists and analysts Selig Harrison, Jim Hoagland, Richard Cohen, and Robert Kagan, all supported the agreement. Former President Jimmy Carter opposed it, writing that 'the proposed nuclear deal with India is just one more step in opening a Pandora's box of nuclear proliferation' (Carter, 2006). Carter also called for prohibiting ENR transfers to India and for India's joining the test ban treaty. Among other major dailies, *The Washington*

Times had three editorials and three opinion-editorials supporting the nuclear agreement, while *The Wall Street Journal* carried one editorial and four opinion-editorials favouring the agreement and one opinion-editorial against it. Prominent supporters included former Defense Secretary William Cohen in *The Washington Times* and *The Wall Street Journal*; Ashton Carter in *Foreign Affairs*; Senator Hagel in *The National Interest*; and Karl Inderfurth in *The Boston Globe*, while prominent opponents included former Senator Sam Nunn in *The Wall Street Journal*.

Overall, while opponents drew attention to non-proliferation issues, supporters highlighted the strategic, economic, and environmental case for the nuclear agreement, and their arguments helped expand the win-set.

The Administration and Congress

The Bush administration adopted several approaches to persuade Congress on the nuclear agreement. The senior-most administration officials engaged Congress; the administration sought to influence key senators and representatives from both parties; it made a general strategic case to members of Congress but also focused on specific details in working with congressional staff; and it released statements outlining its concerns about congressional legislation.[27]

First, very senior administration officials engaged Congress. President Bush met the House and Senate foreign policy leaders when he returned from India in March 2006. Secretary Rice testified and made the administration's case before the SFRC and HIRC on 5 April. And Undersecretaries Burns and Joseph briefed the SFRC on 29 March. Just as importantly, Undersecretary Burns met every member of the SFRC, and nearly every member of the HIRC, to personally explain the administration's strategic, economic, and environmental case for the nuclear agreement.

Further, in June and July, Secretary Rice and senior State Department and NSC officials phoned or met with key members of the House and Senate (Rice focused on the Senate, while National Security Advisor Hadley focused on the House). Subsequently, in late 2006, Secretary Rice again called the majority and minority leadership in the SFRC and HIRC, urging them to advance the India legislation (the administration was concerned that Congress would not have time for the India legislation because it also had to act on major appropriation bills during its lame-duck session).[28]

Second, the administration focused on persuading the House and Senate committees (the State Department worked with these committees), the House and Senate party leadership (the White House engaged these leaders), and particular members of Congress. Principally, the administration sought to convince the majority and minority chairs in the SFRC and HIRC, because other members of these committees were likely to defer to their chairs. Beyond the committees, the White House reached out to the overall leadership of the Republican and Democratic parties. In addition, the administration targeted influential representatives and senators, including those who were presidential contenders. Here, it engaged Senators Clinton and Obama, with Senator Biden helping the administration reach out to these senators. And the administration was responsive to the concerns of each key senator and representative. For example, it explained to Senator Obama the environmental benefits of the nuclear agreement, drawing upon arguments made by experts such as David Victor. Moreover, the breadth of the administration's arguments helped its case: while Republicans looked favourably upon the strategic argument for the nuclear agreement, Democrats found the environmental argument appealing.

Third, the administration took a general, as well as a specific, approach to persuading Congress. While senior administration officials made the general strategic and economic arguments for the nuclear agreement, other officials worked with congressional staff on specific technical items in the House and Senate bills.

Illustrating this, in June 2006, when the HIRC marked up legislation and introduced amendments that the administration had not previously seen, administration officials engaged congressional staff on technical details in these amendments. Later, in November and December, NSC and State Department officials similarly worked with Senator Lugar's staff on specific items in the conference bill. Moreover, administration officials such as Assistant Secretary Rademaker explained to congressional staff that the administration's preferred language for a bill would have the same impact as congressional language. In addition, administration official Richard Stratford's interventions with Congress had considerable credibility because of his non-proliferation background. Overall, the administration showed a worker-level willingness to discuss with Congress how different parts of congressional legislation and its own agreements with India would work together, and this approach strengthened its case.

The administration's detailed answers to dozens of congressional questions also illustrate the specific approach. These answers strengthened the administration's case in three ways. For one, they enabled congressional supporters to counter claims made by opponents that the nuclear agreement had not been extensively debated. In addition, once Congress received the administration's answers and could hold future administrations accountable to these, it was more confident of moving ahead with the legislation. Finally, the administration gave no answers that derailed its case.

Fourth, and again related to the specific approach, the administration released several statements informing Congress about its specific concerns with the House and Senate bills. Thus, on 26 July, ahead of the House vote, an administration statement expressed concern with items in the House bill. It noted, for example, that the administration would 'oppose any amendment conditioning cooperation with India upon India's policies towards Iran, which would be beyond the scope of our July 2005 commitments' (The White House, 2006b). Similarly, on 16 November, ahead of the Senate vote, the administration objected to specific provisions in the Senate bill, such as those mandating only one approach to safeguards in perpetuity and singling out India for bans on sensitive technology transfer (The White House, 2006c). And, on 30 November, Secretary Rice sent a letter to the HIRC chair outlining nine concerns with the Senate and House bills.[29]

Fifth, administration officials and supportive members of Congress echoed India's concerns, thereby making the case that certain provisions in the legislation would fall outside India's win-set. For example, during the 16 November Senate vote, Senator Lugar noted that 'India will regard this [Bingaman amendment] as "moving the goalposts," an unacceptable renegotiation of the deal, and a bad-faith effort on our part' and 'as a consequence, this is a deal-killer'.[30] Similarly, Secretary Rice's 30 November letter to the HIRC chair mentioned India's concerns with legislative provisions on export controls, Iran, and fuel supply assurances (Congress eventually modified language on the first two issues).[31]

Other Developments

Some additional developments helped expand the win-set on the nuclear agreement. First, the administration sought to ensure that negative developments would not affect the congressional vote. Thus, it waited until after the House passed legislation in July 2006 to announce sanctions on two Indian firms alleged to have transferred missile-related parts to Iran: had it made this announcement ahead of the House vote, fewer congressmen may have supported the bill (alternatively, members of Congress may well have delayed and added stronger provisions to the bill).

Second, India's reactions to the Hyde Act created difficulties, but also strengthened the administration's case, with Congress. On the one hand, the Indian government's position with domestic audiences, that it retained the right to conduct nuclear tests, hurt the administration's case with Congress. Yet, India's opposition to the Hyde Act also enabled the administration to credibly argue that, contrary to the points made by non-proliferation groups, congressional legislation was having a non-proliferation impact on India's nuclear program.[32]

In the end, a number of factors influenced the US win-set. The non-proliferation arguments made in congressional hearings, in outreach efforts by non-proliferation groups, and in the press, all contributed to reducing the win-set so that the administration's March 2006 bill remained outside the win-set. On the other hand, the arguments by strategic affairs and regional affairs experts, mobilization by the India lobby, and the administration's engagement of Congress also shaped the win-set so that the Hyde Act fell within, but killer amendments stayed outside, the win-set.[33]

India's Domestic Politics

In 2006, as legislation made its way through the House and Senate, India's domestic polity mobilized against the legislation. This domestic mobilization and political opposition reduced India's win-set. It also influenced India's government to spell out its red lines (that is, its win-set) during Prime Minister Singh's 17 August statement to the Parliament. In the end, the Hyde Act remained outside India's win-set, but India's government could still move ahead with the nuclear agreement. Mobilization by proponents, the government's defence of its case, endorsement from the Congress Party and its allies, and the left's not withdrawing support for the government enabled the government to proceed to the next stage of negotiations on the agreement.

Domestic Mobilization

India's strategic affairs experts, nuclear experts, and foreign policy commentators extensively debated congressional legislation as well as the overall desirability of the nuclear agreement.

First, writing in the press, experts closely scrutinized the 10 non-proliferation issues in congressional legislation. Thus, on fuel supply assurances and terminating nuclear cooperation in the event of nuclear testing (issue 2), a senior nuclear scientist noted that 'these [congressional] bills also contain clauses which totally contradict the earlier [March 2006] assurances of the PM [prime minister] and the US administration on uninterrupted fuel supply to India' (Gopalakrishnan, 2006c).[34] Others added that 'The most contentious part or provision in the bills of both the chambers is the provision for termination of the agreement after India conducts nuclear tests in the future' (Institute for Defence Studies and Analyses [IDSA], 2006). And, on ENR restrictions (issue 4), commentators stated: 'When India expands its civilian nuclear program manifold, it expects to take advantage of global advances to gain the best economics and operating reliability...Hence the exclusion of these [reprocessing] technologies not foreseen in the July 2005 and March 2006 agreements violates the spirit of these agreements' (*The Hindu*, 2006).

Second, beyond their writings in the press, India's ex-governmental senior nuclear scientists highlighted their concerns in three ways. First, in a 14 August letter to the Parliament, seven senior scientists noted that Congress had 'modified, both in letter and spirit, the implementation [of the July 2005 Joint Statement]'; that India should not make concessions that affected its nuclear deterrent ('India should continue to be able to hold on to her nuclear option as a strategic requirement'); that safeguards should be 'strictly restricted to those facilities and materials imported from external sources'; and that 'Our R&D [that is, nuclear research and development] should not be hampered by external supervision or control'.[35] Second, on 26 August, these senior scientists held a 90 minute meeting with the prime minister, the national security advisor, the principal secretary to the prime minister, the DAE secretary, and the principal scientific advisor to the prime minister.[36] Third, some senior scientists briefed India's opposition parties about their objections (see *The Indian Express*, 4 September 2006).

Third, analysts debated the overall utility of the nuclear agreement. In 10 pieces in *The Asian Age*, from March to December 2006, Bharat Karnad repeatedly stated that the agreement restricted India's ability to conduct nuclear tests and to acquire fissile material for its nuclear arsenal.[37] Others asserted that the nuclear agreement would not contribute significantly to India's energy security.

On the other hand, many analysts supported the nuclear agreement and downplayed the impact of congressional legislation. They argued that the benefits of lifting technology embargoes on India were worth the costs, and that the costs were not substantial because India already had a minimum deterrent and did not need additional testing.[38] Reflecting these views, C. Raja Mohan noted, 'as it considers the many pinpricks that have been attached to the nuclear legislation in the House and the Senate, India should remain focused like a laser beam on the basics [that is, the benefits]' (Mohan, 2006c). Similarly, The Times of India stated, 'These [items in congressional bills] are irritations which should not obscure the larger picture' (The Times of India, 2006e). And K. Subrahmanyam noted that, in terms of the larger picture, 'Now, on offer is the lifting of this technology apartheid. What is involved is not just a nuclear deal between India and the US but a restructuring of the international system incorporating India in the global balance of power' (Subrahmanyam, 2006).

In the end, India's leftist and right-wing parties drew upon points made by domestic critics to oppose the Hyde Act, but mobilization by supporters helped India's government to still proceed with the nuclear agreement.

The Left and the Right

India's political left and right strongly opposed congressional legislation and pressed for a sense of Parliament resolution on the nuclear agreement.

India's leftist parties raised concerns about technical nuclear issues, particularly about congressional issue 2 (fuel reserves) and issue 4 (ENR restrictions, which were framed as restrictions on 'full' nuclear cooperation); political process issues; foreign policy issues, especially those related to issue 5 (Iran); energy issues; and overall cost–benefit issues. Thus, on the political process, at a 22 July meeting, the left sought a resolution that would reflect parliamentary opinion on the nuclear agreement. On foreign policy issues, it noted, 'The statements of policy contained in the [House] bill are highly objectionable as they seek to bind India not only on nuclear issues but [also on] broader [US] foreign policy goals' such as Iran (Karat, 2006). And, on technical and strategic nuclear issues, it was concerned that, as a result of congressional legislation, there were 'doubts in seven areas', which included full civilian nuclear cooperation, fuel supply assurances, and India's stand on the FMCT. The left also argued that the nuclear agreement had low energy benefits but high costs in terms of constraining India's independence in foreign policy. Reflecting this, Sitaram Yechury noted that 'by the year 2015, this [nuclear share] would still be only 5 per cent of India's projected capacity generation then. So, for this 5 per cent of the projected capacity generation, are we going to tie down our country's strategic interests?'[39]

The BJP called attention to technical and strategic nuclear issues (related to issues 1 and 2 in congressional legislation); the inequality of the US and Indian obligations; the low energy benefits; and, based on these points, argued that the nuclear agreement had an unfavourable cost–benefit ratio (a theme that it had not highlighted earlier).

Highlighting these issues, former Prime Minister Atal Behari Vajpayee cautioned about the nuclear test conditions in the March 2006 bill. He noted that 'The obligations under this Bill are far more stringent than those under the CTBT'.[40] And Jaswant Singh noted that 'several serious questions arise from a detailed study of the Secretary of State's [5 April] testimony', as well as from Senator Lugar's 82 Questions for the Record.[41] Singh was concerned that India had not attained the status of a nuclear weapons state and that it had forfeited its right to test. He added that such strategic costs of the nuclear agreement were not worth the small energy and economic benefits: 'What the government has offered to the US results in a significant erosion of our strategic space…[such as] placing 90% of our nuclear plants on surveillance by an intrusive IAEA regime; and all this for just about 8% of our energy requirements of around 2025…only if all goes well.'

Other BJP leaders such as Arun Shourie and Yashwant Sinha, and the BJP's allies (the All India Anna Dravida Munnetra Kazhagam [AIADMK], Shiv Sena, and Telugu Desam Party [TDP]), repeated these points in a parliamentary debate in August as well as in the press.[42]

To summarize, the BJP and the left raised major concerns about congressional legislation. Eventually, however, the left did not withdraw support for India's government.[43] It did not want to be seen as aligning with the BJP, nor did it want to bring down India's government, especially when, in late July and August, India's defence minister and the Congress Party president separately informed the left that any sense of Parliament resolution could jeopardize the government's future.

India's Government Defends the Nuclear Agreement

India's government countered the position of the BJP and the left and also defended the nuclear agreement within the Congress Party and in the Parliament.

In a 7 March statement to the Parliament, the prime minister defended India's separation plan, affirmed that it would not impact India's strategic nuclear program and its nuclear research, and highlighted the foreign policy and energy benefits of the nuclear agreement. That same week, the Congress Party Working Committee and the Congress Party president backed the prime minister.[44] Congress Party leaders thereby addressed concerns within their party about the overall desirability of the nuclear agreement.[45]

For the next four months, from mid-March to mid-July, India's government did not publicly comment on congressional legislation. Thereafter, however, it expressed concerns with the House and Senate bills but still defended the nuclear agreement and countered the opposition's points. Reflecting this, in July, India's minister of state for external affairs informed the Congress Party that India had not forfeited its strategic autonomy through the nuclear agreement. And, at the 23 July UPA–Left coordination committee meeting, Prime Minister Singh informed the left that his government would not make concessions to the US beyond those outlined in his 7 March parliamentary speech; he added that he had conveyed this position to President Bush during the G8 summit in St. Petersburg.

Most significantly, Prime Minister Singh defended the nuclear agreement in his 17 August statement to the Parliament. Here, he responded to nine points raised by the left and the right and by Indian nuclear scientists in their 14 August letter. He noted that, on issue 1 in congressional legislation, the 'adequacy of fissile material' for India's nuclear deterrent would not be affected. He added that 'The integrity of our 3-Stage nuclear program', including 'fast breeder reactors and the thorium program', would not be affected, meaning that these programs would not be subject to international restrictions. He further noted that, on issue 4 in congressional legislation, his government would 'seek the removal of restrictions on all aspects of cooperation and technology transfers', including those on reprocessing and enrichment technology. The prime minister concluded by outlining India's red lines on congressional legislation: 'we will not accept any conditions [in the legislation] that go beyond the parameters of the July 18, 2005 Joint Statement and the March 2, 2006 Separation Plan'. Finally, other members of India's government reinforced the prime minister's points and also addressed the issues of fuel supply assurances and testing.[46]

To summarize, India's government made a strong case for the nuclear agreement to the Congress Party and to its UPA allies. They, in turn, affirmed their support for the government; for example, in early August, RJD leader Lalu Prasad Yadav confirmed that his party stood behind the government. Simply put, as long as the government's advancement of the nuclear initiative did not cause the left to withdraw support for the government and result in national elections, the Congress Party and its UPA allies stood behind India's government. Further, the left accepted that the prime minister's 17 August parliamentary statement could substitute for a sense of Parliament resolution. All these factors helped India's government to move ahead with the nuclear agreement. At the same time, India's government repeatedly conveyed its concerns to the Bush administration.

India Conveys its Stand to the Bush Administration

India's government issued several public statements, aimed at domestic audiences and at the Bush administration, outlining its concerns with the House and Senate bills.[47] It also directly took its case to representatives, senators, and senior Bush administration officials.

First, India's foreign secretary and Undersecretary Burns discussed congressional legislation in several meetings, including those in London on 23 May, Paris on 13 July, and New York in September.[48] Moreover, in July 2006, India's government handed a 12-page dossier to the US outlining how the House and Senate bills deviated from the July 2005 Joint Statement and the March 2006 separation plan. Second, Prime Minister Singh conveyed India's concerns to President Bush at their 17 July meeting in St. Petersburg, and in phone calls on 16 October and 16 November.

Third, Indian officials discussed their position with congressional leaders. For example, during his 29–31 March visit to Washington, India's foreign secretary met Senators Biden and Obama and Representatives Hyde, Lantos, Ackerman, Wilson, and Faleomavaega. The foreign secretary cautioned against changing the 'very delicate balance' of obligations in India's separation plan and noted that congressional concerns about India's relations with Iran were 'completely misplaced'.[49] On this point, New Delhi strongly objected to legislation mandating that its policy on Iran should conform to US preferences, and the administration asked Congress to change such language (congressional staff responded with language that Indian policy on Iran conform to UN Security Council resolutions).[50]

Fourth, other senior US and Indian officials discussed the issue. On 7 August, India's foreign secretary informed Assistant Secretary Boucher that if congressional legislation were seen as deviating from the Joint Statement, it could cause major problems in India.[51] Further, Secretary Rice discussed congressional legislation with Defence Minister Mukherjee when they met in New York on 21 September. Later, in a phone conversation in early November, Rice informed Mukherjee (who had by then been appointed India's Minister for External Affairs) that the administration was pressing for a Senate vote and for restricting the number of amendments in the Senate bill to between five and seven.[52]

Finally, Indian officials met Undersecretary Burns on 8 December and outlined their concerns about fuel supply, testing, and other issues in the conference bill.[53] Burns was then visiting India for US–India bilateral dialogue meetings and he reassured Indian officials about these issues. He informed India's external affairs minister and national security advisor that Washington would honour all its commitments to New Delhi, including those on fuel supply. He also noted that the bill's final language on Iran accommodated India because it did not mandate action by India but instead asked the executive branch to write reports to Congress on this issue.[54]

In the end, despite US reassurances that the Hyde Act's statement of policy sections were not binding on the administration, India's government still objected to some of its clauses, especially on fuel supply assurances and on restricting ENR technology. The Hyde Act therefore fell outside India's winset (which remained at the same level it had been during negotiations for the separation plan, extending from points 9–5 in Figure 2.1). Yet, India's government did not reject it because, despite its shortcomings, it had exempted India from Section 123(a), 128, and 129 of the Atomic Energy Act and thereby permitted nuclear cooperation with India. New Delhi instead sought to address the shortcomings through a presidential signing statement and through the Section 123 Agreement. Outlining these points in a 21 December phone conversation with President Bush, Prime Minister Singh stated that 'India still has some concerns, though many have already been addressed in the president's signing statement' (Government of India, 2006). The prime minister also 'expressed the hope that [India's] remaining concerns will be addressed in the next stage of negotiation', which was the Section 123 Agreement.

Endnotes

1   This point was noted in a statement by Senator Lugar at the SFRC, 26 April 2006.
2   The discussion in this section and the next section is drawn from author interview D1, 9 July 2010; author interview D2, 31 August 2011; author interview N1, 13 October 2011.

3   Section 123(a) of the Atomic Energy Act requires US civilian nuclear cooperation agreements to include full-scope safeguards in the recipient country unless exempted by the president and approved by a joint resolution of Congress. Section 128 requires recipient states to have full-scope safeguards, while Section 129 requires them to not have detonated a nuclear explosive nor to be involved in the manufacture of nuclear devices.

4   This point was noted in a statement at the American Enterprise Institute, 11 May 2006.

5   HR 4974 attracted a gradually increasing number of co-sponsors from April to June but then stalled. It had eight co-sponsors, including four Democrats, by 30 April (compared with 21 for House Conference Resolution 318); 31, including 11 Democrats, by 30 May (compared with 22 for Resolution 318); and 41, including 17 Democrats, by 30 June (compared with 23 for Resolution 318).

6   Explaining why Congress cited GOV/1621, Senator Biden subsequently noted: 'the IAEA document makes a real contribution to our understanding of safeguards [in] perpetuity...GOV/1621 of 20 August 1973...makes clear that safeguards on nuclear material will extend until that material no longer has any possible nuclear weapons use'. See Senator Biden's statement in *The Congressional Record-Senate*, Vol. 152, Part 8, 8 December 2006, p. S23729.

7   See Senate Amendment S.AMDT.5183 to Bill S.3709, found at the Library of Congress, available at http://thomas.loc.gov/cgi-bin/bdquery/z?d109:SN03709:

8   Ibid., see Senate Amendment S.AMDT.5174 to Bill S.3709.

9   Ibid., see Senate Amendment S.AMDT.5187 to Bill S.3709.

10 See *The Congressional Record-Senate*, Vol. 152, Part 17, 16 November 2006, p. 22162.

11 Ibid., p. 22163.

12 See Senate Amendment S.AMDT.5178 to Bill S.3709.

13 Author interview N1, 13 October 2011.

14 These issues, and more details of the lobbying effort, are covered in Mistry (2013). For other perspectives on the lobbying effort, see Vickery (2011) and Weiss (2007).

15 The experts are listed in Table 2.1. Congressional staff selected the experts based on their areas of specialization and ties with representatives and senators. Thus, Ashton Carter and Ron Lehman had previously worked with Senator Lugar. Further, among non-proliferation specialists, Ron Lehman balanced the stronger line adopted by Henry Sokolski and Michael Krepon. Also, at the 11 May hearing in the House, Leonard Weiss took a strong non-proliferation approach, while Fred McGoldrick, a mentor to administration official Richard Stratford, asked important non-proliferation questions but did not oppose the strategic case for the nuclear agreement.

16 These points were made in a statement by Senator Lugar at the SFRC, 26 April 2006.

17 These points were made in a statement by Daryl Kimball at the HIRC, 11 May 2006.

18   These points were made in a statement at the SFRC, 26 April 2006.

19   Ibid.

20   Ibid.

21   These points were made in a statement at the Senate Energy Committee, 18 July 2006.

22   These points were made in a statement at the SFRC, 26 April 2006.

23   Ibid.

24   Author interview M2, 25 February 2010.

25   This discussion draws from author interviews with members of the lobbying Coalition; author interview X1, 10 March 2010; and author interview X2, 18 November 2009.

26   Data compiled by author from a database hosted by FARA, Department of Justice.

27   This section is based on several author interviews: author interview D2, 31 August 2011; author interview I2, 16 September 2011; author interview O1, 7 September 2011; and author interview N1, 13 October 2011.

28   Further, in internal debates within the administration, Secretary Rice and Undersecretary Burns made the India legislation a top priority for the congressional session in November; the White House had given greater priority to a trade agreement with Vietnam.

29   For details, see the 'Letter to House Foreign Relations Chairman Henry Hyde from Secretary of State Condoleeza Rice', 30 November 2006.

30   See the statement by Senator Lugar listed in the *Congressional Record, 109th Congress (2005–2006)*, p. S11001.

31   Secretary Rice's 30 November letter noted that the House bill's provision on ending nuclear cooperation if India violated NSG and MTCR guidelines is 'viewed in India as "moving the goalposts" of the US–India joint statements' (the conference bill then modified this language). On another provision in the House bill, calling for the president to press other countries against supplying fuel to India if it conducted a nuclear test, the letter noted that 'India has taken the position that this is a deal-killer'. And, on the Senate bill's requiring India's 'full and active participation' versus Iran, the letter stated that this 'would be viewed in India as adding additional conditions to the July 2005 and March 2006 understandings' (the conference bill then changed this to a reporting requirement).

32   Author interview O1, 7 September 2011.

33   The statements of two senators illustrate how they were influenced by these arguments. Senator Kennedy extensively cited non-proliferation points raised by Brent Scowcroft, Robert Gallucci, Sam Nunn, Zbigniew Brzezinski, and Jimmy Carter to explain why he opposed the Hyde Act. He noted, for example, that 'Zbigniew Brzezinski points out that this deal "will complicate the quest for a constructive resolution of the Iranian nuclear problem"' and also cited Jimmy Carter's point that 'there is no doubt that condoning avoidance of the NPT encourages the spread of nuclear weaponry'. See the *Congressional Record, 109th Congress (2005–2006)*, p. S11023.

On the other hand, Senator Reed supported the Senate bill because it addressed two non-proliferation concerns. He noted that, first, 'Probably the most important of the determinations in section 105 is the fifth which states, "India is working with the United States to conclude a multilateral treaty on the cessation of the production of fissile materials."' Second, 'Section 106 of S. 3709 would prohibit the export of equipment, materials and technologies related to uranium enrichment, spent nuclear fuel reprocessing, and the production of heavy water.' He added that the two-step process would enable him to re-examine his stand after the Section 123 Agreement with India was negotiated: 'I will carefully examine any 123 Agreement to ensure that it adequately addresses vital proliferation concerns.' See Ibid., p. S11024.

34 For additional concerns, including about issue 9 and the National Nuclear Security Administration's involvement in any US–India cooperative threat reduction program, see Gopalakrishnan (2006e, 2006f).

35 These points were noted in an 'Appeal to Parliamentarians on Nuclear Deal', 14 August 2006.

36 The scientists involved in the meeting included three former chairmen of the Atomic Energy Commission – H. N. Sethna (chairman from 1972–83); M. R. Srinivasan (chairman from 1987–90), and P. K. Iyengar (chairman from 1990–93) – along with A. Gopalakrishnan (former chairman of the Atomic Energy Regulatory Board), A. N. Prasad (former director of the BARC), Y. S. R. Prasad (former chairman of the Nuclear Power Corporation of India), and Placid Rodriguez (former director of the Indira Gandhi Centre for Atomic Research). The first six of these scientists had signed the letter on 14 August. See Gopalakrishnan (2006d).

37 Brahma Chellaney made similar arguments, for example, in the *Hindustan Times* (18 July 2006) and *The Asian Age* (20 May 2006).

38 For such views, see pieces by C. Raja Mohan (*Indian Express*, 29 June 2006), Arun Bajpai (*Hindustan Times*, 12 May 2006), and R. Rajaraman (*Hindustan Times*, 21 November 2006); see also editorials in *The Times of India* (2006c) and *The Telegraph* (2006).

39 These points were noted in a statement by Sitaram Yechury in the Rajya Sabha, 17 August 2006.

40 See a 'Statement Issued by Shri Atal Behari Vajpayee on Implementation of Indo-US Nuclear Deal', 6 April 2006.

41 See the press statement by Jaswant Singh, 'India–US Nuclear Agreement', 21 April 2006. In additional conversations, Singh noted that Washington and New Delhi should not emphasize the nuclear agreement over other bilateral initiatives, and he cautioned against exaggerated energy expectations from the agreement. The US Embassy, New Delhi, cable, 13 April 2006.

42 See, for example, three pieces by Arun Shourie in *The Indian Express* on 22, 23, and 24 August 2006.

43 In May, emboldened by state election victories in West Bengal and Kerala, the left clarified that it would not withdraw support for India's government but

still highlighted the government's deficiencies in implementing the UPA–Left common minimum program.

44 See, for example, *Congress Sandesh* (2006) and Gandhi (2006).

45 Congress Party members were concerned that the nuclear agreement could cost them the support of Muslim voters, especially because, ahead of and during President Bush's visit to India, some Indian Muslim groups, the left, and the SP had held protests against the nuclear agreement.

46 For example, in his 23 August speech in the Parliament, India's minister of state for external affairs responded to criticism about issues 2 and 3 in congressional legislation (covering fuel supply assurances, testing, and safeguards). He noted that the IAEA safeguards pact 'will be India specific…the Safeguards Agreement will also have a multi-layered fuel supply guarantee. There will be uninterrupted fuel supply.' Further, he mentioned that the government's position on testing was no different from that of the BJP: 'the then honorable Prime Minister [in the BJP government] had made an offer in the UN General Assembly to convert the unilateral [testing] moratorium into a de jure one, which virtually amounted to signing the CTBT'.

47 See the 'Statement by Mr. Anand Sharma, Minister of State for External Affairs, on US–India Nuclear Cooperation Promotion Act of 2006', 26 July 2006; and Gentleman and Shanker (2006).

48 The US Embassy, New Delhi, cable, 13 July 2006.

49 See the 'Transcript of the Press Conference by Foreign Secretary Mr. Shyam Saran at the Embassy of India, Washington, DC', 31 March 2006.

50 Author interview N1, 13 October 2011.

51 The US Embassy, New Delhi, cable, 11 August 2006.

52 The US Embassy, New Delhi, cable, 8 November 2006.

53 Just after Congress approved the Hyde Act, the Indian press carried many pieces against it and this reinforced New Delhi's case for a presidential signing statement. For example, M. R. Srinivasan expressed concerns about 'the suspension of all cooperation were India to conduct a nuclear test'; he was also concerned about 'the assurance of fuel supply' and about 'the scope of "full civilian nuclear energy cooperation"…India had assumed that this term encompassed the fuel cycle, namely enrichment of uranium and reprocessing of spent fuel' (see a piece by M. R. Srinivasan, *The Hindu*, 14 December 2006). Others making similar points included A. N. Prasad (*Deccan Herald*, 18 December 2006) and Brahma Chellaney (*The Asian Age*, 9, 10, 16, and 18 December 2006).

54 The US Embassy, New Delhi, cable, 11 December 2006; author interview O1, 7 September 2011.

CHAPTER SIX

Negotiating the Section 123 Agreement

In early and mid-2007, after Congress passed the Hyde Act, Washington and New Delhi completed negotiations on their Section 123 Agreement for civilian nuclear cooperation. The Bush administration sought an agreement that would be consistent with the Hyde Act, while New Delhi sought to counter the Hyde Act and to adhere closely to its March 2006 separation plan and the July 2005 Joint Statement. Initially, both sides were unable to bridge their differences. As a result, in April 2007, US officials observed that 'there is a fair degree of frustration in Washington that the Indian government has not engaged seriously enough or quickly enough with...the United States'.[1] President Bush ultimately intervened to break the negotiating deadlock, after which US and Indian officials finalized a Section 123 Agreement with relatively low-to-moderate non-proliferation provisions.

Domestic politics considerably influenced negotiations for the Section 123 Agreement. In the US, congressional involvement and mobilization by the non-proliferation lobby made it hard for Washington to make major non-proliferation concessions to New Delhi. Still, senior US policymakers were willing to accept some of India's positions, and this allowed for negotiating compromises. In India, bureaucratic resistance from the nuclear establishment and mobilization by opponents prevented India's government from accepting any agreement with relatively high or even moderate non-proliferation provisions. However, political power considerations and mobilization by advocates helped India's government to conclude an agreement having relatively low-to-moderate non-proliferation provisions.

Multiple Rounds of Talks

Washington and New Delhi began talks on the Section 123 Agreement in 2006 and completed them in July 2007. They focused on six main issues: references to an Indian nuclear test as a condition for terminating nuclear cooperation; Washington's right to demand the return of technology transferred to India if it conducted a nuclear test; India's desire for fuel supply assurances to maintain the uninterrupted operation of its reactors; the transfer of enrichment and reprocessing (ENR) technology to India; consent for India to reprocess US-origin spent fuel; and legal issues about the Section 123 Agreement overriding the Hyde Act.

Both sides initially discussed the Section 123 Agreement in 2006. They exchanged multiple drafts between March and August, and further discussed the agreement during a 6–8 November meeting in Delhi. Here, Washington was disappointed that the Indian team had not been prepared to negotiate the text of an agreement. New Delhi was unwilling to finalize any text before Congress passed enabling legislation. It also expressed concerns about items in congressional legislation such as fuel supply restrictions in the House bill, ENR transfer restrictions in the Senate bill, and the issue of reprocessing consent (New Delhi eventually sought to address these concerns in the Section 123 Agreement).[2] Further, it drew attention to Washington's unwillingness to refine its thinking on various Indian proposals.

US–India negotiations then resumed in February 2007. During a 21–24 February visit to the US, Foreign Secretary Shivshankar Menon gave US officials a 14-clause draft agreement. Washington assessed this to be 'a completely inadequate counter-draft to the 123 Agreement – authored by the skeptics in India's nuclear establishment who remain concerned about U.S. efforts to "entrap" India and constrain its strategic program'.[3] Undersecretary Burns asked Foreign Secretary Menon to provide a more workable basis on which the US and India could continue talks. Thereafter, Washington wanted the negotiating teams to quickly settle the basic issues so that 'one to three points at the most, that may remain after the negotiating process, could then be discussed at senior levels'.[4]

The two sides next held talks in Delhi (25–27 March) and Cape Town (16–19 April, at the sidelines of an NSG meeting), but they could not resolve their differences. At this time, given that they had other foreign policy priorities such as Afghanistan, Iraq, and Iran, US officials questioned whether they should divert high-level attention to the Section 123 Agreement.[5] Eventually, the negotiations advanced only because of such high-level attention.

First, during a 1 May meeting in Washington, Undersecretary Burns and Foreign Secretary Menon sought to reach an accord by not mentioning some areas of disagreement. Undersecretary Burns anticipated signing such an accord during a 21 May visit to Delhi. However, the compromise was rejected by the Indian Prime Minister's Office (PMO). Accordingly, Undersecretary Burns delayed his visit to Delhi, and US and Indian negotiators met instead in London on 21–22 May. Second, in meetings in Delhi on 1–2 June, Undersecretary Burns confirmed a compromise on the contentious reprocessing issue.

Third, on 6–8 June, Prime Minister Singh met President Bush at the G8 summit in Germany and the two leaders discussed advancing the nuclear agreement. In a 9 June meeting, the US and Indian national security advisors followed up on the issue. They agreed to a negotiating solution based on a dedicated Indian reprocessing facility ('we agreed it was an eminently suitable proposition'); they noted that Prime Minister Singh and President Bush had also discussed this compromise; and they looked into the issue of fuel reserves for India's reactors.[6] They then decided to meet in July.

Thus, in mid-June, the senior-most US and Indian officials sought to complete the Section 123 Agreement by July so that they could focus on a broader range of deliverables for an August summit between Prime Minister Singh and President Bush (this summit eventually did not take place). US officials then assessed the situation as one where 'the Indian government now believes [the] 123 Agreement has boiled down to two issues: advance consent right for reprocessing and immunity of the strategic reserve'.[7] They added that 'the perceived positive US reception [to compromises] on both matters…has garnered the attention of the Indian leadership, which now thinks that an end is in sight'.

Fourth, US and Indian negotiators settled the outstanding issues during talks in Washington from 17 July to 20 July. India's government sent a strong delegation to these talks. It included the former joint secretary (Americas) in the Ministry of External Affairs (MEA) who led the Indian negotiating group in prior months, the new joint secretary (Americas), a PMO representative, the DAE's director of strategic planning, and at more senior levels, the national security advisor and the foreign secretary. Further, the DAE secretary was available for consultations: although he did not participate in the negotiations, he expedited them by quickly reviewing and accepting the negotiating compromises.

After slow progress for one-and-a-half days, the two sides advanced the dialogue during a 18 July meeting between their national security advisors. At this time, 'the two basic issues of reprocessing and right of return… were finalized' (Khare and Varadarajan, 2007a). India's national security advisor and foreign secretary then continued the discussions with their US counterparts: as India's national security advisor noted, 'I had two rounds with [National Security Advisor] Hadley entirely one to one. And a two-hour round with myself, [Undersecretary] Burns, and Hadley. We had altogether eight hours involving Hadley' (ibid.). Eventually, on the morning of 20 July, Undersecretary Burns informed India's foreign secretary that the talks would have to conclude that day because he had other engagements in the evening, and both sides reached a final compromise by mid-afternoon.[8]

The Main Negotiating Issues

Four general principles affected US–India negotiations on the Section 123 Agreement.[9] First, Washington sought firm restrictions on areas that enhanced India's nuclear weapons capabilities: areas such as testing and reprocessing. Second, New Delhi sought to avoid any repeat of the Tarapur experience, and therefore insisted on fuel supply assurances.

Third, India's red lines were those outlined in the prime minister's August 2006 and earlier speeches to the Parliament, which affirmed that India would only accept positions from the Joint Statement and from its separation plan. For much of 2006 and 2007, Indian officials were concerned that Washington was negotiating beyond these red lines. Thus, US negotiators were unable to extract concessions from New Delhi because it was rigid about not exceeding the boundaries mentioned in the prime minister's parliamentary speeches (it considered these to have the force of law). At the same time, Indian negotiators were not rigid about US laws and US Section 123 Agreements with other countries, but instead selected portions of these laws and agreements that would benefit India.

Fourth, Indian officials had read the US' Section 123 Agreements with other countries and they sought clauses from these agreements in the US–India Section 123 Agreement. Relatedly, New Delhi wanted to be treated like Europe and Japan, but Washington noted that India was new to the area of civilian nuclear cooperation and therefore needed to demonstrate a good record before the US could offer it the same terms that it gave Japan and Europe.

These basic principles influenced negotiations on the issues of terminating cooperation, the right of return, fuel supply assurances, ENR technology, reprocessing consent, and international law.

Terminating Cooperation

The Hyde Act and the March 2006 US draft of the Section 123 Agreement mentioned that Washington would terminate nuclear cooperation if India detonated a nuclear device. New Delhi responded that 'such a provision has no place in the proposed bilateral [Section 123] agreement and that India is bound only by what is contained in the July 18 Joint Statement, that is, continuing its commitment to a unilateral moratorium on nuclear testing' (*The Times of India*, 2006d).[10] Both sides then looked at three approaches to resolving this issue.

First, they examined language whereby India would undertake to not detonate a nuclear weapon using US-supplied materials or technology (this language was in the Atomic Energy Act). New Delhi was willing to accept this in the February 2007 discussions, but Washington sought alternative language (Varadarajan, 2007a).

Second, Washington then suggested language about terminating nuclear cooperation if an event occurred that 'jeopardizes supreme U.S. national interests', and it included this language in its April 2007 draft (Varadarajan, 2007d). Yet, Indian officials considered this to be even more dangerous than a reference to nuclear testing (Varadarajan, 2007b).

Third, both sides eventually excluded any mention of an Indian nuclear test as well as any language on 'supreme national interests'. Their compromise, outlined in the final Section 123 Agreement, simply noted that 'Either Party shall have the right to terminate this Agreement'. It added that the parties would 'take into account whether the circumstances that may lead to termination or cessation [of the Agreement] resulted from a Party's serious concern about a changed security environment or as a response to similar actions by other States which could impact national security'. Thus, the Section 123 Agreement had relatively low non-proliferation provisions on this item: it mentioned that either party could terminate the agreement, but it required the parties to consider the security-related circumstances that could possibly prevent termination, circumstances such as testing by other countries.

The Right of Return

The right of return clause was an important way to deter an Indian nuclear test. The Atomic Energy Act mentioned that Washington must seek the return of items transferred to a country if that country detonated a nuclear device. The conference report accompanying the Hyde Act confirmed that such provisions would apply to India.[11]

Washington and New Delhi could not resolve their differences over this issue in 2006 and early 2007. Indeed, in April 2007, it was the main obstacle in talks, because the US draft mentioned that India would be required to return imported items, which could include its nuclear fuel stockpile; Indian officials opposed this because it would negate the fuel supply assurances mentioned in its separation plan (Varadarajan, 2007d).

Eventually, both sides reached a compromise. The final Section 123 Agreement gave the US the right of return, but it also had a one-year period before the agreement could be terminated and the right could be exercised. It had four other provisions that made it hard to exercise the right of return.

First, both parties 'recognize[d] that exercising the right of return would have profound implications for their relations'. Second, the parties would give 'special consideration to the importance of uninterrupted operation of nuclear reactors' while invoking the right of return. Third, the party acquiring the returned technology would 'compensate promptly that Party for the fair market value thereof and for the costs incurred as a consequence of such removal'. Fourth, as noted earlier, before terminating the nuclear cooperation agreement, Washington would 'take into account...[any] serious concern about a changed security environment'.

Thus, the Section 123 agreement had relatively low-to-moderate non-proliferation provisions on the right of return. Representing a moderate position, it explicitly gave Washington this right, but, diluting it to accommodate India, the right would only be exercised after extensive consultations that would consider Indian security concerns.[12]

Fuel Supply Assurances

The conditioning of fuel supply assurances was another way to deter an Indian nuclear test. The separation plan allowed India to build up fuel reserves and take corrective measures to ensure the uninterrupted operation of its reactors if nuclear cooperation were terminated. However, the Hyde Act mentioned that such fuel reserves were not intended to help India override sanctions in the event of a nuclear test (though the presidential signing statement considered this section of the Hyde Act to be advisory but not legally binding). New Delhi opposed these provisions.

Ahead of the February 2007 talks, Washington had proposed fuel supplies for just one extra core of a reactor, while New Delhi sought uninterrupted fuel supplies for up to 40 years, which was the operating life of a reactor. New Delhi also insisted on maintaining the fuel supply arrangements of its separation plan (Varadarajan, 2007b). In early June, India's prime minister informed Undersecretary Burns that India's Parliament would only accept an agreement that insulated India's reactors from fuel supply disruptions. Still, Washington would not provide the strongest fuel supply assurances to New Delhi because it could not undermine the Atomic Energy Act and it could not mandate that industry vendors supply fuel to India.[13]

Washington and New Delhi eventually resolved this issue in the July meeting between their national security advisors. Here, India's national security advisor informed his US counterpart that 'you cannot derogate a commitment [on fuel supply assurances] that has been made because it is linked to safeguards in perpetuity': this point referred to India's separation plan which linked fuel supply assurances to safeguards in perpetuity (Khare and Varadarajan, 2007a). The Section 123 Agreement then adopted language identical to that in the separation plan. Washington agreed to provide fuel supply assurances to New Delhi in four ways, and to allow India to take corrective measures, and New Delhi accepted safeguards in perpetuity (Varadarajan, 2007f).[14] Thus, on this issue, the Section 123 Agreement had the same relatively low-to-moderate non-proliferation provisions as the separation plan.

ENR Technology

The Hyde Act barred ENR technology transfer to India with minor exceptions. India objected to this provision, arguing that 'While the Indian side does not realistically expect controls to be eased on…actual reprocessing or enrichment plants, it must be able to buy dual-use list items for use in civilian reprocessing and enrichment facilities'.[15]

Washington took the position that, because India had the capability to reprocess, it did not need such technology from abroad.[16] It further explained to New Delhi that the US did not transfer ENR technology even to close allies, and therefore the prohibition on ENR technology would treat India on par with such US allies. It added that, because the Joint Statement mentioned that India would not support ENR programs in other countries, it assumed that India would not seek ENR exceptions for itself.

Washington and New Delhi eventually agreed that ENR technology 'may be transferred under this Agreement pursuant to an amendment to this Agreement'. Thus, the Section 123 Agreement had relatively moderate-to-high non-proliferation provisions on this issue. It was in some ways moderate because it mentioned the future possibility of ENR transfers to India. Yet, it was high in practice, because negotiating the amendments to allow such transfers would be very difficult.

Reprocessing Consent

India's three-stage nuclear program entailed the reprocessing of spent fuel from its first-stage reactors to fuel the second-stage breeder reactors. However, the Atomic Energy Act did not permit reprocessing of US-origin fuel without prior US approval. Washington therefore sought to adopt the same approach that it took in the Hyde Act, which was to not mention reprocessing. When New Delhi pressed the issue, Washington indicated that it was willing to use 'forward looking language' that would be similar to the US–China Section 123 agreement (where Washington had committed to 'consider...favorably' any Chinese request for reprocessing) (Varadarajan, 2007e).

In May, both sides sought a compromise by 'not including some of the contentious issues with regard to reprocessing of spent fuel' (Haniffa, 2007). However, India rejected this formula. Thereafter, the US was willing to give India reprocessing consent on terms similar to those that applied to Japan and the EU: by establishing a new reprocessing facility, with Washington closely involved with the IAEA in framing the safeguards (Ramachandran, 2007). US negotiator Richard Stratford informed his Indian counterparts about this approach, but Indian officials were reluctant to accept US inspectors for their reprocessing plants.[17] Eventually, New Delhi accepted IAEA oversight of its new reprocessing plant. It then agreed to this compromise during Undersecretary Burns' 1–2 June talks in Delhi.

In mid-June, Washington and New Delhi further discussed the reprocessing facility. Indian officials explained that the dedicated facility would reprocess spent fuel originating from all countries, rather than from just the US, because, on economic grounds, India did not want the facility to remain idle. They added that, while the US had suggested that the facility could be part of the international Global Nuclear Energy Partnership (GNEP), India did not necessarily see a connection between the facility and GNEP, but instead considered it to be a national rather than a multinational facility.[18]

In the end, the Section 123 Agreement noted that 'the Parties grant each other consent to reprocess' and that 'to bring these rights into effect, India will establish a new national reprocessing facility'. Further, to avoid delays, it stated that 'consultations on arrangements and procedures [for reprocessing] will begin within six months of a request by either Party and will be concluded within one year'.

To summarize, the Section 123 Agreement had relatively low-to-moderate non-proliferation provisions on reprocessing consent. It was moderate because it allowed reprocessing only at a dedicated national facility, but lower because it accommodated India with a reasonable one-year timeframe to negotiate reprocessing rights.

International versus Domestic Law

In the Section 123 Agreement, New Delhi sought affirmation that it would only have to accept this agreement (that is, international law) and not the Hyde Act (that is, US domestic law). Accordingly, Indian negotiators had a line in all their drafts that was similar to Article 2.1 of the China–US 123 Agreement (Varadarajan, 2007h). This mentioned that 'the parties recognize…the principle of international law that provides that a party may not invoke the provisions of its internal law [such as the Hyde Act] as justification for its failure to perform a treaty'. Yet, US negotiators noted that Congress would not accept such a provision.

Eventually, the Section 123 Agreement included a compromise sentence. It stated that the Agreement 'shall be implemented in good faith and in accordance with the principles of international law'.[19] Thus, the Section 123 Agreement had relatively moderate non-proliferation provisions on this issue, because it indirectly, though not specifically, accommodated New Delhi's position.

To summarize, the final Section 123 Agreement had relatively low-to-moderate non-proliferation provisions overall, and represented an A6 arrangement shown in Table 6.1. It had relatively low provisions on terminating cooperation; low-to-moderate provisions on the right of return, fuel supply assurances, and reprocessing consent; moderate provisions on the issue of international law; and moderate-to-high provisions on restricting ENR technology transfers to India. It excluded relatively high non-proliferation provisions on the issues and therefore remained within India's win-set, and it excluded relatively low non-proliferation provisions on most issues and therefore remained within the US win-set.

Table 6.1 Alternative Arrangements for the Section 123 Agreement

Type	Example	Non-proliferation Provisions
A1	Very strong non-proliferation position	*Very high non-proliferation provisions on all issues*
A3	Strong position sought by the US non-proliferation bureaucracy	*High non-proliferation provisions on all the issues*
A4	Closer to April 2007 draft and equivalent arrangements	*High non-proliferation provisions on about half and moderate provisions on the other half of the issues*
A5	Closer to May 2007 compromise and equivalent arrangements	*Moderate non-proliferation provisions on almost all the issues*
A6	Section 123 Agreement	*Moderate nonproliferation provisions on about half and low provisions on the other half of the issues*
		*Terminating cooperation (low): either party has a right to terminate cooperation taking into account India's security concerns
		**Right of return (low-to-moderate): Atomic Energy Act provisions and *several* mitigating counter provisions
		***ENR technology transfer (moderate-to-high): allowed with amendments to agreement, but difficult to implement
		****Reprocessing consent (low-to-moderate): in a dedicated national facility, and with consultation on the facility within one to two years
		*****International law (moderate): 'in accordance with the principles of international law'
		******Safeguards/fuel assurances (low-to-moderate): permanent India-specific safeguards and significant fuel assurances and corrective measures
A7	Closer to position of India's nuclear establishment	*Low non-proliferation provisions on all issues*
A9	Ideal position of India's nuclear establishment	*Very low non-proliferation provisions on all issues*

Notes: The non-proliferation provisions are coded from very high to very low as follows:

1. *Terminating cooperation: immediately upon (very high) or within weeks of (high) India's detonating a nuclear device; if an event jeopardizes the US supreme national interests (moderate); either party may terminate cooperation taking into account India's security concerns (low); no mention of terminating cooperation (very low)

2. **Right of return: The US has the right with no (very high) or almost no mitigating provisions (high); with some mitigating counter provisions (moderate); conditional upon mitigating counter provisions (low); no mention of the right of return (very low)

3. ***ENR technology transfer: banned entirely (very high); banned with minor exceptions (high); allowed with amendments to the agreement (moderate); allowed as per terms of the agreement (low); no barriers to ENR transfers (very low)

4. ****Reprocessing consent: none (very high); none with minor exceptions (high); in dedicated national facility, but consultation on the facility can take a long time (moderate); in any facility, and with consultation on the facility within one to two years (low); allowed with little further consultation required (very low)

5. *****International law: internal laws entirely apply (very high) or usually apply (high); 'in accordance with the principles of international law' (moderate); more indirect, saying that a party 'may not invoke the provisions of its internal law' (low); direct mention that Section 123 Agreement will override internal laws (very low)

6. ******Safeguards/fuel supply assurances: IAEA's standard permanent safeguards and no (very high) or limited (high) fuel supply assurances; permanent safeguards and significant fuel assurances but no corrective measures (moderate); permanent safeguards and significant fuel assurances and corrective measures (low); voluntary safeguards and extensive fuel assurances and strong corrective measures (very low)

US Domestic Politics

Bureaucratic factors, congressional activism, and domestic mobilization influenced the US negotiating position on the Section 123 Agreement. At the bureaucratic level, the senior-most policymakers were willing to accommodate India on the principal non-proliferation issues, thereby enlarging the win-set. In terms of congressional activism, Congress repeatedly indicated that it would reject any Section 123 Agreement that was not consistent with the Hyde Act, thereby reducing the win-set. Finally, substantial mobilization by non-proliferation groups heightened congressional awareness of the non-proliferation issues. At the same time, mobilization by advocates, especially on commercial issues, reinforced the administration's strategic and economic case for the overall nuclear agreement and helped expand the win-set. This enabled the Bush administration to accept a Section 123 Agreement that had low-to-moderate rather than moderate or high non-proliferation provisions.

Bureaucratic Factors

Bureaucratic factors affected Washington's position on the Section 123 Agreement in three ways.[20] First, although Section 123 Agreements are almost exclusively negotiated by non-proliferation specialists (from the Department of Energy and the State Department's bureau of international security and non-proliferation), regional and strategic affairs experts (from the State Department's South Asia bureau, Undersecretary Burns' staff, the US Embassy in India, and the Department of Defense) also participated in Section 123 talks with India. Indian negotiators persuaded these experts to accommodate New Delhi on issues that were not the most sensitive.

Second, in contrast to its position on less sensitive issues, the US negotiating team did not offer New Delhi concessions on the most sensitive issues of ENR transfers and reprocessing. This was because non-proliferation specialists were well-represented on the US negotiating team and regional and strategic affairs experts also accepted the need to protect certain non-proliferation red lines.

Third, while the US negotiating team did not offer India concessions on sensitive issues, more senior US officials did. Here, it should be noted that while a non-proliferation specialist (Richard Stratford from the State Department's bureau of international security and non-proliferation) led the US negotiating group, he reported to Nicholas Burns, the undersecretary for political affairs, rather than to Robert Joseph, the undersecretary for arms control and international security (also, Joseph had left his position in March 2007). Eventually, Undersecretary Burns and even more senior officials handled the negotiating deadlocks. And, since the undersecretary for arms control and international security did not participate in talks with India, there was no high-level non-proliferation representation in senior-level US decision making on the issue.

The senior-most US officials eventually took important decisions to advance talks with India. Thus, after talks stalled in April and May 2007, President Bush allowed India the consent to reprocess, and National Security Advisor Hadley and Undersecretary Burns then worked with their Indian counterparts to finalize arrangements on reprocessing.

Overall, while the president, secretary of state, undersecretary for political affairs, and national security advisor are not normally involved in Section 123 talks with other countries, they were involved in breaking negotiating deadlocks with India. These senior officials gave priority to advancing the strategic partnership with India. Their involvement allowed Washington to make compromises towards India's position and kept a Section 123 Agreement with relatively low-to-moderate non-proliferation provisions within the US win-set.

The Congressional Position

Congressional activism reduced the US win-set on the Section 123 Agreement in four ways. First, the Hyde Act had outlined the terms for nuclear cooperation with India and the Bush administration had to incorporate these in the Section 123 Agreement. Further, in 2007, Democrats held a majority in Congress, and they were less likely than Republicans to accept any Section 123 Agreement that did not adhere closely to the Hyde Act.

Second, especially because of the above-mentioned considerations, the Bush administration kept Congress informed about negotiations for the Section 123 Agreement. It explained to Congress how its negotiating position met the requirements of the Hyde Act and the Atomic Energy Act.[21]

Third, Congress directly conveyed its concerns to the Bush administration. Illustrating this, a letter from Representative Markey, signed by 22 additional representatives, stated that 'we write to underscore the necessity of abiding by the legal boundaries set by Congress for any such cooperation [with India]'.[22] It added that the Section 123 Agreement should adhere to certain 'minimal conditions under US law'.

Fourth, Congress informed India's government of its position. In an early April 2007 meeting in Delhi with India's foreign secretary and former foreign secretary, congressmen noted that their support for the Section 123 Agreement should not be taken for granted; contrary to any Indian government thinking, Congress would not change the Hyde Act; and the US could not pursue civilian nuclear cooperation with countries that conducted nuclear tests.[23] Subsequently, members of Congress raised additional issues. They expressed concerns about India's ties with Iran and about its technology procurement activity in a 19 April letter signed by eight senators and in a 2 May letter signed by seven representatives. These drew upon a 19 March *Defense News* article mentioning an India–Iran defence group and a 2 April Justice Department indictment of individuals assisting India in procuring missile-relevant technology. While such issues were not part of the Section 123 Agreement, they were covered in the Hyde Act, and congressional activism on the issues signalled that Congress would uphold the terms of the Hyde Act.

To summarize, congressional concerns about India's conforming to the Hyde Act, and about the Section 123 Agreement being consistent with the Hyde Act, reduced the US win-set on the Section 123 Agreement. Congress drew upon points raised by non-proliferation groups.

Non-proliferation Groups

Non-proliferation groups highlighted the main non-proliferation issues in the Section 123 Agreement in several ways. In December 2006, non-proliferation experts outlined their concerns about the Hyde Act and called for addressing these in the Section 123 Agreement (Kimball and Cirincione, 2006). Later, in a May 2007 letter, 14 experts urged Congress 'to communicate to the White House that you will oppose any proposed [Section 123] agreement for nuclear cooperation with India that does not explicitly meet all the requirements outlined in U.S. law' (ACA, 2007). The letter specifically mentioned concerns in the areas of 'Nuclear Testing and Termination of U.S. Assistance', 'Permanent, Unconditional Safeguards', and 'Reprocessing and Enrichment Prohibitions'. And the Lawyers Alliance for World Security outlined similar concerns.[24] All these initiatives ensured that Congress did not neglect the principal non-proliferation issues in the Section 123 Agreement.

The Advocacy Coalition

While the Section 123 Agreement was negotiated, US business pursued several efforts to advance defence and nuclear cooperation with India. In December 2006, assisted by the US-India Business Council (USIBC) and Confederation of Indian Industry (CII), 258 business executives from 200 US firms visited India, including 30 executives from the nuclear sector. Further, from January to June 2007, USIBC hosted many meetings on strategic and nuclear cooperation with India. These included a 19 January round table with Undersecretary Burns, events on 30 January and 23 March with Undersecretary of Commerce Franklin Levin, and a 27 June 'Global India' event where Secretary Rice was the keynote speaker.

These business initiatives influenced Washington's stand on the Section 123 negotiations in two ways. First, they indirectly widened the US win-set by indicating that American business would lobby for the nuclear agreement even if the Section 123 Agreement did not have the strongest non-proliferation conditions. Second, they directly conveyed Indian concerns – which were also the concerns of US business – about specific items in the Section 123 Agreement. On this point, Indian government officials informed US business executives that US firms would be less competitive in India's nuclear sector if the Section 123 Agreement did not satisfy India on reprocessing.[25] American business conveyed this information to the US government. Thus, US business, both indirectly and directly, influenced the US government to accommodate India in the Section 123 Agreement.

The Press

In early and mid-2007, the major US dailies carried 10 editorials and opinion-editorials on the nuclear agreement, of which eight supported and advocated moving ahead with the Section 123 Agreement.

Thus, reflecting the administration's stand, an opinion-editorial by Undersecretary Burns highlighted the strategic and commercial benefits of a partnership with India (Burns, 2007a). Echoing a similar sentiment, *The Washington Times* endorsed movement on the Section 123 Agreement (Boyle et al., 2007). It argued that Washington could accommodate New Delhi on reprocessing because this could be part of the GNEP program. Reflecting a further supportive position, former Defense Secretary William Cohen wrote that the nuclear agreement 'finally removes the cinder from the eye, ending decades of misunderstanding and distrust about India's nuclear intent and capabilities' (Cohen, 2007).

On a related note, Washington and New Delhi had an understanding to not negotiate through the media. As a result, there were no leaks from the US side and little press coverage of the Section 123 talks in the US media. This lessened domestic mobilization against the agreement in the US.

To summarize, the US media, along with US business, favoured advancing the nuclear agreement with India and this helped expand the US win-set on the Section 123 Agreement.

India's Domestic Politics

Domestic political factors affected India's position on the Section 123 Agreement in various ways. Bureaucratic resistance from India's nuclear establishment, opposition from the left and the right, and mobilization by critics, all reduced India's win-set so that an agreement with relatively moderate non-proliferation provisions fell outside the win-set. Still, mobilization by advocates helped expand the win-set so that India's government could accept a Section 123 Agreement having relatively low-to-moderate non-proliferation provisions.

Bureaucratic Factors

Bureaucratic differences between DAE and MEA, as well as similarities in their positions on some issues, reduced India's win-set on the Section 123 Agreement.

In terms of similarities, DAE and MEA both held the view that Washington was changing the terms of the Joint Statement in the Hyde Act. They, therefore, sought to address these issues in Section 123 talks with Washington. In terms of their differences, MEA rather than DAE had more knowledge of the US' Section 123 Agreements with other countries and it brought up these in Section 123 talks with Washington. The DAE was more influenced by the legacy of technology denial regimes against India, and therefore sought a more thorough lifting of technology restrictions. Further, DAE was more affected by the Tarapur experience (though MEA rather than DAE had, in prior decades, negotiated the Tarapur issue with Washington), and therefore sought provisions to counter hypothetical future situations where nuclear cooperation with India could be curtailed.[26] These bureaucratic factors affected India's negotiating position on a number of occasions.

First, DAE's approach to India's February 2007 draft of the Section 123 Agreement set back talks with Washington. The press surmised that 'clearly, the Department of Atomic Energy broadened the area of divergences through this draft' (Samanta, 2007). Second, in April, DAE again appeared to oppose some negotiating solutions. Commenting on this, the press noted that 'the arms of the government that are negotiating this deal are at war with each other. While the diplomats want to continue working to find a way out, the scientists are on an all-or-nothing mode' (Rajghatta and Bagchi, 2007). Third, in May, the Government of India's overall 'all or nothing' stance influenced it to reject any Section 123 arrangements that excluded the contentious issues; accordingly, 'the compromise [of mid-May] was rejected when it was presented to the prime minister's office' (*The Telegraph*, 2007a).

To summarize, bureaucratic factors reduced India's win-set on the Section 123 Agreement and, in the end, India's national security advisor had to bridge the gap between MEA and DAE to keep compromises within India's win-set.

Opposition from the Left and the Right

From December 2006 to July 2007, India's leftist and right-wing parties repeatedly raised concerns about the Hyde Act and called for addressing these in the Section 123 Agreement.

Reflecting these concerns, after a meeting on 10 December 2006, BJP leaders Atal Behari Vajpayee, L. K. Advani, Rajnath Singh, Jaswant Singh,

Yashwant Sinha, and Arun Shourie criticized the Hyde Act. They raised the same technical and strategic nuclear issues that they had mentioned in prior months (that the Hyde Act restricted India's ability to test and to build a credible deterrent); they raised new nuclear issues such as ENR restrictions; they repeated their argument about the net high costs and low benefits of the nuclear agreement; and they continued to highlight political process issues.[27] On this point, as Section 123 talks advanced, the BJP called for a parliamentary statement from India's prime minister. It stated that 'it is incumbent upon the Prime Minister to satisfy both Houses of Parliament...that the assurances he had given [to the Parliament in August 2006] have been fulfilled [in the Section 123 Agreement]'.[28]

The left expressed even stronger concerns with the Hyde Act and with the overall nuclear agreement. It observed that the Hyde Act 'is grossly violative of the assurances made by the prime minister in the Indian parliament' (*People's Democracy*, 2006). As Section 123 talks progressed, it called for India's prime minister to make a parliamentary statement. It also objected to the 19 April and 2 May letters signed by US congressmen that had criticized India's ties with Iran; India's Parliament adjourned on 7 May when the left and the right both opposed these letters (*People's Democracy*, 2007a). Finally, it asked the government 'not to proceed with the 123 bilateral negotiations without the United States changing some of the provisions of the Hyde Act' (*People's Democracy*, 2007b).

India's government had to take into account the left's opposition, especially in early 2007, because of its political weakness. It had lost state elections in Punjab and Uttarakhand (Uttaranchal) in February, and the Congress Party leadership was extremely concerned about the May 2007 elections in Uttar Pradesh.[29] It was concerned that any perception of a pro-US foreign policy could cost them the Muslim vote in these elections. It therefore urged cautious approaches on economic reforms and foreign policy, including on the nuclear agreement. As a result, reformers such as Prime Minister Singh were politically weakened and the old-line Congress Party and the left were politically empowered. These developments hindered India's government from making compromises on and pressing ahead with a Section 123 Agreement in early 2007.

To summarize, opposition from the left and the right reduced India's winset as it negotiated the Section 123 Agreement. India's political parties drew upon domestic mobilization on the issues.

Domestic Mobilization

India's strategic affairs experts, nuclear experts, and commentators mobilized for and against the nuclear agreement in a number of ways. Some of them briefed India's political parties about technical issues in the Hyde Act; for example, in the spring of 2007, leaders of the left met strategic affairs experts and discussed the Hyde Act and the Section 123 Agreement.[30] Others expressed their concerns to the DAE leadership; on 15 December 2006, senior ex-governmental nuclear scientists met the DAE secretary to outline their concerns. In addition, experts and analysts wrote extensively in the Indian press.

First, supporters highlighted the overall strategic benefits of the nuclear agreement and argued that, despite the Hyde Act, India should move ahead with the Section 123 Agreement.[31] On the other hand, opponents highlighted legal concerns about the Hyde Act overriding the Section 123 Agreement. They noted that 'no 123 agreement – however diplomatically worded – can release India from the Hyde Act's obligations. An earlier 123 accord over Tarapur, signed in 1963, was abandoned by Washington in 1978 simply by enacting a new domestic law that retroactively overrode the bilateral pact' (Chellaney, 2007).[32]

Second, the press drew attention to the main issues in the Section 123 Agreement. Some analysts noted the need to maintain India's right to conduct nuclear tests (Karnad, 2006, 2007). Others sought to inform Indian policymakers about the issues: 'India must absolutely insist on getting lifelong nuclear fuel assurances under this deal…and the waiver from having to return any prior supplies we might have received' (Gopalakrishnan, 2007a). Still others noted that: 'If there is no 'full' cooperation [on ENR technologies] at the end of the negotiating tunnel and if the U.S. succeeds in converting India's voluntary test moratorium into an involuntary one…the political fallout [in India] will be substantial' (Varadarajan, 2007c).

To summarize, the Indian press highlighted the principal issues in the Section 123 Agreement, but also supported moving ahead with this agreement.

Indian Business

Indian business pursued a number of initiatives that influenced India's government to advance the Section 123 Agreement. As noted earlier, in late 2006 and early 2007, Indian business and their US counterparts held several events exploring commercial opportunities in India's nuclear and defence sectors. And US officials reinforced the case that Indian business would benefit from the nuclear agreement. For example, on 26 June 2007, Undersecretary of Commerce Franklin Lavin informed Indian business that 'The United States nuclear industry frankly has more to offer the Indians than the competition'.[33] Such initiatives resulted in Indian business mobilizing in favour of the nuclear agreement.

Further, Indian business continued to sponsor track-2 initiatives. For example, at the January 2007 CII-Aspen dialogue, participants discussed bilateral US–India economic and military ties, and also held private meetings with Prime Minister Singh, External Affairs Minister Mukherjee, and Finance Minister Chidambaram. Through such interaction, US and Indian business leaders and strategic elites affirmed to the senior-most Indian policymakers their support for, and the importance of moving ahead with, the nuclear agreement.

Summing Up

In the end, mobilization by some strategic affairs analysts and nuclear scientists reduced India's win-set on the Section 123 Agreement, but mobilization by supportive experts and by Indian business helped expand the win-set. Such mobilization, along with political power considerations (related to the left's not withdrawing support for India's government), enabled India's government to move ahead with the Section 123 Agreement in mid-2007.

The eventual Section 123 Agreement contained relatively low-to-moderate non-proliferation provisions that kept it within Washington's and New Delhi's respective win-sets. Still, in the US, non-proliferation advocates and even some neutral observers took the view that Congress and the NSG should seek tougher non-proliferation conditions from India. Reflecting these concerns, *The New York Times* noted that the nuclear agreement had 'been made even worse by a newly negotiated companion agreement [the Section 123 Agreement]. Congress should reject the agreement and demand that the administration, or its successor, negotiate a new one' (*The New York Times*, 2007a). And *The Washington Post* noted that the Section 123 Agreement would not deter an Indian nuclear test. It stated that 'the United States committed to helping India accumulate a nuclear fuel stockpile, thus insulating New Delhi against the threat, provided for by U.S. law, of a supply cutoff in the unlikely event that India resumes weapons testing' (*The Washington Post*, 2007a).

India's opposition parties took a very different position: they argued that New Delhi went too far in accommodating Washington. They, therefore, blocked movement on the nuclear agreement for the next several months.

Endnotes

1   These remarks were cited in Rajghatta and Bagchi (2007).
2   At this meeting, participants recognized that India sought firm assurances on these issues to avoid a recurrence of the Tarapur experience, while Washington noted that any Indian nuclear tests would kill the political will in the US for the civilian nuclear initiative. The US Embassy, New Delhi, cable, 13 November 2006.
3   The US Embassy, New Delhi, cable, 13 March 2007.
4   The US Embassy, New Delhi, cable, 22 March 2007.
5   Author interview Y1, 2 November 2011.
6   The US Embassy, New Delhi, cable, 18 June 2007.
7   Ibid.
8   Author interview D4, 25 October 2011.
9   This discussion draws from author interview F1, 2 September 2011; author interview O1, 7 September 2011; and author interview U1, 26 November 2011.
10 New Delhi also took two other positions on termination. First, it argued that termination should only be linked to a violation of the Section 123 Agreement and not to issues outside the agreement such as nuclear testing. Second (this was relevant to the right of return), it was only willing to accept prospective termination that would apply to future nuclear cooperation, but it would not accept retrospective termination for prior nuclear cooperation since this would require it to return imported materials.
11 New Delhi opposed the right of return by making the argument that, in the July 2005 Joint Statement, it had not agreed to accept penalties such as returning imported items if it conducted a nuclear test; it also noted that, in the Joint Statement, the Bush administration had committed to changing the US laws to facilitate nuclear cooperation with India, but that, in subsequent months and years, the Bush administration made no attempts to change parts of the Atomic Energy Act that mandated the right of return if India conducted a nuclear test.
12 Commenting on this issue, K. Subrahmanyam noted that the Section 123 Agreement 'strengthens India's position on testing compared to the situations in 1974 and 1998…Indian diplomats have secured the country's right to test if the security environment deteriorates and if the US or any other nuclear weapon power were to test' (Subrahmanyam, 2007).
13 Author interview U2, 13 September 2011.

14 On corrective measures, Washington had taken the position that it could accept Indian corrective measures short of termination of safeguards, while New Delhi pressed for the original understanding of the term 'India-specific' safeguards, that is, permanent safeguards that were linked with fuel supply assurances and corrective measures.

15 New Delhi drew upon incidents involving US export control regulations to make its case for dual-use items. It noted that Washington had indicted Indian individuals for importing what it considered to be obsolete chips, and that, in a similar manner, any future Indian purchases of civilian reprocessing items might also lead to sanctions.

16 Author interview T1, 25 October 2011. In India's view, Washington's 'assurances provided during the 123 Agreement negotiations [were] that, while the U.S. would not transfer ENR to India, we [the US] would not stand in the way of others doing so'. The US Embassy, New Delhi, cable, 12 February 2009.

17 Author interview I2, 16 September 2011; author interview U2, 13 September 2011.

18 The US Embassy, New Delhi, cable, 18 June 2007.

19 This was a reference to the Vienna Convention on the Law of Treaties, which states that 'A party may not invoke the provisions of its internal law as justification for its failure to perform a treaty'.

20 This discussion draws from author interview F1, 2 September 2011; author interview I2, 16 September 2011; author interview O1, 7 September 2011; author interview U2, 13 September, 2011; and author interview Y1, 2 November 2011.

21 Author interview I2, 16 September 2011.

22 Though it was dated 25 July, after the Section 123 Agreement was completed, the letter reflected congressional concerns while the agreement was being negotiated.

23 The US Embassy, New Delhi, cable, 9 April 2007. Indian officials replied that 'any perception that the Indian side is trying to change what Congress has in mind is not an accurate reflection'.

24 On these concerns, see publications by the Lawyers Alliance for World Security (2007a, 2007b).

25 Author interview L2, 26 July 2010. During a 5 March meeting in India with USIBC executives from the nuclear sector, Indian officials mentioned that Russia had given India reprocessing consent, thereby suggesting that US firms would be less competitive versus their Russian counterparts if Washington did not give India such consent. The US Embassy, New Delhi, cable, 6 March 2007.

26 Author interview T1, 25 October 2011.

27 For these issues, see the 'Joint Press Statement of Yashwant Sinha and Arun Shourie on the Indo-US Nuclear Deal', 10 December 2006; and Arun Shourie's pieces in the *The Indian Express* on 20, 21, 22, and 23 December, 2006.

28 See 'Statement of Shri Atal Bihari Vajpayee on the Indo-US Nuclear Deal', 28 May 2007. Later, in a 6 July statement, Vajpayee expressed concerns about a task force set up by the PMO to review Indian nuclear policy.

29   The US Embassy, New Delhi, cable, 6 March 2007. Indian and US officials also speculated that because of electoral defeats in February, some Congress Party members wanted to stall the Section 123 Agreement, with some even suggesting an 18-month freeze in nuclear discussions. As a result, US officials noted in early March that 'the only way to move the nuclear deal forward may be to make a decisive play at the senior political level'.

30   Author interview M1, 5 November 2009.

31   See, for example, pieces by K. Subrahmanyam (*The Indian Express*, 12 December 2006), Raj Chengappa (*India Today*, 25 December 2006), G. Balachandran (*The Times of India*, 27 December 2006 and *The Indian Express*, 19 December 2006) and R. Rajaraman (*Hindustan Times*, 30 April 2007).

32   Chellaney also made similar and additional points in *The Times of India*, 9 January 2007 and the *Hindustan Times*, 28 May 2007.

33   These points were noted by Franklin Lavin at an event of the USIBC–CII Joint Task Force on Commercial Nuclear Cooperation, Washington, DC, 26 June 2007.

CHAPTER SEVEN

India's Domestic Politics

On 7 August 2007, days after the US and India announced the details of their Section 123 Agreement, India's leftist parties declared that they were 'unable to accept' the agreement.[1] They also called upon India's government 'not to proceed further with the operationalizing of the agreement'. The left thereby blocked India's government from negotiating a safeguards pact with the IAEA and sending it to the IAEA board for approval.

India's government then made three attempts to advance the nuclear agreement. First, from August to November, it sought to persuade both the left and the right to accept the agreement. In mid-November, the left allowed the government to begin safeguards talks with the IAEA. Second, from late November 2007 to May 2008, India's government again made its case to the left and the right. Yet, they both still rejected the government's overtures. Therefore, while India's government negotiated a safeguards pact with the IAEA, it could not forward the pact to the IAEA board. Third, in June and July 2008, India's government attained the backing of a regional party, the SP, so that it could remain in office despite leftist opposition. This enabled India's government to send the safeguards pact to the IAEA board and thereby move ahead with the nuclear agreement.

Initial Efforts to Overcome Domestic Opposition

In the fall of 2007, India's government asked the left and the right not to block movement on the nuclear agreement. Mobilization by supporters and US initiatives reinforced the government's efforts. Still, the left and the right opposed the agreement on the grounds that it affected India's nuclear weapons program, its three-stage nuclear energy program, and its pursuit of an independent foreign policy. Eventually, however, the left accepted a limited compromise: in mid-November, it allowed the government to pursue safeguards talks with the IAEA.

Government–Left Interactions

India's government interacted extensively with the left in August and September 2007. On 7 August, left leaders – Prakash Karat (from the CPI(M)), A. B. Bardhan and D. Raja (both from the CPI), Abani Roy (from the Revolutionary Socialist Party [RSP]), and G. Devarajan (from the All India Forward Bloc [AIFB] – had met and discussed the Section 123 Agreement. They issued a statement raising technical concerns with the agreement and seeking a review of US–India strategic relations. India's government countered the left's technical points and also highlighted the broader strategic, energy, and geopolitical benefits of the nuclear initiative.

First, non-political government officials addressed technical concerns about the nuclear agreement. Thus, at a 27 July press conference, the national security advisor, foreign secretary, and DAE secretary outlined the main features of the Section 123 Agreement. Soon thereafter, on 10 August, the principal scientific advisor to the Government of India, R. Chidambaram, further commented on the issues (Khare and Varadarajan, 2007b). On the broader strategic and energy issues, he noted that the nuclear agreement was consistent with 'three boundary conditions. There will be no effect on the [Indian] strategic program, there will be no deceleration in our three-stage nuclear power program…and there will be no effect on our advanced R&D program'. On the technical issue of nuclear testing, he noted that 'there is nothing in the agreement which prevents us from testing'; that 'based on the tests [of 1998] we can build weapons [with yields] from sub-kiloton to 200 kilotons'; and that 'we [also] have a considerable computer simulation capability'. Further, on 11 August, the DAE secretary provided similar reassurances on these issues. For example, on the technical issue of fuel supplies for India's reactors, he affirmed that 'there will be no interruption in their operation', and that, if the nuclear agreement was terminated, 'we can still run the [reactor] systems using the strategic reserve of fuel' (Subramanian, 2007).

Second, India's political leaders defended the nuclear agreement. In a 10 August interview, Prime Minister Manmohan Singh outlined the case for the nuclear agreement. He added that in his conversations with the left, he had said that they could 'do whatever they want to do, if they want to withdraw support [for the government], so be it' (Chatterjee, 2007). The prime minister also quoted R. Chidambaram's above-mentioned points on the three boundary conditions: 'I cannot improve on what he [Chidambaram] has said. He has said that all three conditions have been met' (ibid.).

On 13 August, the prime minister defended the nuclear agreement in the Parliament. On the strategic, economic, and energy issues, he noted that: 'we have ensured that the autonomy of our strategic program is fully maintained'; the nuclear agreement would address 'the twin challenges of energy security and environmental sustainability'; it would remove 'the technology-denial regimes that have, for decades, been a major constraint on our development'; and 'the commitments I had made to Parliament, including those on August 17, 2006, have been fully adhered to'.[2] He also discussed technical points that the left had raised on 7 August. Thus, he noted that India would maintain fuel reserves for its reactors, and he affirmed that the nuclear agreement 'does not in any way affect India's right to undertake future nuclear tests'.

Senior leaders of the Congress Party backed the prime minister. On 14 August, Congress Party President Sonia Gandhi defended the nuclear agreement in a Congress Parliamentary Party meeting. Other members of the Congress Party endorsed the agreement in the press.[3]

While affirming its intentions to advance the nuclear agreement, India's government still reached out to the left. On 7 August, the prime minister had a phone conversation with Prakash Karat, A. B. Bardhan, and D. Raja. From 14 August to 30 August, senior Congress Party members (Prime Minister Singh, External Affairs Minister Mukherjee, Defence Minister A. K. Antony, Party President Sonia Gandhi, and political secretary to the party president, Ahmed Patel) held several meetings with CPI(M) leaders, Prakash Karat and Sitaram Yechury, and CPI leaders, A. B. Bardhan, D. Raja, and Gurudas Dasgupta. India's government also appealed to left leaders from West Bengal: the prime minister hosted a dinner for the West Bengal chief minister when he was in Delhi for a CPI(M) politburo meeting on 17–18 August.

Despite the government's overtures, the left opposed movement on the nuclear agreement. Thus, after outlining its technical and political concerns on 7 August, the left privately noted, in a 9 August meeting with the US Embassy, that it would oppose the Section 123 Agreement in the Parliament, but that it would not join the BJP in demanding a parliamentary vote (because this could bring down the government).[4] On 14 August, it reiterated that 'The Prime Minister's [13 August] statement in Parliament does not shed any new light on the India–US Nuclear Agreement'.[5] Eventually, in late August, the government and the left agreed to form a committee to assess the Hyde Act and the Section 123 Agreement. The committee had 15 members, six each from the Congress Party and the left and one each from UPA constituents: the RJD, the DMK, and the NCP.

The UPA–Left Committee

The UPA–Left committee held its first four meetings on 11 September, 19 September, 5 October, and 9 October. It discussed broader geopolitical and energy issues behind the nuclear agreement as well as technical issues that were mentioned in the left's 7 August statement. The left submitted very detailed notes on these issues (dated 14 and 19 September and 2, 5, and 20 October) and the UPA submitted its responses (dated 17 and 24 September, 5 and 8 October, and 16 November).

First, the left questioned the necessity of importing reactors and the high price of imported reactors; the government affirmed the case for nuclear energy imports.[6] Second, the left argued that the Hyde Act overrode the Section 123 Agreement; the government took the opposite view. Third, on the technical issue of 'Full Nuclear Cooperation', the left note of 14 September stated that 'Sections 104(d)(4)(A)(i) and 104(d)(4)(B) [of the Hyde Act] together deny the export' of ENR technology to India. The UPA response of 17 September stated that 'such [ENR] technology can be accessed from other NSG countries as well and is not prohibited under the 123 Agreement'.

Fourth, on the technical issue of 'Fuel Supply Assurances', the UPA response of 17 September stated that India's separation plan had outlined multiple ways to assure fuel and that 'this has [also] been achieved in Article 5.6(a) of the 123 Agreement which specifically provides for reliable, uninterrupted and continual access to fuel supplies to Indian reactors'. The left took the opposite view: its 19 September rejoinder stated that 'Sections 103(b)(10) and 104(g)(2)(F)(iii) of the Hyde Act stand in the way of India accumulating adequate nuclear fuel reserves for imported reactors'.

Fifth, the two sides discussed IAEA safeguards, and also discussed fuel supply assurances in the IAEA safeguards context. The UPA response of 17 September stated that 'We have agreed to apply safeguards in perpetuity in return for assurance of fuel supply. These will be reflected appropriately in our [IAEA] Safeguards Agreement.' The UPA response of 24 September added that 'The early conclusion of the India-specific Safeguards Agreement with the IAEA would further clarify matters'.

This last point highlights a recurring theme in the Indian government's dialogue with the left: the government argued that the left's technical concerns would be addressed at a subsequent stage of international negotiations (in this case, in the IAEA safeguards pact) and that the left should therefore allow the government to proceed to that stage.

The October Impasse and November Compromise

India's government and the left could not bridge their differences at the first four UPA–Left meetings through early October. Further, West Bengal left leaders, who had made statements supporting nuclear power and who sought a compromise via an expert panel to review the nuclear agreement, could not persuade the left leadership to change its position: partly because West Bengal held only four of the 17 seats on the CPI(M) politburo (Chaudhry, 2007). At the 9 October UPA–Left meeting, the left rejected the government's renewed request to allow it to pursue safeguard talks, though it did not object to Prime Minister Singh's meeting with the visiting IAEA Director General, Mohammed El Baradei. India's government then gradually retreated.

The Congress Party decided, in a core committee meeting, to hold back on the nuclear agreement rather than face national elections that would follow if the left withdrew support for the government. While some Congress Party members such as Kapil Sibal and P. Chidambaram had defended the nuclear agreement in the press, others such as A. K. Antony, Pranab Mukherjee, Arjun Singh, and Shivraj Patil were cautious. The party also wanted to wait until December to focus on state elections in Gujarat. Further, its UPA allies – the NCP, DMK, and RJD – all advised against national elections (George, 2007). Subsequently, on 12 October, at the *Hindustan Times* Leadership Summit in Delhi, Prime Minister Singh and Congress Party President Sonia Gandhi both stated that they would not push ahead with the nuclear agreement. On 15 October, when President Bush called Prime Minister Singh, the prime minister informed the president that 'certain difficulties' were slowing India's government from advancing the agreement.[7]

Subsequently, between the fifth (22 October) and sixth (16 November) UPA–Left committee meetings, India's government and the left reached a compromise. The left affirmed that it would not seek a parliamentary voting resolution on the nuclear agreement and the government agreed to a parliamentary debate on the issue. Thereafter, at their 16 November meeting, both sides outlined a larger compromise: 'The government will proceed with the talks [with the IAEA] and the outcome will be presented to the [UPA–Left] Committee for its consideration before it finalizes its findings'.[8] This comprise also enabled the Congress Party and the left to avert a political confrontation ahead of the Gujarat elections.

Overtures to the BJP

While it reached out to the left, India's government simultaneously made overtures to the BJP. Some BJP leaders indicated flexibility on the nuclear agreement, but the BJP ultimately opposed the agreement.

On 26 July, India's government briefed the BJP leadership about the Section 123 Agreement.[9] In a meeting at the prime minister's residence, it discussed the issue with Jaswant Singh, Yashwant Sinha, Rajnath Singh, Arun Shourie, Atal Behari Vajpayee, and Brajesh Mishra. External Affairs Minister Mukherjee explained the political rationale for the nuclear agreement, while the national security advisor, DAE secretary, and foreign secretary discussed the technical issues in the Section 123 Agreement. They noted that the agreement would not impact India's strategic weapons program and its three-stage energy program, and that it addressed India's concerns about fuel reserves and reprocessing. The BJP leaders asked how India would respond if, after international vendors made large investments in India's nuclear sector, Washington pressured India by halting nuclear commerce and disrupting nuclear projects. The government replied that such interdependence was inherent in any international trade transaction and that it had secured fuel supply assurances to prevent disruptions in the operation of India's reactors. When the meeting ended, Prime Minister Singh privately informed former Prime Minister Vajpayee that he had completed a process that Vajpayee had started, and the two leaders shook hands. After the meeting, BJP leaders noted that Indian negotiators had done a 'superb job' in the negotiations, but they still did not endorse the Section 123 Agreement.

On 3 August, after the text of the Section 123 Agreement was released, Atal Behari Vajpayee, Yashwant Sinha, Jaswant Singh, and L. K. Advani (who was not at the 26 July meeting but was briefed by India's national security advisor on 1 August) discussed this agreement and came out against it. In a 4 August press release, Yashwant Sinha and Arun Shourie elaborated upon the BJP's objections. They highlighted their arguments from prior months about technical issues and overall cost–benefit issues.

Thus, on specific technical points, they argued that, first, the implementation of the Section 123 Agreement would be governed by the Hyde Act. Second, the Hyde Act and the Section 123 Agreement restricted ENR transfers and did not provide full nuclear cooperation. Third, these arrangements had a 'right of end-use verification [and therefore]…American inspectors will "roam around our nuclear installations"'. Fourth, fuel supply assurances were 'vague and futuristic'. Fifth, India would not have the freedom to conduct nuclear tests. Arun Shourie elaborated upon these and related points in *The Indian Express* on 17, 18, and 19 August.

Despite these objections, however, two members of the right suggested a compromise. First, in a 27 August interview in *The Indian Express*, L. K. Advani noted that he would not have 'any problem with the 123 Agreement' if the government introduced legislation that would offset the provisions of the Hyde Act.

Second, in late October, Brajesh Mishra conditionally supported the nuclear agreement. Mishra was somewhat assured by the Indian government's 26 July briefing and his subsequent conversations with strategic and nuclear experts.[10] He then stated: 'Perhaps one way out is for the government to provide credible guarantees about its devotion to the [Indian] strategic nuclear weapons program and the ready supply of fissile material now and in the future for weapons purposes. Given such guarantees, some of the opponents of the deal should think of supporting it' (*DNA*, 2007).

He repeated this point on 25 October, stating that 'If I were to get credible guarantees from the government…then I would say, personally, to go forward with the deal' (*The Indian Express*, 2007b).

In the following weeks, India's government again made its case to the BJP. Prime Minister Singh met Atal Behari Vajpayee and L. K. Advani in mid-November. Further, while other BJP leaders informed Vajpayee that their party had taken a decision against the nuclear agreement, Mishra's statements suggested a way for the BJP to reconsider its stand. In addition, on 3 and 4 November, India's national security advisor and the DAE secretary met Rajnath Singh and L. K. Advani. In the end, however, despite these efforts, which were backed by US initiatives, the BJP continued to oppose the nuclear agreement.

US Initiatives

US non-governmental groups and government officials made several attempts to persuade the left and the BJP to accept the nuclear agreement, and they also urged India's government to advance it.

First, US non-governmental groups made their case to India's opposition parties. Thus, a US–India Political Action Committee delegation visited India on 22–24 October. The prime minister asked the delegation to inform the BJP that he was willing to have a parliamentary debate on the nuclear agreement, while the BJP informed the delegation that it sought a joint parliamentary committee to look into the Hyde Act. Subsequently, in early November, a US–India Friendship Council member met left leaders from West Bengal and outlined the benefits of the nuclear agreement. At this time, Henry Kissinger also met L. K. Advani and West Bengal left leaders. Finally, in mid-November, former Defense Secretary William Cohen met Indian government officials, left leaders, and the West Bengal chief minister. He called attention to deadlines on the US congressional calendar that would require India's government to act on the agreement by the spring of 2008.

Second, the US ambassador urged the BJP to support the nuclear agreement. From 24 to 30 October, the ambassador met separately with L. K. Advani, Rajnath Singh, and Brajesh Mishra, and, on November 5, he met separately with Yashwant Sinha and Jaswant Singh.[11] In these interactions, Brajesh Mishra backed the nuclear agreement but stated that the Congress Party leaders, rather than the foreign secretary, should reach out to the BJP, and that the government should brief the BJP about India's strategic program. Rajnath Singh sought a joint parliamentary committee to examine the Section 123 Agreement and the Hyde Act. Jaswant Singh noted that he had asked the prime minister to not rush the nuclear initiative. Yashwant Sinha outlined the BJP's technical concerns, such as the fact that the nuclear agreement would 'put an embargo on nuclear testing' and would impact both the size and quality of India's deterrent.[12]

Third, US government officials discussed the nuclear agreement with India's government and with the left. Treasury Secretary Henry Paulson met the prime minister and the West Bengal chief minister, while Secretary Rice called India's external affairs minister to discuss the issue. At the same time, US government officials as well as US business executives did not publicly press India to act on the nuclear agreement because they recognized that any such statements could be politicized by the left and the right.

Fourth, the US media encouraged India's political establishment to advance the nuclear agreement. *The Washington Post* took note of Prime Minister Singh's domestic difficulties and also endorsed the nuclear agreement (*The Washington Post*, 2007b). *The Washington Times* noted that 'India could hardly have expected a sweeter deal [but]…Shockingly, the deal is being jeopardized by politicians in India…that either can't recognize India's interests or isn't committed to pursuing them' (*The Washington Times*, 2007). *The Wall Street Journal* questioned the left's opposition to the nuclear agreement: 'How this [opposition by the left] benefits India is anyone's guess' (Kissel, 2007). Relatedly, Undersecretary Nicholas Burns discussed the merits of the nuclear agreement in a November 2007 article in *Foreign Affairs* (Burns, 2007b).

To summarize, US governmental and non-governmental initiatives sought to persuade India's right and the left to not block the nuclear agreement. They augmented similar efforts by Indian supporters of the agreement.

Domestic Mobilization

India's strategic affairs experts, foreign affairs commentators, leading dailies, nuclear experts, and business executives, all came out in support of the nuclear agreement, though some sections of these constituencies continued to oppose it. They drew attention to broad strategic and energy issues as well as specific technical issues behind the agreement.

First, strategic affairs experts such as K. Subrahmanyam and Raja Mohan highlighted the strategic benefits of the nuclear agreement, arguing that it enabled India to avail of civilian nuclear cooperation without giving up its nuclear weapons program.[13] Siddharth Vardarajan also cautiously endorsed the agreement. On 17 August, he argued that of the three concerns India's opposition parties had about the agreement – its impact on India's nuclear weapons program, on India's three-stage nuclear energy program, and on Indian foreign policy – the Section 123 Agreement 'goes some way towards addressing the first two concerns' (Varadarajan, 2007g). He further suggested that, to address the left's concerns about India having to return any imported fuel or technology if the US terminated nuclear cooperation, 'Parliament could enact an amendment to the Atomic Energy Act of 1962 as well as a change in the Special Chemicals, Organisms, Materials, Equipment and Technologies (SCOMET) guidelines making it illegal for nuclear material or equipment to be transferred out of the country if the transfer would disrupt the continuous operation of our power reactors or pose an environmental or security risk' (ibid.). BJP leader L. K. Advani mentioned this point in his 27 August interview.

At the same time, two other strategic affairs experts continued to oppose the nuclear agreement. Bharat Karnad repeated his earlier concerns about the Hyde Act and the Section 123 Agreement, while Brahma Chellaney mentioned similar concerns in three pieces on 8, 9, and 10 September and another piece on 14 September that outlined 15 questions for the UPA–Left committee.[14]

Second, several ex-diplomats, retired military officials, commentators, and analysts endorsed the nuclear agreement. They included former Ambassador to the Conference on Disarmament Arundhati Ghose; former Ambassador to the US K. Shankar Bajpai; former Indian space agency Director K. Kasturirangan; former Foreign Secretary Jagat Mehta; former Foreign Secretary Muchkund Dubey; and former Army Chief V. P. Malik, who noted that 'India's strategic autonomy has not been compromised...the Agreement does not impinge on India's military strategic programs' (Malik, 2007).[15] Further, on 14 November 2007, 23 experts (including six retired senior military officers, four members of the scientific enclave, as well as strategic affairs experts and diplomats) sent an open letter to Members of Parliament (MPs) supporting the nuclear agreement. Several other commentators and analysts also endorsed the agreement.[16]

In contrast, a small number of commentators were neutral towards or opposed to the nuclear agreement. The neutral perspectives noted that the energy benefits of the agreement could not be easily calculated, and they cautioned against moving ahead without a domestic consensus.[17] Among the stronger opponents, ex-Prime Minister V. P. Singh questioned the energy benefits of the agreement. He wrote: 'the maximum contribution from imported nuclear plants will be around 5 per cent [of India's electricity requirements]. With the same outlay of more than Rs 1,00,000 crore [about $20 billion at then-prevailing exchange rates] that we are going to make in imported nuclear plants, we can get more and cheaper electricity from our own resources' (Singh, 2007).

Third, editorials in major centrist dailies such as the *Hindustan Times*, *The Indian Express*, *The Telegraph*, and *The Times of India* endorsed the nuclear agreement and highlighted its strategic and energy benefits.[18] And *The Indian Express*, writing soon after L. K. Advani's interview, also commended 'Advani's reworking – in this newspaper on Monday – of the BJP's nuclear policy position' (*The Indian Express*, 2007a).

Further, the left-leaning newspaper, *The Hindu*, temporarily reversed its opposition to the nuclear agreement. On 6 August, its editorial page noted that 'It is a sound and honorable agreement and the assurances provided to Parliament by Prime Minister Manmohan Singh in 2006 have been fulfilled virtually in their entirety' (*The Hindu*, 2007b). Subsequently, the newspaper's editor conveyed this supportive line to India's prime minister, but then met CPI(M) leader, Prakash Karat, who noted that the left would still oppose the nuclear agreement. Thereafter, on 20 August, *The Hindu* urged a cautious approach in an editorial titled, 'Put the Nuclear Deal on Hold' (*The Hindu*, 2007c). On 22 August, it elaborated upon the issue. It then accepted some technical points made by India's government, noting that 'The newspaper's editorial assessment of the key provisions of the 123 agreement is that they do provide adequate protection for both fuel supply to the nuclear power reactors and for the strategic program' (Ram, 2007). It still sought a political process that addressed the left's concerns, stating that 'the nuclear deal should be put on hold and that the government could pursue the deal by scheduling an earnest round of all-party discussions'.

Fourth, a number of nuclear experts supported the nuclear agreement. Former AEC Chairman M. R. Srinivasan noted that the Section 123 Agreement addressed India's basic concerns (*The Hindu*, 2007e). He also wrote several pieces on the benefits of nuclear power, especially because he desired to, but could not, brief the UPA–Left committee on this issue.[19] In addition, several former governmental scientists (who were not associated with the senior scientists group that had been raising concerns about the nuclear agreement since 2005) issued a statement favouring the agreement.[20] In contrast, three (but only three) of the seven senior scientists who had written the August 2006 letter to the Parliament still had reservations about the nuclear agreement. They maintained their concerns about fuel supply assurances, reprocessing consent, full nuclear cooperation, and energy issues.[21]

Fifth, Indian business executives strongly endorsed the nuclear agreement. They met with MPs whom they knew personally or professionally to make the case for the agreement.[22] As press reports subsequently noted, '[business] leaders were the chief spokesman for the government during the negotiations with the Opposition on the Indo-US nuclear deal' (*The Economic Times*, 2010a). And India's leading industrialist, Ratan Tata, supported the agreement in a 25 August interview on CNN-IBN.

To summarize, domestic mobilization in favour of the nuclear agreement bolstered the Indian government's position as it engaged the left and the right. Relatedly, because critical views were largely relegated to just two major dailies – *The Hindu* and *The Asian Age* – India's government made the case to other dailies and to its supporters that these criticisms were political in nature. Thus, India's government shifted from a defensive position of having to justify the nuclear agreement to an offensive position of arguing that the opposition's case was more political than technical.

A Second Round of Domestic Efforts

From late November 2007 to May 2008, India's government made further efforts to persuade the left and the right to support the nuclear agreement. Domestic mobilization and international initiatives again reinforced the government's position. Still, both the left and the right opposed the agreement.

Government–Left Interactions

In late 2007 and 2008, India's government and the left affirmed their respective positions for and against the nuclear agreement.

First, in a parliamentary debate on 28 November and 4 December 2007, both sides stood by the points they had made in the UPA–Left committee in prior weeks. Second, in January and February 2008, India's government further defended the nuclear agreement and also emphasized its multilateral rather than its US-centric features. At the time, it had discussed civilian nuclear cooperation ventures with the UK, France, China, Australia, Canada, and Russia. On 18 February 2008, in a talk at the India International Centre, the prime minister's special envoy for nuclear affairs (former Foreign Secretary Shyam Saran) affirmed that 'Our objective is not merely to seek the U.S. as a partner. Our objective is to enable India to have a wide choice of [international] partners in pursuing nuclear commerce and high technology trade'.[23] India's government stressed this multilateral aspect to persuade the left to accept the nuclear agreement, but the left rejected this argument. It instead favoured nuclear cooperation with countries other than the US and sought to 'work out a mechanism to ensure that the nuclear fuel market opens up for India but the deal with the U.S. is not operationalized' (*The Economic Times*, 7 January 2008).

Third, from March onward, after it finalized the IAEA safeguards pact, India's government asked the left to let it send this to the IAEA board.[24] However, on 7 March, in a letter to Prime Minister Singh, the left warned that 'Should the government decide to push ahead with the deal…We will then be left with no option but to withdraw our support to the government' (*The Hindu*, 2008b). Both sides then reached a partial compromise at the 17 March UPA–Left committee meeting. The government briefed the left on the safeguards pact and it agreed to hold another UPA–Left meeting on the issue. At this 6 May meeting, participants discussed in detail the safeguards pact (but the government did not disclose its actual text). The left sought clarifications on four areas: uninterrupted fuel supply; transfer of technology; reciprocity; and the implications of the Hyde Act for India's pursuit of an independent foreign policy.[25] The government agreed to provide its responses ahead of the next meeting, which was scheduled for late May but was eventually held in late June. The government also repeated its earlier position that, after the IAEA and NSG processes were complete, it would take the sense of the House before formalizing the nuclear agreement. Still, the left did not allow the government to send the safeguards pact to the IAEA board.

The BJP's Continued Opposition

The BJP affirmed its objections to the nuclear agreement during the November–December 2007 parliamentary debate as well as in subsequent months. In February 2008, it noted that Secretary Rice's 15 February statements vindicated its position that the Hyde Act would override the 123 Agreement. On 5 June, L. K. Advani highlighted his concerns about nuclear testing, remarking that the BJP would have no objection to the nuclear agreement if it was renegotiated to permit testing.

It should be clarified that BJP leaders themselves had varying opinions on the nuclear agreement. L. K. Advani's views were shaped by the fact that, if he became India's prime minister, he might have to make a nuclear test decision similar to that taken by the previous BJP-led government in May 1998. Arun Shourie and Yashwant Sinha opposed the nuclear agreement for a broader set of reasons. Jaswant Singh had, in his 1998–2000 dialogue with Strobe Talbott, shown flexibility on the test ban treaty, and was therefore presumably willing to accept testing constraints. The BJP President, Rajnath Singh, remained ambivalent, partly because he expected to succeed L. K. Advani as a prime ministerial candidate.

India's government recognized these differences as it reached out to the BJP, and it also appealed to the BJP's elder statesman who could bridge these differences: former Prime Minister Atal Behari Vajpayee. In a 5 March 2008 speech in the Parliament, Prime Minister Singh urged Vajpayee to support the nuclear agreement. Further, India's government sought an understanding with the BJP where it would place a sense of the House resolution in the Parliament and the BJP could oppose it without seeking a vote of confidence. Still, the BJP's leaders rejected this approach.

Other Domestic Options

In early and mid-2008, even as it sought support from the left and the right, India's government was considering other ways to advance the nuclear agreement.

In January, Indian government officials strategized that they could wait until July to assess whether the monsoon harvest brought down food prices and improved their electoral prospects; if it did, then the government could call for elections and send the safeguards pact to the IAEA board despite the left's objections.[26] In March and April, analysts speculated that India's government would present an electorally friendly budget in early May and then break with the left; others noted that the government would wait until the late May elections in Karnataka before advancing the nuclear agreement; still others noted that Congress Party President Sonia Gandhi and Prime Minister Singh would make a final decision irrespective of the timeline.[27]

In the end, however, India's government was unwilling to risk its downfall just to complete the nuclear initiative. It remained unsure of its prospects in national elections, especially because it had lost several state elections in 2007 and 2008.[28]

US and International Initiatives

In late 2007 and 2008, US business groups, Bush administration officials, members of Congress, and other countries, all urged India's government to advance the nuclear agreement and they also asked India's opposition parties to accept it.

First, US business continued its outreach efforts in India. A group of nuclear-related firms, sponsored by USIBC, visited India on 10–11 December 2007. India's government assured them that it would purchase US reactors; it discussed giving them a letter of intent to confirm such purchases; and it clarified that it would enact relevant nuclear liability laws.[29] Subsequently, in February 2008, another USIBC delegation led by former Defense Secretary William Cohen visited India. Indian government officials informed them that domestic politics would determine the fate of the nuclear initiative and they cautioned against imposing time pressure on India's government.[30]

Second, Bush administration officials discussed the nuclear agreement with India's government. In late November 2007, Foreign Secretary Menon met Undersecretary Burns in Madrid: Burns did not travel to India and the meeting in Madrid was not publicly disclosed because India's government wanted to avoid a confrontation with the left (Nayar, 2008). By early 2008, however, US officials were more outspoken about the agreement. Thus, in a 9 February interview on CNN, Ambassador Mulford noted that if the agreement was 'not processed in the present [US] Congress it is unlikely that this deal will be offered again to India' (CNN-IBN, 2008). Also, in a 29 February interview in *The Times of India*, just before he left office, Undersecretary Burns emphasized the multilateral aspects of the agreement, noting that 'this agreement between the United States and India is really an agreement between India and the world community'. He added that 'There is a calendar and there is a clock ticking...this agreement would have to get to the US Congress by May or June'. Further, during a 4–5 March visit to India, Assistant Secretary Boucher noted the importance of completing the IAEA process by May (*The Times of India*, 2008e).

Third, members of Congress affirmed the same timeline for the nuclear agreement. In a 29 December 2007 meeting with Prime Minister Singh, a congressional delegation asked whether there was political support in India to complete the nuclear initiative.[31] More significantly, during a 20 February 2008 visit to India, Senators Joseph Biden, John Kerry, and Chuck Hagel discussed the nuclear agreement with Prime Minister Singh. They noted that any future Democratic administration would not likely offer India a similar agreement, and this influenced Indian governmental thinking on advancing the agreement. At the same time, Indian officials privately informed the senators that the chances of the agreement advancing through Indian domestic politics were only about '50 percent'.[32] After the meeting, the senators publicly stated that India should act on the agreement so that it reached the US Congress by June or July.

Fourth, US officials asked India's right not to block the nuclear agreement. During his 27 February visit to India, Defense Secretary Robert Gates asked India's government to move ahead with the nuclear agreement, and also met BJP leader L. K. Advani. More significantly, in a 8 May meeting, Ambassador Mulford urged L. K. Advani to 'exhibit statesmanship and either back the nuclear deal or withdraw opposition to it'.[33] The ambassador also met former President Abdul Kalam on 14 May, after Kalam had met with BJP leaders.

Fifth, other countries reached out to the left. In late February, the French ambassador met the former West Bengal chief minister. He outlined a proposal for a strategic partnership between India and France and suggested that any India–France nuclear cooperation agreement would have fewer restrictions than those in the Hyde Act.

To summarize, a number of US and international initiatives reinforced the Indian government's attempts to advance the nuclear agreement.

Domestic Mobilization

In early and mid-2008, ex-national security officials, strategic affairs experts, political commentators, nuclear experts, and Indian business, all endorsed the agreement.

First, two prominent national security officials who were associated with the BJP's nuclear decisions – former National Security Advisor Brajesh Mishra, and former President Abdul Kalam – backed the agreement. In late February and again in early May 2008, Mishra repeated and went further than his October 2007 endorsement of the agreement (rediff.com, 2008). And, in late March and May, Kalam affirmed that the agreement would help India's energy sector.

Second, strategic affairs experts urged movement on the nuclear agreement. Thus, K. Subrahmanyam asked India's right to accept the nuclear agreement, stating that BJP leaders should 'consult the nuclear scientists – Srinivasan, Chidambaram, and Kakodkar – [as well as] former foreign secretaries and ex-ambassadors to the US and former chiefs of staff of the armed forces to arrive at a realistic assessment of our nuclear situation…Many of them had served with distinction during [the BJP-led] NDA regime' (Subrahmanyam, 2008a).

Third, additional commentators endorsed the nuclear agreement, and some criticized the left and noted that its opposition benefited China.[34] Editorials in major dailies also urged the government to move ahead.[35]

Fourth, the Indian press again published the views of supportive nuclear scientists. For example, a piece by M. R. Srinivasan repeated his earlier energy-related arguments, stating that India 'must have some 30,000 to 50,000 MW of the first stage program (using natural and enriched uranium) to allow us to exploit the thorium resources in a significant manner', and this would only be possible if 'India can import some 20,000 to 30,000 MW of Light Water Reactors (LWRs)' (Srinivasan, 2008a). In contrast, India's major dailies did not publish the writings of the three senior scientists who had expressed reservations about the nuclear agreement. Also, the one outlet that had previously published their views, *The Asian Age*, carried very few pieces against the nuclear agreement after its editor changed in March 2008.

Fifth, Indian business continued to make the case for the nuclear agreement. On 8 March, a study sponsored by an Indian industrialist, titled 'Liberating India from Technology Denial Regimes', outlined the benefits of the agreement. On 8 April, the Associated Chambers of Commerce and Industry of India hosted an event for business and political leaders who supported the agreement. At this event, a Muslim group (the All India Organization of Imams of Mosques) came out in favour of the nuclear initiative. And, in a 10 April opinion-editorial, the secretary general of the Federation of Indian Chambers of Commerce and Industry countered the left and endorsed the nuclear agreement (Mitra, 2008).

To summarize, domestic mobilization by foreign policy experts, nuclear experts, and business groups reinforced the Indian government's attempts to advance the nuclear agreement. While such mobilization ultimately did not convince the left and the right to reverse their positions, it strengthened the prime minister's hand within the Congress Party. The proponents and the prime minister had been cautious about pressing their party in the absence of domestic support for the nuclear agreement. Yet, the favourable media coverage demonstrated that there was such support, and this allowed the prime minister to credibly ask his party to advance the nuclear agreement in June.

A Third Effort to Break the Domestic Deadlock

In June 2008, India's government informed the left about its intention to advance the IAEA safeguards pact. On 8 July, the government sent this pact to the IAEA board and the left withdrew support for the government. The government still won a parliamentary vote of confidence because it had obtained the backing of the SP.

Parting with the Left

In early June, India's government undertook to go ahead with the nuclear agreement subject to a decision by Congress Party President Sonia Gandhi. It informed the US ambassador of this position after his 11 June meeting with Prime Minister Singh.[36] On 18 June, India's prime minister met the Congress party president and made the case for the nuclear agreement. He sought to ascertain the government's position ahead of his early July meeting with President Bush at the G8 summit, and he expressed reservations about continuing in office if the nuclear agreement did not advance.[37] The government then pressed on with the agreement, but also made a final attempt to persuade the left.

On 16 and 17 June, India's external affairs minister and national security advisor met separately with Prakash Karat, while the Congress Party president met Sitaram Yechury. During the subsequent week, senior Congress Party officials again met with the left and with their UPA allies, and the UPA allies also met separately with the left. In these meetings, and at the 25 June UPA Left committee meeting, the Congress Party and its UPA allies informed the left that the prime minister was determined to move forward with the nuclear agreement. The government asked the left to allow it to complete the IAEA and NSG processes, and it affirmed that it would then bring the nuclear agreement back to the Parliament for a sense of the House resolution. The left rejected this approach. It argued that 'There was also the understanding that till that [UPA–Left committee] finding was made the government would not proceed [to the IAEA]. Now, the Congress leadership wanted to bypass that understanding' (Ramakrishnan and Ramachandran, 2008). As a result, the 25 June UPA–Left committee meeting ended in a deadlock, though both sides agreed to another meeting to finalize the findings of the committee.

Eventually, the two sides did not hold such a meeting. Instead, from 29 June to 4 July, the Congress Party confirmed that it had the backing of the SP. On the evening of 4 July, the government decided to send the safeguards pact to the IAEA board, and it informed the US ambassador of the issue on 5 July.[38] On 7 July, as he was departing for the G8 summit, the prime minister stated that the government 'will, very soon' approach the IAEA (*The Hindu*, 2008d).

On 8 July, the left withdrew support for the government. It stated that 'the text of the Safeguards Agreements negotiated with the IAEA Secretariat, has not been made available to the [UPA–Left] Committee. Without the text, the Committee cannot come to any findings.' It added that 'the Left parties had decided that if the government goes to the IAEA Board of Governors, they will withdraw support. In view of the prime minister's announcement, that time has come.'[39] However, the government could still remain in office because it had obtained the backing of the SP.

Bringing Abroad the SP

The SP had opposed the nuclear agreement until early 2008, but shifted its position in the spring. It recognized that, after its loss in the 2007 Uttar Pradesh elections, it needed to work with the Congress Party to defeat its state rivals, the BSP and the BJP. The Congress Party then secured the SP's backing from May to early July.

On 23 May, SP General Secretary Amar Singh attended a reception hosted by Prime Minister Singh. He observed that his party could reconsider its position if the government briefed it on the nuclear agreement. In June, India's government engaged Amar Singh after he returned from a 20-day health-related visit to the US. On 30 June, Amar Singh stated that the SP would revisit its stand on the nuclear agreement and that he would consult his party colleagues, meet the left, and take a decision at a 3 July meeting of the United National Progressive Alliance (UNPA).[40]

On 1 July, SP leaders, Mulayam Singh Yadav and Amar Singh, met left leader Prakash Karat. They wanted the secular forces – the left, the Congress Party, and the SP – to remain united in their opposition to the religious right and the BJP. They also informed the left that, in any vote against India's government, the SP could not align with the BJP, not just because this would hurt it with Muslim voters but also because the BJP sided with the SP's state rival, the BSP.[41]

On 2 July, Amar Singh and SP MP, Ram Gopal Yadav, met India's national security advisor. He responded to the SP's questions about the nuclear agreement, including about how it would affect India's ties with Iran (this was an issue that resonated with the SP's Shiite Muslim supporters). Amar Singh then asked for the prime minister to publicly address the left's apprehensions. The PMO responded within hours. It pointed out that the nuclear agreement 'did not and would not affect the autonomy of decision-making in regard to foreign affairs' and that, on Iran, 'no outside influence or pressure could force

India to deviate from this path [of maintaining relations with Iran]'.[42] It also discussed technical issues such as fuel supply assurances and, without quoting the text of the IAEA safeguards pact, mentioned some of its provisions.

On 3 July, the SP and its UNPA partners discussed, but were divided on, the nuclear agreement. They sought expert opinion on the points mentioned by the PMO. Former President Abdul Kalam provided this opinion. The SP had played an important role in getting Kalam considered for the position of India's president in 2002, and Kalam now gave the SP the expert endorsement it needed, especially one that would have credibility with Muslim voters. Thus, Kalam met Mulayam Singh Yadav and Amar Singh on 3 July. He informed them that the nuclear agreement was in India's national interest, and the SP quoted Kalam when it outlined its support for the agreement.

On 4 July, Mulayam Singh Yadav and Amar Singh met Prime Minister Singh and the Congress Party President Sonia Gandhi. The SP leaders then noted that the briefings by the national security advisor and by former President Kalam had helped 'clear their doubts', and they announced their support for the nuclear agreement.

Securing Additional Votes

India's government needed 272 votes to win a vote of confidence in the lower house of the Parliament. It was counting on the votes of all UPA constituents (who had about 225 MPs) and the SP (that had 37 MPs, excluding two rebel MPs). Still, it was uncertain about the votes of six SP MPs who did not attend their party meeting on 8 July. It was also unsure about support from a UPA constituent, the Jharkhand Mukti Morcha (JMM), which had five MPs and had held discussions with the BJP. The Congress Party, therefore, sought the support of additional MPs.[43] It aimed to persuade some 40 opposition MPs, including five from Uttar Pradesh, four from Madhya Pradesh, three each from Gujarat, Maharashtra, and Andhra Pradesh, eight from Karnataka, and five from the north-eastern states.[44] It eventually influenced 21 to side with the government: eight abstained and 13 voted for the government. This enabled the Indian government to win the 22 July vote of confidence by a margin of 275 to 256.

Domestic Mobilization

In June and July 2008, domestic mobilization in the Indian press reinforced the government's case for the nuclear agreement.

First, several strategic experts and commentators wrote in favour of the agreement. For example, Siddharth Vardarajan noted that 'the nuclear deal's contours address most if not all of the major concerns the Department of Atomic Energy (DAE) had raised in the course of the debate over the past two years' (Varadarajan, 2008a). He still opposed the 'short-circuiting of democratic propriety through horse-trading [for the votes of MPs] or worse'.

Second, editorials in the major dailies called for moving ahead with the nuclear agreement.[45] However, countering these views, some strategic affairs experts and nuclear scientists continued to express reservations about the agreement.[46]

Third, India's government publicly defended the nuclear agreement and the Indian press reported the government's new arguments for the agreement. Thus, in a 4 July lecture at the Indian Academy of Sciences, the DAE secretary offered fresh arguments for how nuclear imports could fill a projected gap in India's energy needs. Further, on 12 July, four Indian government officials – the national security advisor, foreign secretary, DAE secretary, and the DAE official negotiating with the IAEA – briefed journalists on the IAEA safeguards pact.

In the end, favourable domestic mobilization bolstered the government's case in the run up to the vote of confidence, and thereby helped it press ahead with the nuclear agreement.

Summing Up

India's government could not advance the nuclear agreement from August 2007 to June 2008 because of basic political power considerations. Neither the left nor the right would support the government if it went ahead with the agreement and, without their support, the government would not have been able to remain in office. A different nuclear agreement – one where India's government passed domestic legislation to offset the Hyde Act, as had been suggested by columnist Siddharth Varadarajan and BJP leader L. K. Advani in August 2007 – could possibly have fallen within India's win-set. Yet, this would have remained outside the US win-set. In the end, India's government did not opt for such an approach because it secured the backing of the SP to win a confidence vote. It then submitted the safeguards pact to the IAEA in July 2008, after which the IAEA, the NSG, and the US Congress acted to complete the nuclear agreement.

Endnotes

1   These remarks were made in a 'Statement by Left Parties on the Indo-US Bilateral Nuclear Cooperation Agreement', 7 August 2007.
2   These points were made in the prime minister's statement to the Lok Sabha, 13 August 2007.
3   See, for example, pieces by M. Veerappa Moily (*The Hindu*, 28 August 2007); Jyotiraditya Scindia (*Hindustan Times*, 12 September 2007); and Kapil Sibal (*Indian Express*, 27 August, 29 August, and 17 September, 2007; the September 17 piece was a response to a set of questions raised by Brahma Chellaney).
4   The US Embassy, New Delhi, cable, 9 August 2007.
5   These points were made in a CPI(M) press release, 14 August 2007.
6   Thus, the left's 14 September note stated that the cost of imported reactors was 'about Rs. 9 crore per MW as against Rs. 6.2 crore per MW for domestic reactors' and 'the cost of power from imported reactors will be at least twice that of equivalent coal-fired plants'. The UPA response on 17 September rejected this argument, stating that 'The current annual average tariff for all seventeen power reactors is about Rs. 2.30 per KWh. These are competitive to tariffs of non-pithead coal thermal power stations.' The left's 19 September rejoinder provided alternative figures to show that electricity from imported nuclear plants was much costlier than that from Indian-built nuclear plants. This discussion and all subsequent quotations are taken from *Left Stand on the Nuclear Deal* (2008).
7   A few days before the president and prime minister spoke, senior Indian officials called and informed their US counterparts that India's prime minister could not go ahead with the nuclear initiative because of domestic opposition. The US officials replied that both sides had put two years of effort into this important strategic initiative and therefore India's government must still try to advance it; they also immediately informed Secretary Rice of these developments. Author interview D4, 25 October 2011.
8   For the full text of this compromise, see *The Hindu* (2007f).
9   Author interview D1, 25 November 2011; see also Gupta (2007); *The Hindu* (2007a); and *The Telegraph* (2007c).
10 Author interview O3, 25 November 2011.
11 The US Embassy, New Delhi, cable, 31 October 2007.
12 The US Embassy, New Delhi, cable, 5 November 2007.
13 See, for example, pieces by C. Raja Mohan (*The Indian Express*, 24 July 2007) and K. Subrahmanyam (*The Times of India*, 20 August, 28 August, 20 September, and 8 October 2007; and *The Tribune*, 10 September 2007).
14 See pieces by Bharat Karnad (*The Asian Age*, 9 August, 25 August, and 24 October 2007) and Brahma Chellaney (*Deccan Chronicle*, 8 September, 9 September, and 10 September 2007; and *The Hindu*, 14 September 2007).
15 See also pieces by V. P. Malik (*The Tribune*, 7 November 2007); Arundhati Ghose (*The Tribune*, 12 and 22 November 2007); Jagat Mehta (*The Indian Express*, 8 September 2007); Muchkund Dubey (*The Statesman*, 16 September 2007);

K. Shankar Bajpai (*Hindustan Times*, 21 October 2007); and K. Kasturirangan (*The Indian Express*, 25 July 2007).

16 See, for example, pieces by G. Balachandran (*The Indian Express*, 16 August 2007), R. Ramachandran, (*The Hindu*, 19 September 2007), G. Parthasarathy (*The Tribune*, 1 November 2007 and *The Pioneer*, 2 November 2007), Prem Shankar Jha (*Outlook India*, 29 October 2007), B. G. Verghese (*The Tribune*, 17 September 2007), Gurmeet Kanwal (*The Tribune*, 14 September 2007), and Raj Chengappa (*India Today*, 10 September 2007).

17 For neutral perspectives on energy issues, see pieces by Ashok Desai (*The Telegraph*, 14 August 2007), Sudha Mahalingam (*Deccan Herald*, 26 September 2007), and Arun Kumar Singh (*Deccan Chronicle*, 9 October 2007); for views on political caution, see a piece by Vir Sanghvi (*Hindustan Times*, 20 October 2007).

18 For such typical editorials, see *Hindustan Times* (2007a); *The Times of India* (2007a, 2007b, 2007c); *The Telegraph* (2007b, 2007d, 2007e).

19 See the pieces by M. R. Srinivasan in *The Hindu* on 2 August, 11 September, 5 October, and 9 October, and his interview in *The Hindu* on 2 November 2007. See also the US Embassy, New Delhi, cable, 4 April 2008.

20 For the text of this statement, see a press release by the Press Trust of India, 'Don't Allow N-Deal to be Hijacked by Opponents: Ex-Scientists', Statement by A. K. Anand, ex-Director, Reactor Projects Group, 30 August 2007. India's government called attention to this statement in the November parliamentary debate, and the Indian press reported it under the headline, 'Don't Allow N-Deal to be Hijacked by Opponents: Scientists', (*Hindustan Times*, 2007b). At this time, some senior nuclear scientists who had signed the August 2006 letter to MPs also opposed the left's blocking the nuclear agreement: see *The Hindu* (2007d).

21 See pieces by A. Gopalakrishnan (*The Asian Age*, 3 August, 4 August, and 11 August 2007); P. K. Iyengar (*The Asian Age*, 17 August 2007); and A. N. Prasad (*The New Indian Express*, 6 August 2007 and *Deccan Herald*, 13 August 2007).

22 Author interview R1, 12 August 2010.

23 These points were made in a presentation titled 'India and the Nuclear Domain', 18 February 2008. At this discussion, Saran also defended the nuclear agreement against domestic criticism.

24 On 4 March, Indian officials informed Assistant Secretary Boucher that they had completed safeguards talks with the IAEA (see the US Embassy, New Delhi, cable, 5 March 2008). In the following days, the left stated that a 2 March parliamentary statement by India's external affairs minister, and a 5 March parliamentary remark by India's prime minister, were both 'unfortunate' because they had 'harp[ed]' on the government's efforts to go ahead with the nuclear deal' (*The Hindu*, 2008a).

25 Illustrating the detailed nature of the discussions, on fuel supply assurances, the left stated that 'its not clear whether the clauses regarding fuel supply assurances and fuel reserves by the IAEA are in the preambular section [of the IAEA

safeguards pact] or binding on the IAEA in any way'. It added that 'it appears that right to withdraw from safeguards would exist at best only for indigenous reactors'. It further stated that, in its analysis, 'all foreign supplies imported by India for civilian reactors till the date of withdrawal would have to remain under perpetual safeguards thereafter'. See *Left Stand on the Nuclear Deal* (2008).

26   The US Embassy, New Delhi, cable, 30 January 2008.

27   The US Embassy, New Delhi, cable, 4 April 2008.

28   The Congress Party had lost state elections in Punjab and Uttarakhand (February 2007), Uttar Pradesh (May 2007), Himachal Pradesh and Gujarat (December 2007), the north-eastern states of Tripura, Nagaland, and Meghalaya (February and March 2008), and Karnataka (May 2008).

29   The US Embassy, New Delhi, cable, 17 December 2007.

30   The US Embassy, New Delhi, cable, 19 February 2008.

31   The US Embassy, New Delhi, cable, 2 January 2008.

32   The US Embassy, New Delhi, cable, 22 February 2008.

33   The US Embassy, New Delhi, cable, 16 May 2008.

34   See pieces by Karan Thapar (*Hindustan Times*, 16 February 2008), Prem Shankar Jha (*Outlook India*, 19 May 2008), Raj Chengappa (*India Today*, 18 April 2008), and G. Parthasarathy (*The Times of India*, 28 February and 9 June 2008).

35   For examples of such typical editorials, see *Hindustan Times* (2008a, 2008b).

36   The US Embassy, New Delhi, cable, 19 June 2008.

37   The US Embassy, New Delhi, cable, 26 June 2008; see also *The Hindu* (2008c) and *The Times of India* (2008a).

38   The US Embassy, New Delhi, cable, 7 July 2008.

39   Responding to the left, the government argued that the IAEA safeguards pact was a 'privileged document' that could not be shared with the left unless it joined the government; it also noted that confidential summaries of the pact were circulated at the UPA–Left committee meetings on 17 March, 6 May, and 25 June. For details of this discussion, see *The Hindu* (2008e).

40   The UNPA included the SP with 37 MPs, the TDP with five MPs, the Assam Gana Parishad with two MPs, the National Conference with two MPs, and the Indian National Lok Dal with one MP.

41   It should be noted that, on 2 July, BJP leader Jaswant Singh met SP leaders, Amar Singh and Mulayam Singh Yadav, just before they met India's national security advisor. Jaswant Singh informed the SP that the BJP and the left could support a centrist-regional coalition headed by the UNPA and, in such a situation, Mulayam Singh Yadav could become India's prime minister.

42   These details were noted in a press release, 'NSA Meets SP Leaders', issued by the PMO, 2 July 2008.

43   This discussion draws from several press reports: Aiyar (2008a, 2008b); Bhatt (2008); Smita Gupta (2008a, 2008b); Kumar (2008); and US Embassy, New Delhi, cable, 17 July 2008.

44   The government also reached out to but failed to secure the support of the Rashtriya Lok Dal (RLD) with three MPs; the Janata Dal (Secular) (JD(S)) with

three MPs (it announced that it would rename Lucknow airport for the RLD leader's father); the Telangana Rashtra Samithi (TRS) with three MPs; some BJP MPs; the Akali Dal with eight MPs (Sikh leaders and businessmen sought to persuade this party to abstain); and the Shiv Sena with 12 MPs (the Maharashtra chief minister and an industrialist from the state sought to persuade Shiv Sena and BJP MPs from the state to abstain).

45 For an example of such editorials, see *The Times of India* (2008a, 2008b).

46 See a letter by P. K. Iyengar, A. Gopalakrishnan, and A. N. Prasad, 24 June 2008. See also arguments by P. K. Iyengar (public statement, June 2008); A. N. Prasad (*Deccan Herald*, 13 July and rediff.com, 15 July 2008), and Ashok Parthasarathi, a former Science Advisor to Prime Minister Indira Gandhi (*The Hindu*, 15 July 2008).

CHAPTER EIGHT

Negotiating IAEA Safeguards

INDIA and the IAEA began discussing a safeguards pact in 2006 and completed negotiations on the pact from November 2007 to February 2008. India then sent the pact to the IAEA board on 8 July. Soon thereafter, once its details were known, non-proliferation specialists expressed serious concerns about the pact. Reflecting these, Representative Edward Markey stated that 'the India–IAEA safeguards agreement is worse than useless; it is a sham… this agreement lays out a path for India to unilaterally remove international safeguards from reactors'.[1] Three weeks later, however, the IAEA board approved the pact. The IAEA director general strongly endorsed it, stating that 'the India Safeguards Agreement could have, if properly implemented, a lot of positive implications…I have been supporting the agreement from day one and am very happy today that I see that my judgment has been certified by the Board'.[2]

The India–IAEA pact required safeguards in perpetuity for India's reactors; it linked these to fuel supply assurances and to India's nuclear cooperation arrangements with other countries; and it mentioned these links in the preamble but not in the main text of the pact. Such an arrangement with relatively moderate non-proliferation provisions was acceptable to the IAEA, to India, and to the US. While the IAEA's practice of taking decisions by consensus would normally have only enabled it to accept a pact with strong non-proliferation provisions, political power considerations also influenced the IAEA. In particular, US and Indian diplomacy persuaded the majority of IAEA members to support a safeguards pact with moderate non-proliferation provisions, and also persuaded the few countries having reservations to not block IAEA approval of the pact.

Initial Talks in 2006

India and the IAEA initially discussed a safeguards pact after India announced its separation plan. An Indian delegation visited Vienna in March 2006, when the secretary of India's DAE met the IAEA director general. An IAEA team continued the talks in Delhi in July. At these meetings, the two sides outlined the basic concepts for the safeguards pact.

The IAEA sought standard INFCIRC-66 facility-specific safeguards (India had such arrangements for its Tarapur, Rajasthan-1 and -2, and Kudankulam reactors). It essentially sought safeguards in perpetuity, and it discussed the IAEA document GOV/1621 as the basis for such safeguards; this was subsequently required by the Hyde Act.[3] New Delhi sought India-specific safeguards that would include key items from its separation plan: fuel supply assurances and the right to take corrective measures if fuel supplies were disrupted.

Negotiations in 2007 and 2008

India and the IAEA continued talks on the above-mentioned issues in late 2007 and early 2008. They held five rounds of talks on 21–23 November and 11–12 December 2007, and 2–5 January, 18–20 January, and 25–28 February 2008, and they also exchanged drafts via e-mail.

In November 2007, India's government expected a safeguards pact to be quickly finalized, especially because the IAEA director general favoured the overall nuclear agreement with India and had met Prime Minister Singh during his October 2007 visit to India. New Delhi also assumed that the non-papers prepared during its 2006 discussions with the IAEA provided the basis for a solution. Eventually, however, although the DAE secretary met the IAEA director general at the November talks, the two sides could not reach an agreement.

In November and December 2007, New Delhi pressed for maintaining the fuel supply provisions from its separation plan and from the Section 123 Agreement (Hibbs, 2007). The IAEA, however, insisted on its standard INFCIRC-66 template. Both sides also discussed having language on fuel supply assurances in the preamble (Hibbs and Horner, 2007). The IAEA accepted this because it considered preambular language to not be legally binding on its verification activities. New Delhi appeared to accept it, but still brought up the issue in every round of talks.

The January 2008 talks remained deadlocked for similar reasons. Washington then observed, in the 2–5 January talks, that New Delhi was going beyond the principle of safeguards in perpetuity that had been established in the Section 123 Agreement.[4] It informed New Delhi that the IAEA board and the NSG would not approve any agreement that allowed India to remove items from safeguards. Indian officials maintained that their position had remained within the terms of the Section 123 Agreement and the Hyde Act, and that the IAEA was not fully informed of these documents.

Subsequently, after the 18–20 January talks, Indian officials held the view that they had settled all technical issues with the IAEA except for those on incorporating the Section 123 Agreement's fuel supply language into the safeguards pact.[5] New Delhi was willing to accept such language in the pact's preamble, but sought a linkage between the preamble and the operational text.[6] It was also concerned that the IAEA had backtracked from previously settled points because of US pressure.

As a result of this impasse, a fifth round of talks scheduled for 29–30 January, and then moved to 10–11 February, was postponed to late February. India then wanted the DAE secretary to meet the IAEA director general to inform him that IAEA negotiators were not reflecting his previous commitments to New Delhi, and to receive a confirmation that the IAEA would keep these commitments.

On 9 February, India's national security advisor and the DAE secretary met the IAEA director general in Munich. The director general accepted that India's IAEA safeguards pact followed from its international understandings (that is, its nuclear cooperation agreements with other countries) and he called the IAEA legal team to inform them of this issue.[7] India and the IAEA then reached an agreement in late February. Both sides kept its text confidential until India submitted it to the IAEA board in July.

The Safeguards Pact

The final India-specific safeguards pact was similar to a standard INFCIRC-66 agreement, with some modifications. It had relatively moderate non-proliferation provisions overall, with relatively moderate provisions on the issues of safeguards in perpetuity, fuel supply assurances, and international legal issues, but relatively low provisions on the Additional Protocol.

First, on safeguards in perpetuity, the main text of the pact referred to the IAEA document GOV/1621. It stated that 'The termination of safeguards on items subject to this Agreement shall be implemented taking into account the provisions of GOV/1621'. At the same time, it diluted these relatively high non-proliferation provisions of perpetual safeguards to a relatively moderate position by linking them with fuel supply assurances.

Second, the pact extensively mentioned fuel supply assurances in its preamble. It stated that, for India accepting the safeguards, 'An essential basis is the conclusion of international cooperation arrangements [with other supplier countries] creating the necessary conditions for India to obtain…reliable, uninterrupted and continuous access to fuel supplies… as well as support for an Indian effort to develop a strategic reserve of nuclear fuel.'

In addition, drawing language from India's separation plan and from the Section 123 Agreement, it stated that 'India may take corrective measures to ensure uninterrupted operation of its civilian nuclear reactors'. Still, by mentioning 'international cooperation arrangements [with other countries]', the safeguards pact accepted the IAEA's position that fuel supply assurances should be covered in arrangements between the seller and the buyer of fuel rather than through the IAEA. Overall, the extensive fuel supply assurances would have represented relatively low-to-moderate non-proliferation provisions, but the safeguards pact increased these to relatively moderate provisions because it only mentioned them in its preamble and not in its main text.

Third, on legal issues, the pact provided India with options in case of a dispute. It noted that 'Nothing in this Agreement shall affect other rights and obligations of India under international law'. Relatedly, it had provisions for consultations with India in the event of a dispute, thereby addressing Indian concerns on this issue.

Fourth, the safeguards pact was not accompanied by an Additional Protocol that the IAEA desired.[8] The IAEA negotiators had suggested a few paragraphs of language on this issue, but India did not accept these terms.

Finally, the safeguards pact accepted India's position on its nuclear status and its energy needs. Its preamble referred to the Joint Statement and the separation plan, thereby acknowledging that India had a military nuclear program outside safeguards. Further, it mentioned India's status as an advanced nuclear state and acknowledged the links between India's nuclear energy plans, its economic development, and global environmental concerns.

The Politics of IAEA Approval

The IAEA Secretariat sent the India safeguards pact to its board on 9 July 2008, and the board approved it on 1 August. Institutional rules, political power considerations, and diplomatic initiatives influenced the IAEA's win-set on the pact.

In terms of its rules, the IAEA board generally took decisions by consensus. This reduced its win-set so that it should only have been able to accommodate a safeguards pact with relatively high non-proliferation provisions. However, political power considerations and diplomatic initiatives expanded the win-set.

In terms of political power (that is, votes on the IAEA board), by mid-2008, over half of the 35 board members supported the US–India nuclear agreement and therefore accepted the safeguards pact negotiated by the IAEA. This was because the most powerful states – four of the five NPT nuclear weapons states as well as major European states – had lobbied other countries since 2005, as noted in the next chapter (Hibbs, 2008c). Still, about one-fourth of the IAEA board had reservations. The strongest critic, Austria, sought to express these in a statement co-sponsored with other concerned states (Sweden, Finland, Germany, Japan, Ireland, Denmark, New Zealand, and Spain), but these states eventually made individual statements.[9] The Austrian statement was then co-sponsored by non-members of the board, namely, Costa Rica, the Netherlands, and Norway. It noted that the India safeguards pact was different from a standard INFCIRC-66 agreement and that its corrective measures and other provisions raised doubts about whether safeguards would apply in perpetuity. Other countries with similar and additional reservations included board members, Ireland, Pakistan, and Switzerland, and non-members, Egypt, Iran, Malaysia, and New Zealand.

Eventually, the countries with reservations did not block the IAEA from approving by consensus the India safeguards pact. They took this approach because they did not have a majority to prevail if they forced a vote; their ties with the US and with India would be set back if they pressed for a vote; and they had another, better, opportunity to address non-proliferation concerns by raising these at the NSG.

Three related diplomatic initiatives in July 2008 kept the compromise safeguards arrangement within the IAEA win-set. First, the US and India undertook diplomatic efforts aimed at IAEA board members (these were part of their broader efforts to influence NSG countries that are reviewed in the next chapter). Illustrating these, on 10 July, US Ambassador to the IAEA Gregory Schulte met the representatives of supportive countries such as Australia, Canada, France, Italy, Russia, South Africa, and the UK.[10] At this meeting, participants observed that briefings by the Arms Control Association, which had raised questions about India's corrective measures and about safeguards in perpetuity, would create difficulties at the IAEA board. Accordingly, they recognized that the US, India, and supportive countries would have to undertake better public diplomacy on these issues.

Relatedly, on 11 July, the chair of the IAEA board, Chilean Ambassador Milenko Skoknic, informed Ambassador Schulte that other countries had informed him of the same concerns and had also sought a list of Indian facilities that would be safeguarded.

Subsequently, on 18 July, India briefed IAEA board members and NSG countries to address these concerns (Hibbs and Horner, 2008). New Delhi stated that: its safeguards pact was similar to an INFCIRC-66 agreement; its conditions for termination were the same as those in an INFCIRC-66 agreement; and India's corrective measures would depend on the specific situation and would involve consultations with supplier countries and with the IAEA. The IAEA Secretariat held a separate briefing on 25 July making similar points. Further, the IAEA circulated a list of facilities that India had agreed to safeguard in its separation plan.

Second, in mid-July, the chair of the IAEA board held bilateral consultations with all 35 board members. He sought to determine their position on the safeguards pact and to discuss any alternative options for approval.

Third, the IAEA director general had endorsed the nuclear agreement with India several times since 2005, and this endorsement had credibility with IAEA board members. The director general again made a statement at the commencement of the 1 August board meeting. He affirmed that: India's safeguards pact was 'an INFCIRC-66-type safeguards agreement'; 'the agreement is of indefinite duration. There are no conditions for the discontinuation of safeguards other than those provided by the [India] safeguards agreement itself' (this addressed concerns about the issues of corrective measures and permanent safeguards); and 'India and the IAEA have already begun discussions on an additional protocol' (this addressed concerns about this issue).[11]

The director general further intervened during the board meeting. He repeated the above points and added that the IAEA could not ignore a country that had one-sixth of the world's population.

To summarize, the above-mentioned diplomatic initiatives by India, the US, the IAEA board chair, and the IAEA director general kept the compromise safeguards pact within the IAEA win-set. The IAEA board then approved the pact on 1 August.

Endnotes

1   For details, see a press release, 'Loopholes in Agreement Contradict Bush Administration Promises, Hyde Act', issued by the Office of Representative Edward Markey, Washington, DC, 10 July 2008.

2   For details, see an IAEA press release, 'IAEA Chief Addresses India Safeguards Agreement', 1 August 2008.

3   The alternative, a 'voluntary offer' arrangement applicable to the five NPT-recognized nuclear weapon states, was opposed by Washington and by other countries. At the G8 and NSG meetings in 2005, Washington made it clear that voluntary offer arrangements would not be defensible from a non-proliferation standpoint, nor consistent with the July 2005 Joint Statement. The IAEA also informed Indian officials that, if they did not accept an INFCIRC-66 agreement, then they would need to negotiate a separate protocol which required IAEA board approval, and this would be difficult and could take much time.

4   The US Embassy, New Delhi, cable, 11 January 2008.

5   The US Embassy, New Delhi, cable, 23 January 2008.

6   The US Embassy, New Delhi, cable, 4 February 2008.

7   The US Embassy, New Delhi, cable, 11 February 2008.

8   Author interview J2, 30 September 2011. The IAEA's other main concern was that India's separation plan had placed eight Candu reactors, that produced a significant amount of plutonium, outside safeguards, but this issue was beyond the scope of safeguards negotiations.

9   On 31 July, these eight states attended a meeting at the Norwegian mission in Vienna as potential co-sponsors of the statement; the Austrian statement itself was drafted by the disarmament department in Austria's Ministry of Foreign Affairs, with Norwegian support. See the US Embassy, Vienna, cable, 31 July 2008.

10   Germany and Japan, who later attended the 31 July meeting discussing the Austrian statement, were also present at this 10 July meeting. The US Embassy, Vienna, cable, 14 July 2008.

11   For details, see an IAEA press release, 'Introductory Statement to the Board of Governors by IAEA Director General Dr. Mohamed El Baradei', 1 August 2008.

CHAPTER NINE

Convincing Nuclear Supplier Countries

ON 6 September 2008, the Indian press carried the headline, 'India Enters N-Club' (*DNA*, 2008). It reported that 'in a major success for India's nuclear ambitions, the Nuclear Suppliers Group (NSG) on Saturday granted it a crucial waiver that will enable it to carry out nuclear commerce, ending 34 years of isolation [on the issue]' (*The Indian Express*, 2008b). The NSG discussed nuclear cooperation with India at eight meetings from 2005 to 2008. In August 2008, it deliberated the terms for nuclear trade with India. It modified and endorsed these in September 2008.

The main issues in the NSG's September 2008 decision concerned India's non-proliferation commitments; a mechanism to review that India maintained these commitments; the termination of nuclear commerce if India conducted a nuclear test; and restrictions on enrichment and reprocessing (ENR) technology transfer to India. The NSG's eventual decision had relatively moderate non-proliferation provisions on these issues. Convincing nuclear supplier countries to accept such an arrangement was difficult because of the NSG's rules of operating by consensus: such rules would normally have led to the NSG requiring strong non-proliferation provisions for nuclear trade with India. However, political power considerations also influenced the NSG. Specifically, US and Indian diplomacy persuaded the majority of NSG members to support nuclear commerce with India. Such diplomacy, along with negotiating compromises that raised the non-proliferation standards of the

NSG decision, also persuaded the few countries with reservations to not block NSG approval.

Initial NSG Discussions

The NSG initially looked into the US–India nuclear agreement at its October 2005 consultative group meeting when Washington began making the case for NSG acceptance of the agreement. Washington stated that it did not seek to undercut the NSG or to amend the NSG's full-scope safeguards requirement for nuclear commerce. Instead, it wanted the NSG to give India an exemption from this requirement because of India's energy needs, its positive export control record, and its non-proliferation commitments. In subsequent meetings, Washington continued to press this argument.

At the March 2006 NSG consultative group meeting, Washington submitted a draft text of the terms for an exemption for India. Thereafter, however, the NSG did not extensively discuss the issue at its June 2006 plenary, its October 2006 consultative group meeting, and its April 2007 plenary. At these meetings, France and Russia joined the US in advancing India's case. France also informed the smaller non-nuclear NSG countries that India's increasing use of nuclear power would help address global environmental and energy concerns. Later, at their November 2007 consultative meeting, NSG countries sought, but were not provided with, more information from France and Russia on their nuclear cooperation talks with India.[1]

In early 2008, some NSG members became more outspoken about the conditions for nuclear trade with India. They sought stronger IAEA safeguards, bans on ENR technology transfers, and the revoking of any NSG exemption if India conducted a nuclear test (these points were drawn from a 7 January 2008 experts' letter sent to members of the IAEA board and the NSG).

To summarize, by early 2008, US briefings at NSG meetings, as well as bilateral US and Indian diplomacy with NSG states (discussed subsequently in this chapter), had persuaded over 30 of the 45 NSG members to accept an exemption for India. Yet, some of these states still wanted meaningful non-proliferation provisions in the NSG exemption, and about 10 NSG members had more substantial reservations.

Securing an Exemption in 2008

In 2008, Washington took four approaches to persuade the states with reservations to not block an NSG exemption for India.

First, in three NSG meetings – the NSG plenary in May and special meetings on 21–22 August and 4–6 September – Washington sought to understand and at least partially address their concerns.[2] Thus, at the 22–23 May plenary, supportive states discussed a smooth NSG process to approve nuclear commerce with India. However, other countries opposed this discussion because they had not seen India's IAEA safeguards pact and they had additional objections on the principal technical issues. The US then incorporated some of the objections into a draft of the terms for an NSG exemption. It discussed this draft with India in late July and early August, and then sent it to the NSG chair (Germany) on 7 August. The chair circulated this draft to NSG members ahead of their 21–22 August meeting.

Second, Washington drew upon a group of supportive countries to convince other NSG members. It looked to the UK and France to make the case to EU countries, South Africa and Brazil to persuade the non-aligned countries, and Russia to persuade China and other countries. It earned their trust by keeping them informed of its own efforts and by treating them as partners in this initiative.

Third, Washington raised the issue to a political level. It made each country's NSG decision a political one taken by national leaders, who looked at the strategic aspects of the nuclear agreement with India, rather than a technical decision that was taken by arms control bureaucrats. It also informed countries that their bilateral relations with India and with the US would be set back if they blocked an NSG exemption for India.

Fourth, President Bush and Secretary Rice met or talked via phone with their counterparts in key states to emphasize the importance Washington placed on the issue.

US Diplomacy in July and August

In July and August 2008, ahead of the 1 August IAEA board meeting and then the 21–22 August NSG meeting, Washington made a strong diplomatic effort to persuade countries to approve nuclear cooperation with India.

First, at the senior-most levels of government, President Bush raised the issue with his G8 counterparts at their 7–9 July summit in Tokyo. The president expressed confidence in Prime Minister Singh's efforts to advance the nuclear initiative.[3] He asked the leaders of Canada and Germany to not hold up the initiative. Canada then agreed to not delay the IAEA board meeting and its prime minister informed his Indian counterpart that he understood the importance of the nuclear agreement (still, Canada objected to placing positive language on India's non-proliferation efforts in the G8 leaders' statement and such language was therefore included in the chair's statement instead). And Chancellor Angela Merkel informed Prime Minister Singh that, as NSG chair, Germany would call for an NSG meeting soon after the IAEA board approved India's safeguards pact.

Secretary Rice also raised the issue at related meetings. In late July, Rice discussed the issue with Asia-Pacific leaders at the Association of Southeast Asian Nations (ASEAN) Regional Forum summit and during her visit to Australia and New Zealand. Thus, in New Zealand, Rice raised the issue with Prime Minister Helen Clark and Foreign Minister Winston Peters, as well as with opposition leader John Key. She emphasized that New Zealand's blocking of an NSG exemption would be of 'serious' concern to the US.[4] In turn, Prime Minister Clark informed Secretary Rice that New Zealand would consult with like-minded countries in deciding its NSG position.[5]

Second, the US ambassador in India took up the issue. On 8 July, the ambassador met with officials from 29 NSG countries. He asked them to support India's case at the IAEA and the NSG, and also noted that their relations with India would be set back if they did not.[6]

Third, in mid-July, the US embassies in countries on the IAEA board (many of whom were also members of the NSG) delivered demarches to the foreign affairs and arms control bureaucracies in these countries. In mid-August, US embassy staff in NSG countries again met with foreign ministry officials from these countries.

At these meetings, many countries were supportive of the US position but some still had concerns. One set of countries sought small changes to the US-drafted terms of the NSG exemption for India. Thus, Australia's foreign minister mentioned that his country would not require further conditions in the NSG exemption, but added that New Delhi might still have to accept modest conditions before all NSG members approved the exemption.[7] Canada sought an NSG review mechanism as well as provisions for a special NSG meeting if India conducted a nuclear test.[8] It also noted that it had 'deliberately avoided proposing improvements [in the US draft]' to not complicate the NSG process. Germany indicated that it would welcome stronger non-proliferation assurances from India such as a firmer pledge to not conduct nuclear tests.[9]

Another set of countries expressed more significant concerns. Reflecting these, New Zealand's Minister for Disarmament, Phil Goff, in a 20 August meeting with the US ambassador, expressed reservations in five areas: Indian nuclear testing; ENR restrictions; a review mechanism every two years; the return of fuel and other technology if India terminated international safeguards; and the Additional Protocol.[10] Japan also voiced concerns about the first two areas (that is, Indian nuclear testing and ENR restrictions).[11] Austria noted that it could not easily scale back its strong non-proliferation position because of domestic political compulsions. And the Netherlands noted that, in their NSG briefings in 2006 and 2007, US officials had indicated that the NSG exemption would include provisions of the Hyde Act and would also suspend nuclear cooperation if India conducted a nuclear test. It added that because the US draft did not include these items, the Netherlands was not ready to support it.[12]

Finally, a few countries had concerns unrelated to India. For example, Brazil supported the NSG exemption for India, but it did not want the issues of the Additional Protocol and ENR technology transfers to be termed a 'nonproliferation commitment' (because Brazil itself had not signed the Additional Protocol and it was actively pursuing enrichment for civilian purposes).[13]

To summarize, by August, the majority of NSG countries favoured an exemption for India, but some still had concerns. The US, along with France, the UK, and other major nuclear vending states, pressed all countries to approve the US draft. They informed the critics that if they sought stronger non-proliferation conditions, domestic political compulsions would cause India to reject the entire nuclear agreement (Hibbs, 2008d). India made a similar argument.

Indian Diplomacy

In July and August 2008, India's government took five main initiatives to advance its case with NSG countries. First, it raised the issue at the highest levels of government. Thus, Prime Minister Singh discussed the issue with G8 leaders at their 7–9 July summit. Further, at a late July meeting of non-aligned countries in Tehran, External Affairs Minister Mukherjee met with his counterparts from IAEA board member Algeria and NSG members Cyprus and Belarus.

Second, at a 14 July meeting in Delhi, India's foreign secretary briefed representatives from 50 IAEA and NSG countries. He stated that the nuclear agreement had benefits for India, for the IAEA, and for the countries themselves, and therefore sought quick IAEA and NSG approval of the agreement. He also observed that the completion of the agreement would benefit India's bilateral relations with these countries, and some countries considered this to be a subtle threat that they not block IAEA and NSG approval.[14]

Third, New Delhi sent 10 envoys to 54 countries to make the case for the nuclear agreement. Among these, Minister of State Prithviraj Chavan visited Beijing on 29–30 July, carrying letters from Prime Minister Singh to President Hu Jintao and Prime Minister Wen Jiabao. India's foreign secretary visited Austria, Germany, and Switzerland. India's former foreign secretary, who served as the prime minister's special envoy for nuclear affairs, visited Asia-Pacific states (Australia, Japan, and New Zealand), Ireland, and Latin American countries (Argentina, Bolivia, Brazil, Chile, Ecuador, and Mexico). And India's national security advisor visited Canada, France, Russia, Turkey, and the UK.

Fourth, New Delhi pursued additional diplomatic strategies with three countries having the strongest reservations: Austria, China, and New Zealand (these are discussed subsequently in this chapter).

Finally, India sent a strong delegation to the August NSG meeting. It included India's foreign secretary, the former foreign secretary, and officials from the DAE, the PMO, and the foreign secretary's office, all of whom had negotiated earlier phases of the nuclear agreement. On 20 August, India's foreign secretary briefed three major NSG countries: Germany (the chair), South Africa (the past chair), and Hungary. On 21 August, the Indian delegation briefed all NSG members. However, this briefing was not entirely successful because the supportive countries asked most of the questions and the countries with objections did not raise them. The Indian delegation also noted that Prime Minister Singh had very little domestic political space to make concessions on the terms of the NSG exemption.

The 21–22 August Meeting

The 21–22 August NSG meeting discussed the draft text of an NSG exemption for India. Some countries such as Belarus, the Czech Republic, and Ukraine backed the draft; others such as Australia and Germany supported it without being overly enthusiastic; and still others raised objections (Varadarajan, 2008c).

Six countries strongly opposed and sought amendments to the draft: Austria, Ireland, the Netherlands, New Zealand, Norway, and Switzerland. Thus, New Zealand noted that its proposed amendments were handwritten by Prime Minister Helen Clark and had to be regarded as 'set in stone', while

Austria and Switzerland stated that their national cabinets had developed their positions and that any changes would require new cabinet instructions.[15] These six states were backed, to varying degrees, by 10–15 others, including Denmark, Finland, and Sweden, who all proposed amendments; US allies Canada (that worked to identify compromise language acceptable to India and to NSG members) and Japan (that made concrete proposals for improvements in the US draft); and China (which only cautiously intervened) (Hibbs, 2008f). These states had concerns about three main issues.

First, they sought to terminate the NSG exemption if India conducted a nuclear test. Some countries sought immediate termination, while others sought a consultation process going beyond paragraph 16 of the NSG guidelines (Varadarajan, 2008d). Second, they sought bans on ENR technology transfers to India. However, some countries suggested that any India-specific ENR decision should be deferred until the NSG changed its ENR guidelines for all countries. Third, they sought a mechanism to review India's compliance with the terms of the NSG exemption. Ahead of this meeting, Washington had drafted language on a review mechanism and participants sought to strengthen this mechanism.

Overall, participants proposed about 50 amendments at the August NSG meeting. In addition to the above-mentioned issues, they sought stronger non-proliferation restraints such as India's accepting IAEA safeguards in perpetuity; accepting IAEA safeguards on all its civilian nuclear facilities; signing an Additional Protocol; and halting military fissile material production (Hibbs, 2008e). Some states also suggested language about India eventually acceding to the NPT and CTBT, though New Zealand noted that while it 'would welcome India's accession to these treaties, we have not included these elements in our package of proposals'.[16]

Given these reservations, the NSG did not agree to an exemption for India at its August meeting.

Further US Diplomacy

Between the 21–22 August and 4–6 September NSG meetings, the US slightly revised the terms of an NSG exemption for India and asked the countries having reservations to accept this revised draft.

First, Washington persuaded New Delhi to accept the revised draft. New Delhi had, in early August, insisted that any qualifications in the NSG exemption would be 'virtually impossible' for it to accept.[17] Yet, Washington was candid about informing India's government that such a position could cause the NSG to not approve any exemption for India. US and Indian officials subsequently discussed this issue during a 25 August meeting in Washington between India's foreign secretary and Undersecretary William Burns, and during a 26 August meeting in Delhi between India's special envoy, Assistant Secretary Boucher, and Ambassador Mulford. The US officials asked their Indian counterparts to be flexible on the NSG text, and also noted that India could help its NSG case by acting on the presidential determination items listed in the Hyde Act.

New Delhi partly agreed with Washington's suggestions.[18] It was willing to accept an NSG review mechanism that was phrased positively as a partnership between India and the NSG; it accepted that countries could end nuclear cooperation with India if it conducted nuclear tests, but insisted that the NSG should not make this automatic for all its members; and it noted that NSG members could express their concerns in the NSG chair's summary or in bilateral agreements negotiated separately with India.

At the same time, New Delhi held firm on some issues. In the 26 August meeting, it stated that it could not accept the proposed amendments in the operative portion of the NSG exemption, especially because these went beyond the terms of the Joint Statement, the separation plan, the Section 123 Agreement, and the IAEA safeguards pact. It also noted that during its outreach efforts in July and August, some countries had expressed concerns about the NSG exemption, but these were not as specific as the points they raised at the August NSG meeting. Further, in a 27 August meeting between the US ambassador and India's prime minister, national security advisor, and special envoy, New Delhi stated that it would find it hard to accept most of the proposed amendments, especially those on testing and the review mechanism. Later, in a 30 August interview, India's national security advisor outlined India's red lines on the issues of testing, review mechanisms, and ENR restraints.[19]

Washington took New Delhi's position into account in its revised draft, which also incorporated some points made by NSG countries at their 21–22 August meeting. It discussed this draft with Indian officials on 28–30 August.

Second, Washington sent a tough message to the six countries that had the strongest objections at the August NSG meeting. On 28 August, the US ambassador in India met his counterparts from these countries. He noted that their delegations had not asked questions at India's 21 August presentation in Vienna. He added that many of their 'concerns' at the August NSG meeting turned out to be killer amendments that had 'shocked' the US and had provoked a sense of betrayal in India.[20] He accordingly urged their governments to take a broader approach; reminded them of the possible damage to their bilateral relations with India; and shared a non-paper outlining each country's economic ties with India. He added that the NSG exemption was a political decision about each country's relations with India. The ambassador also met separately with his counterparts from Canada and Japan because Washington had assessed that the six hold-out countries would be difficult to convince as long as Canada and Japan supported their position.[21]

Third, the US conveyed its message at the highest political level. President Bush and Secretary Rice called their counterparts in the six hold-out countries and in other countries. Overall, Secretary Rice made some 20 phone calls ahead of and during the September NSG meeting (Rice, 2011). Fourth, the US sent a senior diplomat, Undersecretary William Burns, to make the US case at the September NSG meeting.

One other US initiative helped its case: on 2 September, Congress released the administration's answers to a set of Questions for the Record. These answers (discussed in the next chapter) indicated that US policymakers would adopt a tough non-proliferation line on issues such as ENR restrictions and Indian nuclear testing, and this indirectly suggested that the NSG need not be as tough on these issues.

The 4–6 September NSG Meeting

The US went into the September NSG meeting with the assumption that, because of its above-mentioned diplomatic efforts, the six countries having the strongest reservations at the August meeting would not oppose the revised NSG exemption. However, these countries continued to seek tougher non-proliferation conditions. They raised these concerns on 4 September, the first day of the meeting, and participants then recessed into smaller committees, each examining one of the contentious issues. Each committee negotiated draft language that the US officials communicated to the Indian delegation, and this was then modified, accepted, or rejected. This process continued until 11.30 p.m. on 5 September, when the Indian delegation accepted a final version of the NSG waiver. Participants then convened at 2 a.m. on 6 September to approve the exemption for India.[22]

Significant US diplomatic initiatives, along with negotiating compromises, persuaded the six hold-out countries to eventually accept the NSG exemption.

Washington first persuaded two of the six countries: the Netherlands and Norway. US officials held discussions with their delegations on 4 September and President Bush also called the Netherlands' prime minister. The Netherlands sought a political statement from India affirming its non-proliferation commitments. New Delhi initially hesitated and then suggested making a statement at the time of, rather than ahead of, any NSG approval decision. After additional discussions, including talks between the US ambassador in India and India's national security advisor, India's foreign minister made a statement on the morning of 5 September.

India's 5 September statement reiterated its commitments from prior months. It noted that: 'We remain committed to a voluntary, unilateral moratorium on nuclear testing'; 'We affirm our policy of no-first-use of nuclear weapons'; 'We have in place an effective and comprehensive system of national export controls'; and 'we are working closely with the IAEA to ensure early conclusion of an Additional Protocol' (Government of India, 2008).

This Indian statement persuaded the Netherlands and Norway to support NSG approval. Norway's foreign minister then helped write language, that Secretary Rice approved, to persuade other states with reservations (Rice, 2011).

The third hold-out country – Switzerland – eventually accepted the NSG exemption because of India's 5 September statement; because of the diplomatic efforts of Undersecretary William Burns; and because the NSG seemed to accommodate its position on testing. On this point, it noted that 'in the view of Switzerland it is clear that nuclear cooperation must be terminated if India does not uphold its moratorium on nuclear explosions' (*Nucleonics Week*, 2008).

The remaining three countries – Austria, Ireland, and New Zealand – still had reservations. US officials continued discussions with these states on 5 September, after which Ireland, then New Zealand, and finally Austria relented.

Ireland accepted the NSG exemption after President Bush called Ireland's prime minister; because NSG states somewhat accommodated its concerns on ENR issues (Ireland noted that it 'understands that no [NSG member] currently intends to transfer to India any [ENR technologies]'); and with the understanding that NSG states would ensure that India maintained its non-proliferation commitments, including its testing moratorium.

New Zealand eventually acquiesced to the NSG exemption when its concerns on the three contentious issues 'were addressed to a significant degree by India in a formal statement [on 5 September]' and because 'these undertakings [by India on 5 September] are referenced in the NSG state-ment...which also notes constraints on transfer of sensitive [ENR] exports'.[23] It should be noted that both Washington and New Delhi had to make con-siderable efforts to sway New Zealand. President Bush spoke with Prime Minister Helen Clark on 4 September; Secretary Rice also called Prime Minister Clark; Prime Minister Clark spoke with India's prime minister two weeks prior to the September NSG meeting; and Washington and New Delhi had both engaged New Zealand in July and August.[24]

Austria acknowledged that India's 5 September statement 'addresses a lot of concerns' but it still wanted the NSG waiver to include 'auxillary measures' that ensured a net gain for the non-proliferation regime (*The Telegraph*, 2008). Further, it faced domestic political difficulties in accepting an NSG exemption for India. This issue had been politicized ahead of Austria's late September elections, and Austria's government risked political losses if it compromised on its strong non-proliferation position. Austria's NSG decision was then taken by its chancellor, who was above domestic electoral considerations, and the US ambassador to Austria assisted in working out a compromise. In addition, Secretary Rice called and asked Germany's foreign minister to speak with Austrian foreign minister, Ursula Plassnik, on the issue (both were then attending a European foreign ministers' meeting) (Rice, 2011). New Delhi also pursued diplomatic initiatives with Austria. It worked with Austrian diplomat Herbert Traxl, who, when he was Austria's ambassador to India in 1998, had counselled Austria's foreign ministry to understand India's position on its nuclear tests (Menon and Nayar, 2008).

China's position at the NSG meeting is also worth noting. Ahead of the meeting, Indian foreign policy officials had outlined a diplomatic strategy that would make it hard for Beijing to block an NSG decision.[25] Still, China maintained its opposition: its president did not accept a phone call from Prime Minister Singh and, on 1 September, an opinion-editorial in *People's Daily* (which reflects the Chinese communist party line) objected to any NSG exemption for India. At the NSG meeting itself, Beijing wanted the issues raised by the six objecting countries to be adequately discussed. On the evening of 5 September, the head of the Chinese delegation asked for a recess on the grounds of having to consult higher-level national officials. Beijing assumed that this would result in a break in, or even an end to, the negotiations. Yet, US officials noted that the issue was too important to delay and, given the time constraints, they continued the discussions. In response, the Chinese delegates left the NSG meeting, and the two senior delegates remained away from the meeting leaving only junior diplomats to attend its conclusion. Washington also pursued high-level diplomatic efforts with Beijing: Deputy Secretary of State John Negroponte called his Chinese counterpart and President Bush sent an urgent message to China's president, after which the junior Chinese delegates returned to the meeting.

The Terms of the NSG Exemption

The NSG exemption approved on 6 September 2008 had relatively moderate non-proliferation provisions, as shown in Table 9.1. This 730-word document had provisions that were stronger than those in the 430-word draft from March 2006, the 560-word draft that was discussed at the August 2008 NSG meeting, and the 680-word draft going into the 4 September 2008 meeting. It covered the issues of a review mechanism, responding to an Indian nuclear test, ENR transfer restrictions, India's obligations in return for the exemption, and India's nuclear status.

Table 9.1 Alternative Arrangements for the NSG Exemption

Type	Example	Issues and Non-proliferation Provisions
A1	Very strong non-prolifera-tion position	*Very high non-proliferation provisions* *Stronger than A3 arrangement, for example, NSG prohibits ENR transfers to India (similar to the June 2011 NSG decision)
A3	Position of Representatives Markey and Tauscher	*High non-proliferation provisions* *A4 arrangement + terms of NSG exemption based on India signing CTBT and ending fissile material production
A4	Position of six states led by New Zealand, and close to Hyde Act statements of policy	*Moderate-to-high non-proliferation provisions* *Strong review mechanism *Terminate NSG exemption if India conducts nuclear test *Prohibit ENR transfers to India, or at least give high priority to a future decision banning such transfers *Terms of NSG exemption based on A5 items plus India accepting safeguards in perpetuity and a strong Additional Protocol

Type	Example	Issues and Non-proliferation Provisions
A5	NSG exemption of 6 September 2008	*Moderate non-proliferation provisions overall* *Review mechanism as per para 16a of NSG guidelines (moderate) *Response to Indian nuclear test as per para 16 of NSG guidelines (moderate) *ENR restrictions as per paras 6–7 of NSG guidelines (moderate-to-high) *Terms of NSG exemption based on India's 5 September commitments (moderate)
A6-enhanced	NSG draft of 4 September 2008	*Low-to-moderate non-proliferation provisions* *Review mechanism as per para 16a of NSG guidelines *Response to Indian nuclear test as per para 16 of NSG guidelines *ENR restrictions absent *Terms of NSG exemption based on India's updated actions on its Joint Statement undertakings and the US presidential determination items
A6	NSG draft of August 2008	*Review mechanism as per para 16a of NSG guidelines *Response to Indian nuclear test not mentioned *ENR restrictions absent *Terms of NSG exemption based on India's Joint Statement undertakings and the Hyde Act's presidential determination items
A7	NSG draft of March 2006	*Low non-proliferation provisions* *Review mechanism absent *Response to Indian nuclear test not mentioned *ENR restrictions absent *Terms of NSG exemption based on India's Joint Statement undertakings
A9	Terms sought by India	*Very low non-proliferation provisions* *Terms of NSG exemption based on India's Joint Statement undertakings

First, the 6 September exemption had relatively moderate non-proliferation provisions on a review mechanism. The March 2006 draft was weak on this issue because it left the matter entirely to national governments, allowing them to pursue nuclear cooperation with India if they were 'satisfied that India is continuing to meet [its]...non-proliferation and safeguards commitments'.

The August 2008 draft replaced this with language stating that NSG members 'shall maintain contact and consult through regular channels' to periodically review the exemption for India. The 4 September draft and 6 September exemption retained this language, but also accommodated India by stating that the NSG would consult India during any review process.

Second, the 6 September exemption had relatively moderate non-proliferation provisions on responding to an Indian nuclear test. The March 2006 and August 2008 drafts did not mention this issue. The 4 September draft and 6 September exemption included it, noting that 'in the event that one or more Participating Governments consider that circumstances have arisen which require consultations [such as an Indian nuclear test] Participating Governments will act in accordance with paragraph 16 of the Guidelines'. Still, these documents mentioned paragraph 16 as a whole, rather than paragraph 16, subsection 'c', that specifically discusses nuclear testing (and which would have represented a moderate-to-high non-proliferation provision). Also, they did not contain the relatively high non-proliferation provisions of terminating the NSG exemption if India conducted nuclear tests. Washington had informed NSG members that regional security circumstances, such as a war or nuclear testing by China and Pakistan, could cause India to conduct nuclear tests and that such situations required consultation rather than an automatic termination of nuclear cooperation with India (*Nucleonics Week*, 2008).

Third, the 6 September exemption had relatively moderate-to-high provisions on restricting ENR technology transfers to India. This issue was not mentioned in the drafts of March 2006, August 2008, and 4 September 2008. The 6 September exemption then included the issue, noting 'that transfers of sensitive [ENR] exports remain subject to paragraphs 6 and 7 of the Guidelines'. This was a relatively moderate-to-high position because it affirmed the paragraph 6 stipulation that 'Suppliers should exercise restraint' in ENR technology transfers, and because countries with ENR capabilities also separately indicated, at the September meeting, that they did not intend to export these technologies to India. Still, it was not the highest non-proliferation provision because it did not absolutely ban ENR transfers to India.[26]

Fourth, the 6 September decision had relatively moderate non-proliferation provisions on India's obligations and commitments. The March 2006 draft had relatively low-to-moderate provisions on this issue because it simply noted that the NSG exemption was based on India's obligations in the Joint Statement. The August 2008 draft updated these to reflect actual Indian actions (for example, specifying India's actions on export controls and on the IAEA safeguards pact). The 6 September text augmented these by adding India's 5 September statement: it noted that the NSG agreed to the exemption for India 'based on the commitments and actions mentioned above, as reiterated by India on September 5, 2008'.

Fifth, the NSG exemption had relatively moderate non-proliferation provisions on India's nuclear status. Here, it removed the relatively moderate-to-high provisions of the March 2006 draft that had language on the desirability of India ultimately adopting safeguards applicable to non-nuclear weapon states. New Delhi had objected to this in 2006 itself, and it again opposed such language during the July–August 2008 talks with the US. At the same time, NSG countries also removed language on India's nuclear energy needs that would have reflected relatively lower non-proliferation provisions. The March 2006 draft, as well as the IAEA safeguards pact, included such language, but the 6 September draft only generically referred to 'the energy needs of India' rather than specifically to 'nuclear' energy. Further, the 6 September exemption made no mention of India as a state with advanced nuclear technology.

Finally, the NSG agreed to consult India whenever it adopted amendments that India, as an adherent, would be expected to adopt. This point was absent in the March 2006 draft but was included in the August 2008 draft.

International Politics

Institutional rules, political power considerations, and diplomatic initiatives shaped the NSG win-set so that it could accommodate an exemption for India with relatively moderate non-proliferation provisions.[27]

In general, political power considerations (that is, the number of supportive states at the NSG) were more favourable in 2008 than in 2005. This was because Indian and US diplomacy from 2005 to mid-2008, discussed next, had influenced a majority of NSG members to support an exemption for India. However, the NSG's consensus rule still enabled the minority of states with reservations to block an exemption for India: the consensus rule reduced the NSG's win-set and kept the August 2008 arrangement (which was an A6 arrangement with low-to-moderate non-proliferation provisions, as shown in Table 9.1) outside the win-set.

Two initiatives in late August and September then persuaded the few countries with reservations to accept an exemption for India. First, the NSG strengthened the non-proliferation provisions of the exemption for India.

It did this by: (a) adding the compromises reached during and just after its 21–22 August meeting into its 4 September draft; (b) making further adjustments at the September meeting to produce an A5 arrangement with relatively moderate non-proliferation provisions; (c) obtaining from India its 5 September statement; and (d) asking countries with ENR technologies to indicate, at the September meeting, that they did not intend to transfer these to India.

Second, New Delhi and Washington further engaged the hold-out countries, including at the highest levels of government. As discussed previously, President Bush called the leaders of Ireland and the Netherlands and Secretary Rice called the leaders of Austria, New Zealand, Norway, and many other countries. Eventually, these states recognized that their relations with the US and India would suffer if they blocked NSG approval.

To summarize, the above-mentioned initiatives enabled the NSG to approve an exemption for India with relatively moderate non-proliferation conditions.

India's NSG Diplomacy

From 2005 to mid-2008, India's government undertook many diplomatic efforts, both at the highest levels of government and more broadly, to persuade NSG members to support its case.

At the senior-most levels of government, Prime Minister Singh directly asked the leaders of NSG countries for their support. From 2005 to early 2006, the prime minister raised the issue with the leaders of not just the most supportive countries (France, Russia, and the UK) but also of Brazil, Cyprus, Germany, Iceland, Japan, and Norway. Subsequently, the prime minister and senior cabinet ministers continued to press their case with these and other countries. They interacted with the leaders of G8 countries at the G8 meetings; with Brazil and South Africa at the India–Brazil–South Africa (IBSA) meetings; and with major Asia-Pacific, European, and non-aligned states.

India's broader outreach efforts had several dimensions.[28] First, Indian officials briefed the ambassadors and representatives of NSG countries in India. In 2005, they reached out to the Japanese and European missions, and they continued such efforts in subsequent years.[29] Second, New Delhi briefed NSG members on the sidelines of NSG meetings in 2006 and 2007. Third, India pursued nuclear cooperation agreements with France and Russia, giving them a commercial incentive to lobby for India.[30]

Fourth, New Delhi undertook a strong diplomatic campaign in 2007 and 2008. In early 2007, the prime minister's special envoy visited

Australia, Ireland, Japan, New Zealand, Norway, and South Africa and asked them to support – or to at least not stand in the way of – an NSG exemption for India.[31] Later, Prime Minister Singh raised the issue with Chinese leaders during his December 2007 visit to Beijing.[32] And, during their February 2008 visits to India, Prime Minister Singh asked the prime ministers of Denmark, Finland, and Norway to support an NSG exemption for India.[33]

As a result of these efforts, by March 2008, India's special envoy held the view that most NSG countries would support India's case; most would look to the US, Russia, France, and the UK for guidance; Brazil and South Africa had softened their position; Argentina might raise a few questions but would 'do no harm'; Norway had a strong non-proliferation position but also saw a possibility of thorium research collaboration with India; Ireland would uphold its strong non-proliferation stand; and despite Prime Minister Singh's visit to China, Beijing's position remained ambiguous.[34] US officials then suggested that they could again talk with Beijing and that the US and India should also continue efforts to persuade Austria, Australia, Germany, Ireland, and New Zealand. Washington had been diplomatically engaging these states in prior months.

US Diplomacy

From 2005 to 2008, much like India, the US pursued high-level diplomacy and more extensive outreach efforts to persuade NSG countries to support an exemption for India.

At the highest levels of government, President Bush and Secretary Rice raised the issue in bilateral meetings with their Asian and European counterparts, and in multilateral meetings such as the G8 summits. They also encouraged Britain and France to engage other countries. Illustrating this, President Jacques Chirac mentioned the issue in a September 2006 meeting with Chancellor Merkel.[35]

Washington further engaged NSG countries in three ways. First, the US Embassy in India held briefings for its counterparts from NSG countries. For example, it held one such briefing on 3 March 2006, just after India announced its separation plan.[36]

Second, US officials coordinated their position with key countries. Reflecting this, in 2005, US and French officials developed a common argument at the NSG.[37] The same year, US and Russian officials noted that their efforts to persuade the NSG, and to persuade India to develop a credible separation plan, could reinforce each other.[38]

Third, senior US officials raised the issue in discussions with their counterparts. For example, during his December 2007 visit to Australia, Undersecretary Nicholas Burns informed Australia's government that Washington attached high importance to the nuclear agreement with India.[39] He made a similar case to Japan's deputy foreign minister who was then in Australia.[40] The following month, during a visit to Japan, Burns informed Japan's new deputy foreign minister that President Bush sought a strategic relationship with India and that the civilian nuclear accord was a major component of this relationship.[41]

Influencing the NSG

US and Indian diplomacy gradually influenced NSG countries to support an exemption for India. In 2005, only a few NSG members were enthusiastic about the issue. At the October 2005 NSG meeting, the Czech Republic, France, Russia, and the UK backed the US position, but most other countries such as Argentina, China, Greece, Japan, and South Korea awaited details of India's separation plan, and Sweden and Switzerland expressed reservations about any NSG exemption.

In 2006 and 2007, NSG members remained divided on the issue. At the March 2006 NSG meeting, 27 states commented on the US draft circulated at the meeting. Only about one-third supported the US position, while two-thirds were either cautious (and awaited details of the Section 123 Agreement) or critical. By mid-2007, about 15 NSG members (one-third of the group) were more outspoken about their concerns (*Nuclear Fuels*, 2007). Still, the majority of NSG members favoured an exemption for India and, by mid-2008, only eight to 10 countries were strongly holding out. Washington and New Delhi then convinced these states through their diplomatic initiatives in mid-2008, as noted previously in this chapter.

Domestic Politics

Domestic politics shaped the positions of India, the US, and other countries at the NSG. The political power considerations and bureaucratic factors that influenced India's position were discussed in the previous chapter.

Briefly summarized, from August to mid-November 2007, India's government did not have the political power to go ahead with IAEA negotiations that preceded the NSG decision because of opposition from leftist parties. In subsequent months, India's government had to ensure that an IAEA safeguards pact was acceptable to the left as well as to its nuclear establishment. Later, after India's government won a vote of confidence in July 2008, its win-set slightly widened because it did not then need the support of the left. Yet, it still had to accommodate its nuclear establishment as it negotiated an NSG exemption.

India's political parties drew upon domestic mobilization in the Indian press. Here, a few strategic and nuclear affairs experts raised concerns about the IAEA and NSG arrangements (Chellaney, 2008; Karnad, 2008a). For example, Siddharth Vardarajan opposed the NSG placing conditions in its exemption for India, and he also opposed the idea of a 'clean' waiver that was not 'unconditional' (Varadarajan, 2008b). This issue had caught the attention of India's government, which then observed that 'we must be careful with every statement, every word [in the NSG exemption]. Otherwise the press may become trapped on a single word.'[42] Some nuclear experts expressed additional concerns, noting, for example, that in the IAEA safeguards pact, the preamble's language linking safeguards to fuel supplies was inadequate.[43]

Other strategic affairs experts and commentators, however, endorsed the Indian government's position (Subrahmanyam, 2008b, 2008c). Such domestic mobilization in favour of the compromise IAEA and NSG arrangements made it politically easier for India's government to move ahead with these arrangements.

US Domestic Politics

Political–institutional rules, political power considerations, and domestic mobilization significantly influenced Washington's position at the IAEA and NSG.

On political–institutional grounds, the Bush administration needed congressional approval for the nuclear agreement after any NSG decision, but this was far from assured because Democrats held a majority in Congress. For these reasons, the US win-set decreased and the Bush administration could not ignore congressional concerns about the IAEA and NSG decisions. Congress had outlined its position on these decisions in several ways.

First, the Hyde Act mentioned some basic terms for the IAEA and NSG decisions. It required NSG approval by consensus and IAEA safeguards in perpetuity. Second, soon after the Section 123 Agreement was announced, members of Congress noted its weaknesses and sought to overcome these in the IAEA and NSG decisions. Thus, Representative Edward Markey recommended: (a) the NSG suspend nuclear trade with any country that tested a nuclear device; (b) the NSG ban transfers of ENR technologies; and (c) the IAEA safeguards pact with India have permanent and not India-specific safeguards.[44]

Third, on 4 October 2007, the House passed a non-binding resolution, HR 711, which stated that any NSG exemption for India should be 'consistent with the Hyde Act and the Atomic Energy Act'.[45] It added that the NSG exemption should have five provisions: terminating cooperation in the event of an Indian nuclear test; requiring safeguards in perpetuity; banning ENR technology transfer; not granting India the right to reprocess spent fuel except in a safeguarded facility; and a coordinated NSG response to an Indian nuclear test.

Fourth, the same day, Representatives Markey, Ellen Tauscher, and Sam Farr sent a letter to the foreign ministers of NSG countries outlining the above-mentioned non-proliferation concerns. They also urged that the entry-into-force of the CTBT and negotiation of an FMCT should be a condition in any NSG exemption for India.

Fifth, on 5 August 2008, Representative Howard Berman sent a letter to Secretary Rice that reinforced congressional concerns.[46] The letter referred to HR 711 and its five provisions.

Eventually, some of the congressional concerns were reflected in the IAEA and NSG decisions. In turn, Congress and NSG members drew upon points made by the non-proliferation lobby.

The Non-proliferation Lobby

Non-proliferation groups undertook extensive efforts to influence Congress and NSG members on the exemption for India.

Within the US, non-proliferation groups highlighted the principal issues in the NSG and IAEA decisions. In a February 2008 press release, soon after Secretary Rice's statement at the HIRC, ACA raised non-proliferation issues that were mentioned in HR 711 and in the Hyde Act. It stated that 'in response to [Secretary] Rice's comments, we expect the member states of the NSG to insist that' any exemption for India ban ENR technology transfers and that any NSG exemption 'would be revoked if that nation [that is, India] resumes nuclear testing' (ACA, 2008a). ACA again raised these issues, and pointed out weaknesses in the IAEA safeguards pact, at a 30 July press conference; the Stimson Center raised them at an 18 August briefing; and ACA raised them at a 2 September briefing.

The New York Times echoed the above-mentioned non-proliferation concerns. In October 2007, just after HR 711 was announced, it noted that 'Now it's up to Congress and other countries to try to limit the damage [to the non-proliferation regime]' (*The New York Times*, 2007b). Later, in an August 2008 opinion-editorial, Representatives Tauscher and Markey called on the NSG to seek strong conditions, going beyond those in the Hyde Act and in HR 711, for nuclear trade with India: 'First, India must sign the Comprehensive Nuclear Test Ban Treaty…Second, India must agree to halt production of nuclear material for weapons' (Tauscher and Markey, 2008). *The New York Times* (2008a) also endorsed the stand by New Zealand and the other countries seeking stronger nuclear restraints from India.

Outside the US, non-proliferation groups further sought to influence NSG members. For example, the Parliamentarians for Nuclear Non-proliferation and Disarmament (PNND) introduced the US–India nuclear agreement into legislative debates in Belgium, Germany, Japan, and the Netherlands.[47] The PNND also distributed the October 2007 letter written by Representatives Markey, Tauscher, and Farr in 30 countries. The Abolition 2000 network (comprising 2,000 non-governmental and other organizations in about 90 countries) pursued similar efforts. It distributed a briefing paper on the US–India nuclear agreement at the 2007 NPT Preparatory Committee meetings. It sent letters to the Australian government (on 28 June 2007), to countries on the IAEA board (on 10 September 2007), and to the heads of governments of NSG members (on 14 August 2007). On 7 January 2008, it sent an influential letter, signed by 120 experts and non-governmental organizations, to NSG and IAEA members. And it was active at the 2008 NPT Preparatory Committee meetings.

Non-proliferation groups intensified their efforts in August and September 2008. On 15 August, they sent a letter highlighting the principal non-proliferation concerns, signed by 160 experts and organizations from 24 countries, to the foreign ministers of NSG countries (ACA, 2008b). On 13 August, the Global Security Institute and the Middle Powers Initiative wrote to NSG members that 'a legitimate position [for the NSG] might be that which was expressed by Congresswoman Ellen Tauscher, Congressman Sam Farr and Congressman Ed Markey, who, in a letter to you dated October 4, 2007, urged that entry-into-force of the CTBT and negotiation of a Fissile Material Cut-Off Treaty become necessary conditions of the deal' (Global Security Institute, 2008).

On 27 August, Abolition 2000 sent letters to 13 governments that referred to *The New York Times* piece by Representatives Markey and Tauscher.

To summarize, non-proliferation groups pressed Congress to take the position, in HR 711 and in the months after this resolution was passed, that any NSG exemption for India should contain strong non-proliferation conditions. They also lobbied key NSG members to require such conditions.

Domestic Politics in NSG Countries

A comprehensive review of domestic politics in NSG member countries is beyond the scope of this book. Still, it should be noted that in several NSG countries, three factors influenced bureaucratic and inter-ministerial debates on the NSG exemption for India.

First, non-proliferation groups urged foreign affairs diplomats (especially those in the arms control bureaus of national foreign ministries) and national legislatures to seek stronger non-proliferation conditions in any NSG exemption for India.

Second, nuclear-vending industries and national business federations, who interacted with US and Indian business, pressed their economic and industrial ministries to support an NSG exemption acceptable to India. Relatedly, industries in several countries had specific interests in the agreement with India: for example, Swedish firms were interested in arms sales to India, while the Japanese corporations Hitachi and Toshiba were partners of the US firms General Electric and Westinghouse that intended to sell reactors to India.

Third, national foreign ministries took into account their overall strategic and economic interests. They were not willing to damage their ties with the US and with India by opposing an NSG exemption for India, especially because Washington and New Delhi had raised the issue at the senior-most levels of government.

In the end, the second and third factors outweighed the first. This influenced countries such as Australia, Canada, Germany, Japan, and Sweden – all of whom were traditionally strong supporters of non-proliferation – to favour an NSG exemption for India. Explained in another way, two factors expanded the win-set in these NSG countries: (a) advocacy by business groups, which influenced economic and industrial ministries; and (b) decisions by national leaders and foreign ministries to not disrupt strategic and economic ties with

India and with the US. This enabled these countries to accept IAEA and NSG arrangements without the strongest non-proliferation provisions.

To conclude, the NSG eventually accepted an exemption for India that had relatively moderate but not higher non-proliferation provisions. In the weeks after the NSG decision, the US Congress made one final attempt to toughen these provisions.

Endnotes

1   For details of the NSG meetings from 2006 to mid-2008, see Hibbs and Horner (2006); additional reports in *Nuclear Fuels*, 10 April 2006, and *Nucleonics Week*, 12 October 2006; Hibbs and Machlachlan (2007); reports in *Nucleonics Week*, 15 November 2007; Hibbs (2008a, 2008b); Hibbs and Saraf (2008).
2   Author interview T1, 25 October 2011.
3   The US Embassy, New Delhi, cable, 10 July 2008.
4   The US Embassy, Wellington, cable, 8 August 2008.
5   The US Embassy, New Delhi, cable, 28 August 2008.
6   The US Embassy, New Delhi, cable, 8 July 2008.
7   The US Embassy, Canberra, cable, 19 August 2008.
8   The US Embassy, Ottawa, cable, 13 August 2008.
9   The US Embassy, Berlin, cable, 14 August 2008.
10 The US Embassy, Wellington, cable, 20 August 2008.
11 The US Embassy, Tokyo, cables, 14 and 19 August 2008.
12 The US Embassy, The Hague, cable, 14 August 2008; the US Embassy, The Hague, cable, 11 July 2008.
13 The US Embassy, Brasilia, cable, 15 August 2008.
14 The US Embassy, New Delhi, cable, 15 July 2008.
15 The US Embassy, New Delhi, cable, 26 August 2008.
16 This point was made in a press release by the Government of New Zealand, 'US–India Civil Nuclear Agreement', 26 August 2008; see also Varadarajan (2008e).
17 India's minister of state for external affairs took this position in a 6 August meeting at the US Embassy. The US Embassy, New Delhi, cable, 8 August 2008. Author interview T1, 25 October 2011.
18 The US Embassy, New Delhi, cable, 26 August 2008.
19 These points were made in an interview with CNN-IBN, 30 August 2008. On testing, India's national security advisor noted that 'testing is a word that we find difficult to adjust with. Not because of anything else but because Parliament has mandated us to do so.' On ENR, he noted, 'we don't want ourselves to be singled out for this' and 'if any country does not wish to give us Enrichment

and Reprocessing technologies and still wishes to have nuclear commerce, we'll draw up our guidelines according to that'. On the periodic review, he noted that nuclear industry investors 'are putting money [into nuclear facilities] for 30 to 40 years so if you have a review at the end of three years and somebody says that oh well this shouldn't be done then nobody is going to invest in this agreement'.

20   The US Embassy, New Delhi, cable, 28 August 2008. In turn, the New Zealand representative noted that Prime Minister Clark was 'faithful to what she told Secretary Rice [on July 26], including her intention to consult with like-minded countries'; that he understood what was at stake with India; and that 'perhaps in fact we are not prepared to give up our nonproliferation goals'.

21   The US Embassy, New Delhi, cable, 4 September 2008.

22   This discussion is drawn from author interviews with officials familiar with the NSG meeting: author interview H1, 3 August 2010; and author interview T1, 25 October 2011. See also Varadarajan (2008f), Bagchi (2008), and other sources listed in this section.

23   These remarks were made in a press statement by Phil Goff, 'Nuclear Suppliers Group Approves Indian Exemption', Government of New Zealand, 7 September 2008.

24   In late July, India's foreign ministry identified New Zealand and Austria as the most difficult cases in the NSG, and it outlined diplomatic strategies to persuade these states. It sent an official to New Zealand one week ahead of the 21 August NSG meeting. He recommended that New Zealand's Governor General, Anand Satyanand, visit India. Satyanand had close ties with former Prime Minister David Lange, who was close to incumbent Prime Minister Helen Clark. See Menon and Nayar (2008) and *New Zealand Herald* (2008).

25   Just ahead of the 21 August NSG meeting, India's foreign minister announced that Chinese Foreign Minister Yang Jiechi would visit India on 7 September. This announcement made it hard for Beijing to oppose an NSG exemption because any such Chinese action would hurt its foreign minister's visit to India. See Menon and Nayar (2008).

26   In June 2011, NSG countries adopted very high provisions when they modified their guidelines to ban ENR transfers to countries not accepting full-scope safeguards. India strongly objected to these NSG revisions, and Washington noted that 'Nothing in the new enrichment and reprocessing transfer restriction [of June 2011]…should be construed as detracting from the unique impact and importance of the US–India agreement and our full commitment to full civil nuclear cooperation [with India]'(Department of State, 2011).

27   The win-set is best understood by referring to Figure 2.1: here, the NSG win-set extended only from point 4 to point 5. Thus, arrangements A1 to A4 fell outside the win-set because Washington rejected them on the grounds that India would not accept them. Also, arrangements A6 to A9 fell outside the win-set because the six NSG hold-out countries would not accept them.

28   India's foreign ministry recognized that it would have to make special efforts to persuade countries that were strict adherents to the NPT, countries that were

less susceptible to US and Indian pressure, and countries such as Argentina, Brazil, and South Africa who had given up their own nuclear programs. Author interview U1, 26 November 2011.

29 The US Embassy, New Delhi, cable, 3 October 2005.

30 Illustrating this, during President Chirac's February 2006 visit to India, India's national security advisor informed French business leaders that after NSG restrictions were removed, French firms could set up nuclear plants in India, and that one French company was undertaking pre-feasibility studies for a plant in Maharashtra. See the US Embassy, New Delhi, cable, 22 February 2006.

31 The US Embassy, New Delhi, cable, 31 March 2007.

32 The US Embassy, New Delhi, cable, 23 January 2008.

33 The US Embassy, New Delhi, cable, 13 February 2008.

34 The US Embassy, New Delhi, cable, 5 March 2008.

35 The US Embassy, New Delhi, cable, 21 September 2006.

36 The US Embassy, New Delhi, cable, 6 March 2006.

37 The US Embassy, Paris, cable, 20 September 2005.

38 The US Embassy, Paris, cable, 21 October 2005.

39 The US Embassy, Canberra, cables, 11 and 12 December 2007.

40 The US Embassy, Canberra, cable, 20 December 2007.

41 The US Department of State, cable, 28 January 2008.

42 The US Embassy, New Delhi, cable, 8 August 2008.

43 See pieces by Iyengar (2008a) and Prasad (2008).

44 These points were made in remarks at the Council on Foreign Relations, 'Courses of Action for Congress and the Nuclear Suppliers Group', 13 September 2007.

45 See the full text of HR 711, titled 'Expressing the Sense of the House of Representatives Concerning the United States–India Nuclear Cooperation Agreement', 4 October 2007.

46 See the full text of the letter from Congressman Berman to Secretary Rice, 5 August 2008.

47 These activities are discussed in various newsletters such as *PNND Update* 19, October–November 2007; *PNND Update* 18, July–August 2007; and Abolition 2000 US–India Working Group, 'Letter Sent to Heads of NSG Governments', 14 August 2007.

CHAPTER TEN

Persuading Congress, Again

I N the fall of 2008, the Bush administration urged Congress to approve the nuclear agreement with India. It faced a race against time and resistance from influential members of Congress. On 5 August, Representative Howard Berman informed the administration that given 'the lateness in the congressional session, it would be better to review these complex matters [related to nuclear cooperation with India] in the next Congress when they can receive a full and serious examination'.[1] Still, having convinced Congress about the merits of the nuclear agreement in 2006, the administration was successful in persuading Congress, again. The House passed legislation approving the nuclear agreement on 27 September, and the Senate followed on 1 October.

Securing congressional approval was not easy for three reasons. First, the legislation required more than a simple majority of the vote: it needed a two-thirds majority in the House and unanimous consent in the Senate.[2] Second, attaining these votes was difficult because Democrats held a majority in both the House and the Senate and some of them opposed any expedited congressional action. Third, lobbying by non-proliferation groups ensured that Congress remained cognizant of the main non-proliferation provisions. For these reasons, Congress would not accept legislation with relatively low-to-moderate non-proliferation provisions.

On the other hand, three additional factors also influenced Congress so that it eventually accepted legislation with relatively moderate non-proliferation provisions. First, the Bush administration extensively engaged Congress on the issue. Second, advocacy groups reinforced the administration's efforts. Third, India's government took a number of diplomatic, commercial, and export control initiatives to strengthen its case for nuclear cooperation.

The Evolution of Legislation

In September 2008, as Congress crafted legislation authorizing nuclear cooperation with India, it discussed the issues of deterring an Indian nuclear test, restricting enrichment and reprocessing (ENR) technology transfers to India, the terms for reprocessing consent, and the Section 123 Agreement's consistency with the Hyde Act. The Bush administration reassured Congress on these issues and pressed it to advance legislation in several ways.

First, it offered Congress important non-proliferation assurances, especially in its answers to congressional Questions for the Record (QFRs), in its 10 September submissions and at an 18 September SFRC hearing. Second, it engaged Congress at the highest levels: Secretary Rice, Undersecretary William Burns, and other administration officials briefed and reached out to members of Congress. Third, it intervened at critical junctures to address congressional concerns. In particular, Secretary Rice called Representative Berman on 25 September to reassure him about ENR issues. Secretary Rice also sent letters to the House on 26 September and the Senate on 1 October, affirming that US fuel supply assurances would not help India override sanctions following any nuclear test. Finally, supportive members of the House and Senate leadership, and from the House India Caucus, as well as an advocacy coalition of non-governmental groups, reinforced the administration's efforts.

The QFR Answers

The Bush administration offered significant non-proliferation assurances to Congress in its QFR answers, which Congress released on 2 September.[3]

First, the QFR answers affirmed that the Section 123 Agreement was 'fully consistent with the legal requirements of the Hyde Act'.

Second, on fuel supply assurances for India, particularly those in the Section 123 Agreement, the answers stated that these assurances 'are important Presidential commitments that the U.S. intends to uphold, consistent with U.S. law'. Thus, it confirmed that US law (that is, the Hyde Act and the Atomic Energy Act) rather than just the Section 123 Agreement would apply to this issue. It added that 'fuel supply assurances are not, however, meant to insulate India against the consequences of a nuclear explosive test'.

Third, on the transfer of ENR technology, the QFR answers noted that 'the U.S. government will not assist' India with any such technology, 'whether under the [Section 123] Agreement or outside the Agreement'. The only exception was that 'potential dual-use transfers could be considered [but] only under the exceptions granted in the Hyde Act'. The administration's subsequent submissions to Congress reinforced these points.

The 10 September Submissions

On 10 September, the Bush administration submitted the Section 123 Agreement to Congress, along with a four-page covering letter, a three-page list of presidential certifications stating that India had fulfilled the seven Hyde Act requirements for nuclear cooperation, a 26-page report required by the Hyde Act, and a 30-page unclassified version of a Nuclear Proliferation Assessment Statement (NPAS).

These documents took a firm non-proliferation position on the principal issues. Illustrating this, the president's covering letter reflected a strong approach on fuel supply assurances. It noted that: 'Article 5(6) [of] the [Section 123] Agreement records certain political commitments concerning reliable supply of nuclear fuel given to India…[but the] Agreement does not, however, transform these political commitments into legally binding commitments because the Agreement, like other U.S. agreements of its type, is intended as a framework agreement.'

In short, the QFR answers and the 10 September submissions took a strong non-proliferation position, but the administration still faced challenges in getting Congress to approve the nuclear agreement.

Initial Engagement and Challenges

In early and mid-September, the Bush administration engaged Congress at the highest levels to make its case for advancing the nuclear agreement. From 8–10 September, Secretary Rice spoke with key lawmakers, including SFRC Chair Joseph Biden, Senate Majority Leader Harry Reid, House Foreign

Affairs Committee (HFAC) Chair Howard Berman, and House Speaker Nancy Pelosi. Just ahead of the 18 September SFRC hearing, Secretary Rice again spoke with lawmakers. At this time, supportive congressmen favoured waiving the requirement that legislation be considered for 30 days, but others opposed such expedited action.

The supporters included not just Republicans but also most of the Democratic leadership, particularly House Speaker Pelosi, Senate Majority Leader Reid, and Senator Chris Dodd, who chaired the SFRC in place of Senator Biden. They also included members of the fairly large India Caucus in the House. On 16 September, a bipartisan letter written by five past and present co-chairs of the India Caucus urged the House to approve the nuclear agreement. Also, after the SFRC hearing, members of the India Caucus urged that legislation be completed ahead of Prime Minister Singh's 25 September meeting with President Bush.

Still, the Bush administration encountered obstacles to advancing any legislation. In the House, HFAC Chairman Howard Berman indicated his opposition by not scheduling hearings on the issue. Further, on 13 September, Representatives Edward Markey, Ellen Tauscher, and John Spratt sent a letter to the HFAC chairman that opposed expedited congressional action. And, in the Senate, the administration faced the challenge of overcoming the 'unanimous consent' requirement.

The SFRC Hearing

At the SFRC hearing on 18 September, senators reviewed the seven presidential certifications and discussed the main non-proliferation issues in nuclear cooperation with India.

First, on the consequences of an Indian nuclear test, senators noted that the administration and India's government had made contradictory remarks. In response, administration officials quoted Secretary Rice's statement of 2006: 'As Secretary Rice said before this committee in April 2006, "We've been very clear with the Indians…should India test, as it has agreed not to do, or should India in any way violate the IAEA safeguards agreements to which it would be adhering, the deal, from our point of view, would at that point be off"'.[4] They added that the administration had also addressed this issue in the NSG.

Second, on ENR issues, the administration stated that, at the September NSG meeting, 'None of the countries that were present at that meeting indicated a desire to, or plan to, supply those [ENR] technologies to India'. Still, Senator Russ Feingold noted that such a gesture was 'not a binding commitment'.[5]

Third, on India's export controls, Senator John Barrasso called attention to a 18 September piece in *The Washington Post* that raised concerns about this issue. Fourth, on the issue of Iran, senators raised concerns about India's defence ties with Tehran. And Senator Barbara Boxer placed on the record a March 2007 *Defense News* article on the issue.

Fifth, on other issues, Senator Dodd noted that India's heavy water reactors could be a source of tritium, which the IAEA did not safeguard. The administration responded that 'the IAEA will put the heavy water under safeguards, and just as if we supply them fuel, everything that is derived in that reactor is subject to our controls'.

Sixth, on commercial issues, senators asked whether US firms were assured of nuclear trade with India. In response, Undersecretary William Burns revealed a US–India understanding on the issue. He stated that 'The Indian government has provided the United States with a strong Letter of Intent, stating its intention to purchase reactors with at least 10,000 Megawatts (MWe) worth of new power generation capacity from U.S. firms'.[6]

Congressional Legislation

Soon after the SFRC hearing, senate staff and Representative Berman's staff worked with Bush administration officials to draft legislation on nuclear cooperation with India. The legislation included items covered in the SFRC hearing and items that had been excluded from the Hyde Act.[7]

On 23 September, the SFRC passed this legislation (S 3548) by a vote of 19–2. On 25 September, Representative Berman introduced legislation in the House. Berman's original bill had sections that were different from S 3548: these sought additional presidential certifications and sought to link nuclear cooperation with India's actions on Iran. They were removed after administration officials, including Secretary Rice, intervened on 25 September. The legislation was then similar to the Senate bill and was adopted as HR 7081. This approximately 2,600-word bill covered the principal issues of fuel supply assurances, reprocessing consent, ENR restrictions, heavy water restraints, the Hyde Act overriding the Section 123 Agreement, and other items.

First, on fuel supply assurances, the bill had three mechanisms to dissuade an Indian nuclear test. One was its statement of policy section which repeated language from the Hyde Act: it stated that any fuel reserves offered to India would be commensurate with reasonable reactor operating requirements and that the US should prevent other countries from assisting India override sanctions if it conducted a nuclear test.

Another was a stipulation that US fuel supply assurances in the Section 123 Agreement would be interpreted according to prior statements made by US officials (Representative Berman clarified that these were the State Department's QFR answers and the president's 10 September letter to Congress). Thus, it declared that the Section 123 Agreement's provisions 'have the meanings conveyed in the authoritative representations provided by the President and his representatives to the Congress and its committees prior to September 20, 2008'. This language was a compromise between the preferences of Congress – which wanted the actual statements by administration officials and the text of the QFR answers to be placed in the legislation, or at least in the preamble of the legislation – and the administration's objections to this position.

A further mechanism was a clarification that if nuclear cooperation with India were terminated, the presidential waiver of this termination could be overridden by a simple majority in Congress. This improved upon prevailing laws that required a harder to attain two-thirds majority. Through these three mechanisms, HR 7081 had relatively moderate-to-high non-proliferation provisions on this issue.

Second, on ENR technology transfers, HR 7081 responded to congressional concerns that this issue was not sufficiently addressed by the NSG. It asked the president to certify that it was US policy to work with NSG members to further restrict ENR technology transfers. Thus, on this issue, the bill had relatively high non-proliferation provisions that went beyond the moderate-to-high provisions in the September 2008 NSG decision; it was just one step short of the very high provisions that the NSG eventually adopted in June 2011.

Third, on reprocessing consent, HR 7081 stated that no reprocessing pact with India could take effect until the president issued a relevant report to the House and Senate foreign relations committees. It added that Congress could reject this reprocessing pact within 30 days, which was an improvement over existing law that gave Congress only 15 days to disapprove. Thus, the bill had relatively moderate non-proliferation provisions on this issue.

Fourth, on the heavy water issue, HR 7081 directed the president to seek international arrangements to address this issue. However, it did not require a formal presidential certification on the issue. Thus, the bill had relatively low-to-moderate provisions on this issue.

Fifth, on US laws taking precedence over the Section 123 Agreement, HR 7081 approved the Section 123 Agreement 'subject to the provisions of' the Atomic Energy Act, the Hyde Act, and other applicable US law. It thus had relatively moderate-to-high non-proliferation provisions on this issue.

Finally, HR 7081 had relatively low non-proliferation provisions on some issues mentioned in the SFRC hearings. It did not seek to constrain India's fissile material production, nor did it augment the Hyde Act's provisions for making nuclear cooperation contingent upon India's actions on Iran and upon its export controls.

In the end, HR 7081 had relatively high non-proliferation provisions on one issue (ENR restrictions), moderate-to-high provisions on two issues (fuel supply assurances and the Hyde Act overriding the Section 123 Agreement), moderate provisions on one issue (reprocessing consent), low-to-moderate provisions on a further issue (tritium), and weaker provisions on other issues. On the average, it had relatively moderate provisions, and represented an A5 arrangement shown in Table 10.1. It was thereby just sufficient to accommodate the concerns of most members of Congress.

Supporting and Opposing Perspectives

In the 26 September House debate and the 1 October Senate debate on HR 7081, proponents argued that the legislation had been adequately debated; they countered the non-proliferation position; and they affirmed the strategic case for the nuclear agreement. For example, Representative Berman noted that the bill addressed his concerns, 'particularly with regard to the potential consequences if India tests another nuclear weapon, and to the legal status of so-called "fuel assurances" made by our negotiators'. And Senator Richard Lugar affirmed that his non-proliferation concerns were addressed, especially on reprocessing, because the legislation enabled Congress to more easily disapprove a reprocessing pact with India. He also stated that the nuclear agreement had adequately debated, including in 'three public hearings with testimony from 17 witnesses' and in '174 written questions for the record [that Congress had submitted since 2005] to the Department of State'.[8]

Table 10.1 Alternative Arrangements on Congressional Legislation

Type	Example	Issues and Non-proliferation Provisions
A1	Very strong non-proliferation position	*Relatively very high non-proliferation provisions* *Stronger than A3 arrangement on all the issues
A3	Bill sought by Representatives Markey and Tauscher	*Relatively high non-proliferation provisions* *A4 arrangement + nuclear cooperation conditional upon India signing the CTBT and ending fissile material production
A4	Bill closer to Representative Berman's initial bill and with Dorgan–Bingaman amendments	*Relatively moderate-to-high non-proliferation provisions* *A5 arrangement + nuclear cooperation linked with India's actions on Iran + additional presidential certification requirements + actual text of administration's non-proliferation assurances and QFR answers on responding to an Indian nuclear test + Dorgan amendment on ceasing nuclear cooperation 'if the Government of India detonates a nuclear explosive device' + Bingaman amendment on utilizing US nuclear-related export controls 'with respect to countries that continue nuclear trade with India' in the event of an Indian nuclear test
A5	HR 7081	*Relatively moderate non-proliferation provisions overall, but moderate-to-high or high on a few issues* *Three measures to dissuade an Indian nuclear test (moderate-to-high) *Reprocessing pact with India could be more easily disapproved by Congress (moderate) *The US would work with the NSG to end ENR technology transfers to India (high)

(Continues)

Table 10.1 Alternative Arrangements on Congressional Legislation (*Continued*)

Type	Example	Issues and Non-proliferation Provisions
		*Approves India 123 Agreement 'subject to the provisions of' the Atomic Energy Act and the Hyde Act (moderate-to-high)
		*Other issues: no constraints on fissile material and no conditioning cooperation to India's actions versus Iran (low)
A6	Bill initially sought by Bush administration	*Relatively low-to-moderate non-proliferation provisions*
		*A5 arrangement without some of the measures on responding to an Indian nuclear test
A7	Bill generally accept-able to India	*Relatively low non-proliferation provisions*
		*A5 arrangement without most of the measures on an Indian nuclear test; with low non-proliferation provisions on ENR transfers, a reprocessing pact, and other issues; and without language that approved the Section 123 Agreement 'subject to the provisions of' the Hyde Act
A9	Ideal bill sought by India	*Relatively very low non-proliferation provisions*
		*No restrictions on Indian nuclear testing, ENR transfers, and a reprocessing pact

On the other hand, opponents highlighted non-proliferation concerns and sought to delay the bill until the next session of Congress. Thus, some members of the House entirely rejected nuclear cooperation with India because it would undermine the non-proliferation regime.[9] Others noted that the legislation contained too many ambiguities. Here, Representative Adam Schiff stated that 'the deal is really no deal at all. The Indian government and the administration have been issuing contradictory statements about it for the past year.'[10]

Prominent senators echoed these and additional concerns. Thus, Senator Byron Dorgan raised two issues. First, he highlighted the bill's weakness in limiting India's fissile material production, and he cited *The New York Times* opinion-editorial on this issue: 'I wish to describe something the *New York Times* wrote yesterday, and I fully agree: President Bush and his aides were so eager for a foreign policy success they didn't even try to get India to limit its weapons program in the future'. Second, he sought more measures to dissuade an Indian nuclear test. Accordingly, along with Senator Bingaman, he proposed an amendment that would terminate nuclear cooperation if India tested a nuclear device, and would use US export control laws to prevent other countries from assisting India in overriding sanctions. The Senate defeated this amendment by a voice vote.

The House and Senate Votes

On 27 September, the House approved HR 7081 by a vote of 298–117, with one answering 'present' (another 17 members did not vote). Given that the bill needed a two-thirds majority to pass, the margin of victory was small: the bill would have failed if the 17 members not voting had voted against the bill and just nine others had switched their votes. Significantly, a substantial 47 per cent of the Democrats opposed the bill, but 95 per cent of the Republicans supported it.

On 1 October, the Senate passed HR 7081 by a vote of 86–13. About 25 per cent of the Democrats voted against the legislation. They included eight of the nine senators who co-sponsored the Dorgan–Bingaman amendments and nine of the 12 senators who had voted against the Hyde Act in 2006.

The Politics of the House and Senate

In late September, much like in mid-September, the administration faced different sets of challenges in the House and Senate.

In the House, the administration's principal challenge was to convince Representative Berman to drop his preferred bill that had some strong non-proliferation provisions. A number of factors eventually swayed Berman on this issue. These included: advocacy by House Speaker Pelosi and members of the House India Caucus; the efforts of the India lobby; negotiations with Bush administration officials such as Undersecretary William Burns and Acting Undersecretary for Arms Control John Rood (who worked with Representative Berman's staff on the legislation); Berman's own recognition, as mentioned previously, that HR 7081 provided for adequate responses to an Indian nuclear test; and assurances from Secretary Rice on the ENR issue. On 25 September, Secretary Rice called Representative Berman to affirm that the US would give the highest priority, at the November NSG meeting, to an NSG decision prohibiting the transfer of ENR technology to states outside the NPT.

The administration's other challenge was to secure the fairly substantial two-thirds of the vote. Here, the administration worked with Representative Gary Ackerman to win some crucial Democratic votes. Further, the administration reassured representatives about their non-proliferation concerns through Secretary Rice's 26 September letter to Speaker Pelosi.

In the Senate, the administration faced obstacles from five Democrats who opposed unanimous consent: Senators Robert Byrd, Jeff Bingaman, Daniel Akaka, Russ Feingold, and Tom Harkin. The administration and the India lobby engaged these senators; it asked other senators to engage them; and it worked out a compromise to address their concerns. Under the compromise, these senators could express their position in a debate, and they could also introduce amendments.

Even thereafter, the administration continued to engage the Senate at the highest levels. On 1 October, Secretary Rice sent a letter to Majority Leader Reid, which responded in detail to Senate concerns about any nuclear testing by India. The administration also made substantial efforts to remove an anonymous hold that had blocked the bill. Secretary Rice called Senator Reid and spoke to President Bush about this issue, and administration officials such as Joshua Bolten (White House Chief of Staff) and David Abramowitz (Chief Counsel to the HFAC) then worked to remove the hold.

To summarize, important initiatives by the administration and by supportive members of Congress influenced key representatives and senators to accept the eventual compromise legislation. These initiatives shaped the win-set, which is best understood by referring to Figure 2.1 and Table 10.1: the win-set began at point 3 and extended to point 5 in Figure 2.1. Thus, efforts by the administration and by supporters moved the outer boundary of the win-set to point 5, so that HR 7081, which was an A5 arrangement, remained within the win-set. They also moved the inner boundary of the win-set outward from point 0 to point 3, so that it excluded A2 and A3 bills with stronger non-proliferation provisions. An A4-type bill with the Dorgan–Bingaman amendments would possibly have remained within the win-set, but the administration convinced the Senate to not adopt this amendment. A significant lobbying effort complemented the administration's initiatives.

Domestic Mobilization

An advocacy coalition, or 'India lobby', pressed Congress to advance legislation on nuclear cooperation with India. It countered arms control groups who sought to block, or to at least add strong non-proliferation provisions to, such legislation.

The India Lobby

The India lobby, comprising Indian Americans, business, strategic affairs experts, the lobbying firm hired by the Indian Embassy, and other constituents, pursued several initiatives to advance legislation on the nuclear agreement.

From July to early September, the lobby's efforts had three main features. First, in early July, the lobby began preparing for an advocacy campaign. USIFC started mobilizing Indian Americans, and it also met with USIBC to reactivate the 2006 Coalition for the Partnership with India. Second, the lobby held several meetings with congressional staff. Third, it interacted with the Bush administration and with India's government. In early August, the firm hired by Coalition (Patton Boggs) and a USIFC group of two dozen Indian Americans held separate meetings with Undersecretary William Burns. The administration briefed them about its plans for the NSG and for subsequent congressional action. Around the same time, the Indian ambassador hosted a dinner for USIFC members and outlined the Indian government's position. Subsequently, officials from the White House, the NSC, and the State Department participated in conference calls with small groups of Indian Americans.

As a result of the above-mentioned interactions, the India lobby developed a clear set of objectives. It focused on overcoming the time constraints and procedural challenges to advancing legislation. It also sought to convince Representative Berman to advance the legislation. Further, it asked the 12 senators who had previously opposed the Hyde Act to not block a vote even though they opposed the legislation. And it sought flexibility from India's government. In mid and late September, the India lobby undertook several initiatives to advance these objectives.

First, Indian Americans held events and met with the congressional leadership. In mid-September, delegations led by the chairman of the Indian Americans for Democrats met Senators Biden and Clinton and House Speaker Pelosi, as well as Senator Charles Schumer and Representatives Ackerman and Crowley. Later, two dozen Indian Americans from a newly formed Indian American Committee organized a lunch event on the nuclear agreement. Representatives Berman, Hoyer, Ackerman, and Pallone (the latter two were former co-chairs of the India Caucus) attended this event, along with Bush administration officials. And, on 23 September, USIFC held an advocacy day for the nuclear agreement. Here, USIBC hosted a group of Indian Americans for a working lunch, after which they met senators and representatives from their home districts, and then attended a reception at the HFAC.

Second, 13 strategic affairs experts wrote a letter to Congress. This 21 September letter stated that the strategic and energy arguments for the nuclear agreement were as strong as ever and that 'This agreement is too important to be defeated by letting the clock run out' (Haniffa, 2008a).

Third, the lobby pursued additional initiatives. Thus, it sent a letter outlining the case for the nuclear agreement to Indian Americans across the US and they, in turn, faxed the letter to their representatives and senators. Further, on 23 September, USIFC placed an advertisement in the congressional *Roll Call*. And, on 24 September, the American Jewish Committee and the US Chamber of Commerce both sent letters to members of Congress urging them to approve legislation on the nuclear agreement.

Fourth, ahead of the Senate vote, the India lobby worked with the staff of the Democratic leadership – Senators Schumer, Clinton, and Reid – to advance the legislation and to defeat the Dorgan–Bingaman amendments.

Fifth, the lobbying firm hired by the Indian Embassy (namely, BGR) undertook additional efforts. In 2008, BGR participated in over 110 meetings and communications, including 35 with officials from the executive branch and 81 with those from the legislature.

In the end, several factors helped the India lobby: the intensity and breadth of its advocacy campaign; its reaching out to new members of Congress who were not present during the 2006 vote; its reinforcement of the case with members who were supportive in 2006; and Indian American ties with prominent members of Congress such as Senate Majority Leader Reid. These factors enabled the India lobby to counter the efforts of the non-proliferation lobby.

The Non-proliferation Lobby

Non-proliferation groups highlighted concerns about congressional legislation in several ways. First, on 30 July, ACA held a press briefing, titled 'Key Issues before the IAEA, NSG and U.S. Congress', and it held a similar briefing 2 September. These focused on the principal non-proliferation issues of safeguards in perpetuity, ENR restraints, and responses to an Indian nuclear test.

Second, in an 8 September paper, the Stimson Center pointed out weaknesses in the NSG decision, especially in the area of dissuading an Indian nuclear test (Krepon, 2008). Third, the same week, an ISIS report raised concerns about India's nuclear procurement practices and its export controls (Albright and Brannan, 2008). This report was cited by *The Washington Post* and by Senator Barrasso at the 18 September SFRC hearing. Fourth, in a 17 September letter, 34 experts expressed concerns about whether safeguards could continue following any Indian nuclear test. They called upon Congress to resolve 'key issues including safeguards and the possible termination of the agreement in the event that India resumes nuclear testing' (ACA, 2008c). Fifth, the non-proliferation lobby was disappointed by Representative Berman's removal of tougher language from HR 7081 and it sent a letter to members of Congress asking them to oppose the resulting compromise legislation.

The above-mentioned efforts influenced congressional legislation in two ways. First, some members of Congress (particularly Representatives Berman, Markey, and Tauscher and a few senators) highlighted non-proliferation concerns in congressional hearings. As a result, some of these concerns, such as the ENR issue, were substantially covered in HR 7081, while other concerns, such as the heavy water issue, were partly addressed in the bill. Second, the non-proliferation lobby influenced the votes of over 100 members of the House, resulting in a very narrow margin of victory for HR 7081; it also influenced five senators who opposed the unanimous consent process until the last possible moment.

The Press

From July to September 2008, five major US dailies carried 15 commentaries on the nuclear agreement (in addition to a few pieces directed at the NSG that were noted in the previous chapter). Ten were supportive and five were critical of the agreement. Among these, *The New York Times* carried two critical editorials (*The New York Times*, 2008b, 2008c). The *International Herald Tribune* published a critical opinion-editorial by former President Jimmy Carter (Carter, 2008). *The Washington Post* editorials were supportive, though its opinion-editorials offered a balanced debate.[11] *The Washington Times* had a supportive opinion-editorial, while *The Wall Street Journal* offered both supporting and opposing perspectives.[12]

In general, supporters highlighted the strategic argument for the nuclear agreement. They noted that 'The agreement has already been amply debated and discussed, and, on balance, it is in America's interest' (*The Washington Post*, 2008b). They added that 'The U.S.–India nuclear pact is an important step in creating a stabler diplomatic alignment in Asia that can support U.S. security interests in the region' (Hawkins, 2008). These supportive perspectives reinforced the arguments made by the India lobby and by the Bush administration. They complemented the Indian government's own initiatives to advance its case.

India's Initiatives

In the weeks before Congress took up legislation on the nuclear agreement, India's government discussed with the Bush administration the steps it needed to take to satisfy Congress. In early July, US embassy officials informed India's government that it had to act on its export controls so that the president could make the determinations required by the Hyde Act.[13] On 10 July, Indian officials informed the US ambassador that they were beginning to act on these issues. On 17 July, the US and Indian national security advisors met in Ankara and the two sides sketched out the issues and timeline for NSG and congressional action.[14] Both sides then had a better understanding of the steps that each would take in the coming weeks. India's government subsequently took three important steps to further its case with Congress.

First, India's government did not publicly criticize the Bush administration's non-proliferation position on congressional legislation. Thus, New Delhi downplayed the significance of the QFR answers. In private, however, it expressed serious concern that the answers were 'tantamount to undoing an agreed text' (Varadarajan, 2008g); Prime Minister Singh also met senior Indian government officials at his residence on 3 September to discuss this issue.

Moreover, India's government welcomed, and did not publicly criticize non-proliferation issues in, the NSG decision to authorize nuclear cooperation with India. However, catering to a domestic audience, the DAE secretary noted that, despite the NSG decision, India retained its right to conduct nuclear tests (*The Times of India*, 2008d).

In addition, India's government did not criticize the administration's 10 September letter to Congress. Instead, it only cautiously noted that it would 'take up the matter with Washington to seek clarity on these [issues in the letter] which have the potential of creating uncertainty over the fuel supplies issue' (*Hindustan Times*, 2008c).

Finally, during his 25 September meeting with President Bush, Prime Minister Singh called for legislation without tough conditions. President Bush responded that the administration would seek legislation to satisfy India: 'we want the agreement to satisfy you and [will work to accordingly] get it out of our Congress' (Haniffa, 2008b).

Second, India's government worked with the Bush administration to award US firms a substantial share of the Indian nuclear market. In a 10 September letter of intent, India offered US firms contracts for reactors generating 10,000 MW of electricity: such contracts would have been worth $40–$50 billion at prevailing prices. The letter further mentioned that India would address US concerns about 'an adequate nuclear liability regime'. In this manner, India's government assured Congress that US firms would obtain commercial benefits from the nuclear agreement, and it gave US industry an incentive to lobby Congress on the agreement.[15] (The letter also accommodated India's position on the price of imported reactors, and on the location of and requirement for seismic surveys at reactor sites, by stating that these would have to be acceptable to India.)[16]

Third, India's government strengthened its export controls. This enabled the Bush administration to make the relevant presidential determinations required by the Hyde Act. Specifically, on the issue of India's support for international efforts to prevent ENR proliferation, New Delhi stated, in an 18 August letter to the IAEA director general, that it would participate as a supplier nation in international fuel banks. On export controls, New Delhi had revised its control lists on 7 September 2007 to make them consistent with the MTCR's 2005 lists, but it had not further updated these lists. US and Indian officials then held talks on 15–16 October 2007, and on 11–12 August 2008, after which New Delhi again updated its control lists. New Delhi formally adhered to the MTCR in a 9 September letter to the MTCR Point of Contact, and it adhered to the NSG in an 8 September letter to the IAEA director general.

To summarize, India's government took important diplomatic, economic, and export control initiatives that advanced its case with Congress. In turn, the Bush administration took steps to address New Delhi's concerns.

The Presidential Signing Statement

The Bush administration addressed India's concerns about congressional legislation in two ways. First, it worked to keep tough non-proliferation provisions, such as those in Representative Berman's original bill and in the Senate amendments, outside the legislation.

Second, the president issued a signing statement responding to India's concerns.[17] In discussions during Prime Minister Singh's late September visit to the US, New Delhi initially wanted the Senate to change its bill, but US officials noted that their executive branch could not demand such action from the legislature.[18] New Delhi then sought a presidential clarification – both verbally, because this would resonate positively with Indian audiences, as well as in writing – that there would be no change in the Section 123 Agreement. Accordingly, the president's verbal remarks on 8 October directly addressed this concern, and about half of the accompanying written statement also addressed this and related issues. The written statement noted that 'The legislation does not change the terms of the 123 Agreement' (The White House, 2008). It added that 'The Agreement grants India advance consent to reprocessing…In addition, the legislation does not change the fuel assurance commitments that the U.S. Government has made to the Government of India, as recorded in the 123 Agreement.' These administration initiatives helped India's government counter domestic mobilization against congressional legislation.

India's Domestic Politics

After India's government won a confidence vote in July 2008, it did not require the support of the left to remain in office. As a result, its win-set widened and congressional legislation with moderate non-proliferation provisions fell within its win-set. Opposition from the left and the right, as well as mobilization by domestic critics, did not prevent India's government from taking the nuclear agreement to its completion.

India's leftist and right-wing parties criticized the legislation as it advanced through the House and Senate. The left, which had issued statements on 2 August in response to the IAEA safeguards agreement, and on 23 August as the NSG discussed the issue, made further detailed arguments on 12, 17, 20, and 30 September in response to congressional legislation. The BJP issued somewhat fewer but just as detailed statements, and BJP leaders also opposed the nuclear agreement at their 12 September meeting. For example, a BJP statement on 3 September noted that the QFR answers confirmed the 'BJP's stand that the 123 Agreement would compulsorily prohibit any future tests by India' (The Indian Express, 2008a). This statement, and the BJP's remarks on 12 September, also raised concerns about fuel supply and ENR issues.[19] The left and the right drew upon the writings of strategic affairs experts and nuclear specialists in the Indian press.[20]

Among India's strategic affairs experts, a typical critical view stated that 'many in India now believe the Prime Minister should go to Washington to bury the 123 [Agreement] and not to praise it'; it added that 'a separate national statement would have to be issued contesting the U.S. reservation [in the 10 September submission and the QFR answers about fuel supply assurances to India]' (Varadarajan, 2008h).[21] India's media echoed similar sentiments: in early September, Indian television channels asked whether President Bush had kept the Indian government in the dark on the QFR answers; and whether India's government had misled the country on the answers (Lakshmi, 2008). However, other strategic affairs experts highlighted the broader benefits of the nuclear agreement. Illustrating this, K. Shankar Bajpai noted that the technical objections based on 'fuel supply uncertainty and ENR (enrichment and reprocessing) ambivalence' were only 'supplementary' issues, and that the bigger issue was that 'the agreement is a means to an end' and 'a step in India's emergence as a major power' (Bajpai, 2008).[22]

In the end, the supportive positions made it politically easier for India's government to formally sign the nuclear agreement in October 2008. At the same time, domestic criticism allowed India's government to more credibly ask the Bush administration to keep strong non-proliferation provisions outside the legislation and to issue a presidential signing statement. It also enabled India's government to argue that domestic political pressures would not allow it to wait indefinitely for congressional approval, and would instead cause it to advance nuclear contracts with France and Russia ahead of similar contracts with US firms.[23]

The US and Indian governments then completed the formal requirements for civilian nuclear cooperation. On 8 October, President Bush signed legislation authorizing such cooperation and, on 10 October, Secretary Rice and Foreign Minister Mukherjee signed the actual US–India nuclear cooperation agreement. On 20 October, the president submitted the two certifications required by the legislation for New Delhi and Washington to exchange diplomatic notes. On 6 December, Washington and New Delhi exchanged these notes which affirmed that they had met the requirements for the Section 123 Agreement to enter into force. Thus, in its final days in office, the Bush administration secured congressional approval and completed the formalities for nuclear cooperation with India.

Endnotes

1   These points were made in the letter from Congressman Berman to Secretary Rice, 5 August 2008.

2   These legislative voting rules were influenced by time constraints. In particular, the Atomic Energy Act required Congress to consider the India legislation for at least 30 days, but Congress was only in scheduled to meet for about 20 days (from 8 September to the end of September) and the Bush administration therefore asked Congress to waive the 30-day rule. Congress agreed on the condition that: (a) the Senate would have to give unanimous consent to waiving the rule; and (b) the House would have to pass any legislation by a two-thirds majority. The time constraints also made legislative passage harder because the administration had to convince Congress that the India legislation was as important as a $700 billion financial bailout package and other major issues in the few weeks available for congressional action.

3   On 5 October 2007, the chairman of the House Foreign Affairs Committee (HFAC) – previously called the HIRC – had sent 45 questions for the record to the State Department. The State Department responded to these on 16 January 2008, but also asked the HFAC to not release its answers, and the committee agreed to do so until it took up legislation on the issue.

4   These points were made in a statement by John Rood at the SFRC hearing, 18 September 2008.

5   See the transcript of the SFRC hearing, 'Agreement for Peaceful Nuclear Cooperation with India', 18 September 2008.

6   Ibid.

7   Author interview N2, 13 October 2011.

8   These points are noted in *The Congressional Record-Senate*, 1 October 2008, 23506–15.

9   Illustrating this, Representative Barbara Lee asked, 'Why should we expect, for example, Brazil or South Korea to continue playing by the rules [for nuclear commerce]…when they see that India receives the benefits while flouting the rules'. See *The Congressional Record-House*, 26 September 2008, pp. H10088–103.

10   For these points, see ibid.

11   For the supportive views, see *The Washington Post* (2008a, 2008b) and Emmott (2008). For the opposing perspective, see Kamdar (2008).

12   For the supportive view, see *The Wall Street Journal Asia* (2008); for the opposing perspective, see Sokolski (2008).

13   The US Embassy, New Delhi, cable, 9 July 2008.

14   Author interview Y1, 2 November 2011; *Radikal* (Turkey), 21 July 2008.

15   However, congressional staff recognized that, because US reactor companies were partly foreign owned, US industry would only partially benefit from reactor sales to India, and they saw greater commercial opportunities in arms deals with India.

16   India's government had discussed such a letter with US business and with the US government for over a year. Thus, in a December 2007 meeting, USIBC and

Indian officials discussed: (a) a government-to-government memorandum of understanding, similar to India's understanding with Russia, that would expedite the planning and construction of nuclear plants by US firms; (b) the letter of intent; and (c) nuclear liability legislation. In March 2008, commenting on a US draft of the letter, Indian officials noted that offering the US 'numbers [on the magnitude of reactor contracts] may be difficult' but they affirmed that US firms would have a major share of nuclear commerce in India. In July, Indian officials stated that they would finalize a letter of intent and address nuclear liability concerns in forthcoming meetings with Undersecretary William Burns. On 25 August, India's foreign secretary shared with Undersecretary Burns India's draft letter of intent. This suggested that Washington would have to complete a reprocessing pact before US firms could undertake nuclear trade with India, but Indian officials removed this provision when US officials objected to it. Washington and New Delhi settled their final differences just after the NSG meeting on 6 September, when New Delhi objected to mentioning the location of US-built reactors and also noted that Indian law required the government to assess environmental and safety issues such as conducting seismic surveys in determining the reactor sites. See the US Embassy, New Delhi, cables, 17 December 2007, 5 March 2008, 10 July 2008, and 26 August 2008.

17   Washington was initially reluctant to issue a signing statement and, in response, India's government expressed its unwillingness to sign the nuclear agreement during Secretary Rice's visit to India. Washington then agreed to the signing statement. See Sikri (2009).

18   This discussion draws from author interview C2, 17 August 2010; author interview H1, 3 August 2010; and author interview Y1, 2 November 2011.

19   See the BJP press release, 'Presidential Speech by Rajnath Singh at the National Executive Meeting, Bangalore', 12 September 2008; see also pieces by Arun Shourie in *The Indian Express* (6 and 8 September 2008).

20   Nuclear experts focused on technical points in congressional legislation. Expressing concerns, P. K. Iyengar noted that 'in the event of a disruption of fuel supply from the US, the Americans will not help arrange for fuel from another country'; he added that ENR restrictions were 'the most disturbing clause in the Bill' (Iyengar, 2008b). On the other hand, defending the government's position, M. R. Srinivasan noted that India could obtain fuel from NSG countries whose laws did not require them to end fuel supplies in the event of an Indian nuclear test (Srinivasan, 2008b).

21   See also related arguments by Siddharth Varadarajan (*The Hindu*, 3 October 2008), Brahma Chellaney (*The Hindu*, 5 September 2008), and Bharat Karnad (LiveMint.com, 18 September 2008).

22   For additional similar views, see Subrahmanyam (2008d).

23   The US Embassy, New Delhi, cable, 12 September 2008.

CHAPTER ELEVEN

Reprocessing and Liability

Iₙ February 2009, the Obama administration asked India's government to take the steps necessary to facilitate US commercial investments in India's nuclear sector. Washington wanted New Delhi to 'follow through on its commitment to set aside nuclear reactor park sites for US firms', as well as to pass legislation on 'domestic liability protection'.[1] In turn, New Delhi sought a reprocessing pact, and it hinted that US reactor sales to India would be held up without such an accord.

Both sides then acted on these issues. From July 2009 to March 2010, Washington and New Delhi negotiated a reprocessing pact. In turn, in October 2009, New Delhi designated two reactor sites for US firms: Mithi Virdi in Gujarat for Westinghouse; and Kovvada in Seemandhra for General Electric. Further, in August 2010, India's Parliament passed a nuclear liability bill. However, the bill channelled liability to the suppliers of nuclear equipment rather than solely to the operators of nuclear facilities. It was therefore not acceptable to US firms and they held back from making investments in India's nuclear sector.

The Reprocessing Pact

In early 2009, New Delhi formally requested the Obama administration to negotiate a reprocessing pact. US and Indian officials then held reprocessing talks in July and October 2009 in Vienna and in November 2009 in Washington. However, they could not reach an agreement ahead of Prime Minister Singh's 22 November visit to the US. They were unable to resolve two main issues: the number of Indian reprocessing facilities; and the conditions under which Washington could suspend reprocessing consent (Varadarajan, 2009). They settled the first issue in subsequent weeks and resolved the contentious issue of suspending reprocessing consent in March 2010 (Varadarajan, 2010). They then reached a reprocessing pact with relatively moderate non-proliferation provisions.

First, the reprocessing pact gave India advance consent to reprocess US-obligated spent fuel so that it would not require US approval each time it sought to reprocess. India's DAE sought such consent to avoid any recurrence of the Tarapur experience.[2]

Second, the reprocessing pact accommodated both Washington and New Delhi on the issue of suspension. In its 2008 answers to congressional questions, the Bush administration had argued that, despite Indian statements that reprocessing rights are 'permanent', the reprocessing pact 'will provide for withdrawal of reprocessing consent' under certain circumstances.[3] Early drafts of the reprocessing pact had just two paragraphs on suspension, and these accommodated Washington's position. During talks in October and November 2009, New Delhi objected to these terms. It noted that any suspension due to 'exceptional circumstances' (a term mentioned in the Section 123 Agreement) should only follow from India's reprocessing-related obligations such as safeguards, physical security, and safety, and not from circumstances unrelated to reprocessing such as an Indian nuclear test. The final reprocessing pact then had eight paragraphs on suspension that addressed India's concerns.

Illustrating this, the reprocessing pact stated that the 'sole grounds' for suspension would be 'exceptional circumstances limited to' three items. These were a determination by either party that continued reprocessing 'would result in a serious threat to the Party's national security', a 'serious threat to the physical protection of the [reprocessing] Facility', or a 'Party's determination that suspension is an unavoidable measure'.

Further, the reprocessing pact made it difficult to implement suspension. It noted that any suspension 'decision shall only be taken at the highest level of Government' and that consultations on suspension would 'give special consideration to the importance for India of uninterrupted operation of nuclear reactors'. It added that for suspensions longer than six months, both parties 'shall enter into consultations on compensation for the adverse impact on the Indian economy due to disruption in electricity generation'.

Third, although the Section 123 Agreement mentioned that India would establish one new reprocessing facility, the reprocessing pact allowed India more than one facility. New Delhi sought, and Washington eventually agreed, that the pact would apply 'to two new national reprocessing facilities established by the Government of India', as well as to 'any additional new national facilities established' by India. This enabled India to lessen the risks of transporting spent fuel between distant sites (for example, between the two sites it had designated for US-built reactors in Gujarat and Andhra Pradesh) by having a separate reprocessing facility at each.

Fourth, the reprocessing pact had provisions for physical protection and storage at India's reprocessing facilities, but Washington and New Delhi differed over the 'consultation visits' by US officials to implement this provision. India's nuclear establishment sought to restrict US access to its nuclear sites. The Agreed Minute then significantly limited the frequency and scope of US consultation visits.

US non-proliferation groups and Indian critics both objected to the reprocessing pact. Non-proliferation groups were most concerned about giving India long-term reprocessing consent because, by doing so, the US was giving a non-NPT country terms that it had only given Japan and the EU. However, non-proliferation concerns were indirectly accommodated on another issue: that of suspending the agreement in the event of an Indian nuclear test. The reprocessing pact enabled Washington to suspend the agreement by making a determination that any Indian nuclear test constituted a serious threat to US national security or was damaging enough that suspension became an 'unavoidable measure' (Hibbs, 2010).

Indian critics objected to several points: that the reprocessing pact only mentioned that Washington would 'consult' with India on compensation without actually being required to compensate it; that the amount of compensation would be determined by Washington rather than by New Delhi; and that India obtained no legally binding fuel supply assurances (Chellaney, 2010). In the end, despite the various concerns, the reprocessing pact remained within both the US and Indian win-sets.

In India, domestic mobilization against the reprocessing pact was negligible: the pact received little coverage in the press; and India's leftist and right-wing parties did not criticize it. Moreover, India's government did not need parliamentary approval for the pact. Finally, India's nuclear establishment did not resist the pact: instead, it actively wanted the pact and was closely involved in its negotiation. These factors expanded India's win-set so that a reprocessing pact with moderate non-proliferation provisions remained within the win-set.

In the US, domestic mobilization was also limited: the reprocessing pact received little attention in the press and among arms control groups. Still, on political–institutional grounds, Congress had the ability to review the pact (specifically, the October 2008 congressional legislation authorizing nuclear cooperation with India gave Congress 30 days to consider and reject the pact) and this reduced the win-set. For this reason, a reprocessing pact without relatively moderate non-proliferation provisions would have fallen outside the US win-set, but the eventual reprocessing pact had such provisions. Further, in much the same manner as in the period from 2006 to 2008, administration official Richard Stratford's interventions with Congress had non-proliferation credibility. Thus, Stratford made a credible case for allowing India to have two reprocessing sites, and Congress accepted this position.[4] For these reasons, the final reprocessing pact remained within the US win-set: Congress did not oppose it and it took effect without a congressional vote.

India's Nuclear Liability Bill

India's government began drafting a nuclear liability bill in 2007–08 and acted on it in 2010. The DAE initially worked on a liability bill in 2007. In July 2008, it circulated a draft bill to several Indian government ministries. The bill drew upon legislation in other countries and conformed to the Convention on Supplementary Compensation for Nuclear Damage (CSC). Thus, it had relatively higher compatibility with international standards and relatively lesser liability for nuclear suppliers. The US government, US business, and Indian business, all urged India's government to adopt the bill.

India's cabinet cleared the bill in November 2009 and the government then reached out to the left and the right to secure their support. India's prime minister met BJP leaders in January 2010, and India's national security advisor also met BJP member Arun Jaitley, leader of the opposition in the upper house of Parliament, and his deputy, S. S. Ahluwalia. Still, the BJP opposed the bill, drawing upon points raised by domestic critics.[5]

In early March 2010, ahead of Prime Minister Singh's April visit to the US, India's government introduced but failed to advance the bill in the

Parliament: largely because political power considerations reduced India's win-set. At the time, the UPA coalition had just over 260 seats in the Parliament, but it was uncertain about the votes of 19 members from the Trinamool Congress (a coalition partner from West Bengal). Further, because of poor floor management, another 30 UPA members of Parliament were absent when the government sought to introduce the bill. This gave the opposition a small chance to defeat the bill (the BJP-led alliance, the left, and other opponents had about 220 seats in the Parliament). India's government then withdrew the bill.

In May, India's government resubmitted the bill to the Parliament but, instead of pressing for a vote on the bill, it allowed the parliamentary standing committee on science and technology to hold hearings on the issue.[6] From June to August, the committee heard testimony from government ministries, civil society experts, nuclear experts, and Indian business.[7] During these deliberations, India's government sought to address opposition concerns. For example, in June, DAE officials explained to the committee that foreign suppliers were not entirely exempt from liability because they would be liable for defective parts in their contracts with the government; that private sector ownership in Indian nuclear plants was possible only up to 49 per cent; and that the government's liability was actually unlimited, irrespective of the caps of Rs 500 crore (which was $100 million at then-prevailing exchange rates of Rs 50 per dollar) and Rs 2,163 crore (a limit that corresponded to 300 million special drawing rights) in the bill.

More importantly, the government again reached out to the BJP. In early August, External Affairs Minister Pranab Mukherjee met BJP leaders L. K. Advani, Arun Jaitley, Murli Manohar Joshi, Jaswant Singh, Yashwant Sinha, and Sushma Swaraj. Later, during a 17 August meeting between Mukherjee, Swaraj, and Jaitley, the government accepted the BJP's suggestions that private operators be entirely excluded from ownership of nuclear plants and that the operator's liability cap be raised to Rs 1,500 crore. In a further meeting with Jaitley, the government again accommodated the BJP and dropped a controversial word, the word 'and' between two sections in clause 17 of the bill (as noted next). India's Parliament then adopted the liability bill.

Overall, the August 2010 bill differed from the version introduced in March in four significant ways. First, it excluded private sector firms from ownership of nuclear plants. Second, it increased the operator's liability to Rs 1,500 crore. Third, it specified the operator's right to seek recourse from suppliers. In clause 17, it noted that the operator 'shall have a right to recourse where (a) Such right is expressly provided for in a contract in writing; (b) the nuclear incident has resulted as a consequence of an act of suppliers or his employees, which includes supply of equipment or material or patent or latent defects or sub standard services'.[8] This language removed the word 'and' between clauses 17(a) and (b), so that clause 17(b) would apply to a supplier even without any recourse provision in a written contract with that supplier. Fourth, in clause 35, it accepted the parliamentary committee's suggestion that accident victims should be able to appeal to a higher court. It also added the words 'save as provided in Section 46' and section 46 allowed legal proceedings against an operator.

To summarize, the August 2010 liability bill had relatively stronger liability provisions sought by Indian civil society and by India's opposition parties. It therefore fell within India's win-set. However, Indian business, US business, and the US government strongly objected to this bill: the bill fell outside the US win-set.[9] American, as well as Russian and French, nuclear vendors were especially concerned about Articles 35, 46, and 17(b), noting that these were incompatible with international standards that channelled all liability to nuclear plant operators rather than to the suppliers of plant equipment.

India's government subsequently sought to accommodate international suppliers. It initially suggested that their concerns could be resolved in their contracts with India's government and by India's signing the CSC (which it did in late October 2010, though it held back on ratifying the convention). It also issued a set of rules to address international concerns about Section 17(b) (*The Indian Express*, 2010). These rules made suppliers liable for any defective equipment for only the first five years of a reactor's operation, and only to a limit of Rs 1,500 crores. Still, international suppliers did not accept this solution. Washington pressed New Delhi to apply another solution based on conformity with the CSC (Haniffa, 2012). It asked India to 'engage with the International Atomic Energy Agency to ensure that India's liability regime fully conforms with the international requirements under the [CSC] convention'.[10] Yet, New Delhi opposed any IAEA vetting of its liability laws.

In late 2012 and 2013, Washington and New Delhi again sought to resolve their differences over India's liability legislation and to advance US nuclear commerce in India. In 2012, Westinghouse signed a memorandum for an early works agreement with the Nuclear Power Corporation of India Limited (NPCIL). Also, op-eds in the Indian press called for changing India's liability laws to better accommodate US and Indian business.[11] In early 2013, Washington and New Delhi worked out the Part 810 assurances which enable the Department of Energy to authorize US firms to undertake civilian nuclear activities in India. In mid-2013, US and Indian officials further discussed India's liability laws. In September 2013, in a legal opinion requested by India's government, India's attorney general noted that NPCIL could opt to not invoke sections of the liability laws in any commercial contract with international suppliers. That month, NPCIL and Westinghouse signed a preliminary early works agreement under which NPCIL would pay approximately Rs 100 crore ($15 million) to Westinghouse for proprietary information needed to set up Westinghouse's reactors in Gujarat.

To summarize, in the early 2010s, India's government did not amend its liability laws to accommodate US preferences: such amendments remained outside India's win-set. New Delhi still sought to work out alternative arrangements that would remain within its win-set while also permitting US firms to realize the commercial rewards of the nuclear agreement.

Endnotes

1   The US Embassy, New Delhi, cable, 12 February 2009.
2   After India's 1974 nuclear test, Washington did not permit New Delhi to reprocess the spent fuel at Tarapur and did not ship the fuel back to the US; India therefore had to accumulate this spent fuel for over three decades.
3   These points were noted by the State Department in its answers to the QFRs (the 'QFR answers'), 16 January 2008.
4   Author interview N2, 13 October 2011.
5   For these points and India's broader domestic mobilization for and against the liability bill, see the website of PRS Legislative Research, available at http://www .prsindia.org/billtrack/the-civil-liability-for-nuclear-damage-bill-2010-1042/.
6   Soon thereafter, domestic mobilization related to the legacy of Bhopal further reduced India's win-set. In June 2010, an Indian court ruled that seven employees of the US firm Union Carbide would be held accountable for the Bhopal disaster, and India's opposition parties then more prominently insisted on holding foreign suppliers accountable in any nuclear liability bill.
7   The committee heard testimony from nuclear experts, P. K. Iyengar, Anil Kakodkar, and A. Gopalakrishnan; ex-government officials, Kanwal Sibal and Satish Chandra; strategic affairs experts, Brahma Chellaney and Bharat Karnad;

and other nuclear and civil society experts such as Prabir Puryakayasta, S. Sen, and Praful Bidwai. It also heard testimony from the government departments of health, environment, agriculture, and water resources, from the home ministry, and from governmental insurance sector representatives.

8   This language was drawn from the Annex to the CSC.

9   The objections of Indian business and US business were noted in numerous press reports, for example, *The Economic Times* (2010a, 2010b, 2010c).

10   These remarks were made at the Brookings Institution, in an event on 'The Future of the U.S.–India Partnership', Washington, DC, 27 September 2011.

11   See Abraham (2012); Srinivasan (2012).

CHAPTER TWELVE

Reviewing and Extending the Argument

Iɴ July 2005, when President Bush and Prime Minister Singh sought to 'transform the relationship between their countries' through a civilian nuclear agreement, Washington and New Delhi expected to complete the agreement within a year. Ultimately, the agreement was only formalized in the fall of 2008, over two years later than either side expected. And in the early 2010s – several years after the agreement was formalized – US nuclear vendors had still not realized commercial rewards from the agreement. The two-level framework, discussed in prior chapters, explains why US–India nuclear negotiations were long and difficult and why the eventual nuclear agreement did not entirely satisfy either side. This chapter begins by reviewing these negotiations. It then extends the argument to additional cases and shows how the two-level framework provides valuable insights into nuclear diplomacy with other countries.

Reviewing US–India Nuclear Negotiations

From 2005 to 2008, as Washington and New Delhi negotiated their nuclear agreement, some key domestic factors – bureaucratic politics, legislative impediments, and domestic mobilization – prevented them from concluding the nuclear initiative within their originally intended timeframe.

These domestic constraints required both sides to proceed step-by-step to realize their nuclear agreement. Moreover, in each step, the two sides only reached arrangements that could 'win' approval domestically. In short, domestic factors considerably delayed, and may have entirely prevented, US–India nuclear cooperation, and they also placed conditions on the terms for cooperation.

Five additional points were prominent in the US–India nuclear negotiations. First, the details of the main US–India arrangements (such as the Joint Statement, the separation plan, and the Section 123 Agreement) mattered considerably. Only arrangements with carefully crafted language fell within both the US and Indian win-sets, and even small changes of a few words to accommodate one side resulted in these arrangements falling outside the other's win-set. Relatedly, New Delhi held out against each arrangement until the final hour of its negotiation and only accepted the arrangement after Washington accommodated it on the last remaining details.

Second, domestic mobilization significantly influenced win-sets in both countries. In the US, a well-established arms control lobby quickly mobilized to seek non-proliferation restraints in the nuclear agreement. The India lobby (comprising American business, Indian Americans, and strategic affairs experts) took longer to mobilize, but when it did, it substantially countered the case made by arms control groups.

India's domestic mobilization had three notable aspects. One was its rapid pace: domestic constituents mobilized within hours of the announcement of the main US–India arrangements. A second was its breadth: the Indian press carried hundreds of commentaries echoing the views of the left, the centre, and the right that were for or against these arrangements. A third was its depth: a handful of scientific and strategic affairs experts made very detailed technical arguments about the fine points, as well as about the larger strategic and energy issues, in the nuclear agreement.

Third, at the bureaucratic level, the US–India talks followed a pattern where their negotiating teams could agree to about 70–80 per cent of an arrangement but could not complete it.[1] Decisive interventions at higher levels of government were necessary to break the negotiating deadlocks. Thus, senior officials who took a broader strategic view of the negotiations – Undersecretary Burns and Foreign Secretaries Saran and Menon – had to resolve most of the remaining differences. Yet, even they could not finalize an agreement. Ultimately, President Bush himself stepped in to give India fuel supply assurances in 2006, and to allow it reprocessing consent in 2007.

The national security advisor then brokered a compromise on these issues and this enabled both sides to reach a final agreement.

The US and Indian national security advisors also played further crucial roles. In particular, they recognized that President Bush and Prime Minister Singh had made the nuclear agreement a priority for their governments, and they therefore followed the negotiations closely and intervened to advance the dialogue when it stalled. In addition, they worked out bureaucratic compromises in their respective countries: India's national security advisor settled differences between India's nuclear establishment and its foreign policy officials, while the US national security advisor helped reconcile differences between US non-proliferation and strategic affairs perspectives.

Fourth, the US–India dialogue advanced because of the personal relationships and trust established during senior-level discussions.[2] In the period from 2001 to 2004, India's national security advisor established a comfort level in interacting with his US interlocutors, Condoleezza Rice and Stephen Hadley, and this helped both sides advance their high-technology dialogue that preceded the civilian nuclear initiative. A similar dynamic was evident from 2005 to 2008. As they interacted with each other, Prime Minister Singh and President Bush, the US and Indian national security advisors, and the US undersecretary of state and India's foreign secretaries, all developed a better appreciation of the other side's perspective. For example, Undersecretary Burns was not an India specialist and was not familiar with his Indian counterparts before 2005. Yet, he eventually took eight trips to India, got to know India's foreign secretaries, met them in cities around the world, held hours of talks and exchanged numerous e-mails with them, and became familiar with other senior Indian officials and members of the Parliament.

Finally, while the foreign secretaries, undersecretary of state, and national security advisors were instrumental in advancing international negotiations, the US and Indian ambassadors helped in building domestic support for these negotiations. The Indian ambassador met with 227 representatives and 46 senators, individually or collectively, to make the case for the nuclear agreement; he also reached out to Indian American, Jewish, African American, and Latino groups, as well as to corporate America, to secure their support for the agreement.[3]

To summarize, domestic factors considerably affected negotiations for the US–India nuclear agreement. Some factors such as mobilization by supporters and interventions by the senior-most US and Indian officials who focused on the larger strategic perspective helped advance negotiations. Other factors such as bureaucratic resistance, contentious executive–legislative relations in both the US and India, the political weakness of India's minority coalition government, and domestic mobilization by opponents hindered the negotiations process. Many of these factors also affect US nuclear diplomacy with other countries.

Nuclear Diplomacy

US–India negotiations on their civilian nuclear agreement were, in some fundamental ways, very different from US nuclear discussions with other countries.[4] Despite these differences, this study's analytical framework can usefully inform US nuclear dialogues with other countries. Its main analytical point is that nuclear diplomacy between two countries is only successful if an international-level arrangement can 'win' domestic approval in both countries and therefore falls within both their win-sets. The win-set, in turn, is shaped by bureaucratic factors, legislative politics, and the mobilization of domestic groups. Further research can apply this framework to explain several important cases.

First, the framework can be applied to Pakistan and Israel.[5] During the 2000s and early 2010s, Pakistan's and Israel's win-sets could well have accommodated an agreement similar to the US–India agreement, where they separated their civilian and military nuclear facilities, permanently safeguarded the civilian facilities, and adopted export controls and nuclear testing restraints. Yet, there was no bureaucratic push in Washington for such an agreement; and therefore, Washington did not even commence a civilian nuclear dialogue with these states. Further research could explore whether Washington's win-set can widen to accept a civilian nuclear agreement with Pakistan and Israel. It could widen if Washington seeks to advance strategic ties or broader regional political objectives involving these states; if senior decision makers and regional and strategic affairs bureaus press for these objectives; and if the legislature and domestic groups support these agreements. Such research could also examine whether alternative arrangements – such as Pakistan's and Israel's membership in the NSG in lieu of civilian nuclear cooperation or their ceasing fissile material production as a condition for civilian nuclear cooperation – would fit within both the US and Pakistani, and the US and Israeli, win-sets.

Second, the framework offers insights into reprocessing talks with South Korea, enrichment discussions with Brazil, and civilian nuclear pacts with other states. Here, because of bureaucratic resistance from their nuclear establishments, and in the case of Brazil, the military, Brazil and South Korea have opposed restrictions on their enrichment and reprocessing programs.[6] If Washington seeks to reaffirm or advance strategic ties with these states, if senior US decision makers and regional affairs and strategic affairs bureaucrats press these objectives, and if Congress and domestic interest groups are supportive, then Washington could accept Brazil and South Korea's respective positions on enrichment and reprocessing. If these conditions do not materialize, then Washington would be unable to reach a settlement on these issues. And if these factors only partially materialize, then Washington may accept alternative limited constraints on enrichment and reprocessing in South Korea and Brazil. Further research could analyze whether such limited constraints would also have bureaucratic and legislative support in South Korea and Brazil.

Third, the framework can be applied to North Korea and Iran. In the case of Iran, the principal negotiating issues are the magnitude of Iran's enrichment capacity (that is, the size and capacity of its enrichment plants); the levels of enrichment (such as 5 per cent and 20 per cent); the stock of enriched uranium that Iran may retain; and transparency and the Additional Protocol. During the 2000s and early 2010s, arrangements requiring Tehran to renounce or substantially limit enrichment were within Washington's win-set but remained outside Tehran's win-set (Parsi, 2011; Sebenius and Singh, 2012–13). Conversely, arrangements permitting Tehran more flexibility in enrichment were within its win-set but remained outside Washington's win-set because the regional, strategic affairs, and non-proliferation bureaucracies all opposed such concessions to Tehran. In 2013, however, Hasan Rouhani was elected to Iran's presidency, and Iran's merchants, industrialists, bankers, and pragmatist politicians convinced the Supreme Leader to allow Rouhani to negotiate on ending sanctions. These bureaucratic shifts widened Tehran's win-set just enough for it to accept some enrichment restraints in return for some sanctions relief under a temporary agreement in November 2013. On the US side, senior decision makers such as the deputy secretary of state and the secretary of state actively worked to secure such a partial nuclear settlement, and Congress did not immediately impose additional sanctions on Tehran that would have disrupted the settlement—this widened Washington's win-set so that it could accept such a settlement.

In the case of North Korea, since its 2003 withdrawal from the NPT, arrangements that enabled it to retain but not enlarge its military nuclear program did not fall within both its win-set and the US win-set.

If bureaucratic preferences among North Korea's political and military leadership change, Pyongyang could accept some nuclear restraints in return for the lifting of international sanctions. On the US side, if senior decision makers and regional and strategic affairs bureaucrats support engagement with Pyongyang, this may expand the US win-set so that it could accept a similar arrangement. (Such an arrangement would also have to 'win' approval in Seoul, Tokyo, and Beijing to be successful.) Until the US and North Korean win-sets overlap, however, no major nuclear agreement between these states may be possible, though limited nuclear dialogues may still fit within each country's win-set.

A Concluding Word

This study has highlighted how domestic politics significantly affected the US–India nuclear dialogue. Its analytical framework can be extended to explain US nuclear diplomacy with other states. Such a framework also enhances our understanding of two broader, non-nuclear areas: the US–India strategic dialogue; and the politics of partnership building. These are beyond the scope of this book but are worth briefly mentioning.

First, domestic factors influenced the US–India dialogue on strategic issues such as India's export controls, its arms purchases from US suppliers, and its policies on Iran. On each issue, New Delhi essentially pursued policies that could 'win' approval domestically; such policies gradually and partially, rather than rapidly and substantially, aligned with US preferences.[7] On export controls, when it announced a civilian nuclear agreement with India in 2005, Washington anticipated that New Delhi would soon adhere to four regimes: the NSG, the MTCR, the Australia Group, and the Wassenaar Arrangement. New Delhi quickly supported the NSG and MTCR, but it held back on the Australia Group and the Wassenaar Arrangement until around 2010. On arms sales, India ordered a substantial $13 billion worth of US arms between 2005 and 2012 (Grimmett, 2012). However, in 2011, it excluded US firms from its single biggest arms deal: a $10 billion contract for 126 medium multi-role combat aircraft. On Iran, New Delhi voted with Washington and against Tehran at the IAEA meetings in 2005, 2006, and 2009. However, New Delhi only slowly complied with US and European oil sanctions against Iran. Thus, it reduced by just 20 per cent its imports of Iranian oil between 2008 and 2012; it then cut such imports by a more substantial 25 per cent during 2012–13. Further research could explore how Indian bureaucratic and legislative politics affected its position on the above-mentioned issues. Such research would shed light a second broader area: that of the politics of partnership building.

On this area, this book offers insights into the puzzle of why two major powers (that is, the US and India) that had strategic interests in building a partnership found it very difficult to do so. It shows how domestic politics hinder democratic states from practising *realpolitik* and pursuing partnerships. It also illustrates that, while legislatures do not excessively intervene in routine foreign policy initiatives, they more actively intervene in major international initiatives such as defence and strategic partnerships. These observations can form the basis for further research on the process of partnership building, and on how domestic factors affect the pace and depth of this process.[8]

To return to the topic of this book, that of nuclear negotiations, this study's analytical framework offers important insights into the US nuclear dialogue with India and with other states. It identifies the main internal variables – bureaucratic factors, legislative politics, and mobilization by supporters and opponents – that influence a country's win-set; it can determine the size of the win-set and the international arrangement that fits within this win-set; and it can assess whether such an arrangement also falls within Washington's win-set, thereby enabling Washington to attain atomic accommodation with its negotiating partners. A better understanding of this framework, and of the domestic dynamics behind international diplomacy, would usefully inform an array of US nuclear and strategic dialogues with India and with other countries.

Endnotes

1   Here, it is worth noting that Washington and New Delhi have very different negotiating styles: while Washington looks for specific answers in talks with India, New Delhi often pursues 'the art of nondiplomacy', meaning that it does 'not say yes or no' (Cohen, 2001).

2   Author interview D4, 25 October 2011; author interview J1, 12 October 2011; author interview O3, 25 November 2011; and author interview Y1, 2 November 2011.

3   Author interview U5, 15 November 2012.

4   On this issue, first, US nuclear dialogues with other countries have not been routes to strategic partnerships with those countries. Second, while Congress is sometimes involved in nuclear negotiations with other countries, it is not as deeply involved as it was in the negotiations with India; this is largely because

negotiations with other countries do not involve major changes to the Atomic Energy Act and most do not require legislative ratification. (The one exception is US–Russia arms control treaties, where the Senate is required to ratify, and has therefore closely scrutinized, such treaties.) Third, the legislatures of other countries have not been as strongly involved as India's Parliament was in negotiations with the US; therefore, governments in these countries have not had to win legislative votes of confidence to advance nuclear agreements. Still, in future cases where nuclear negotiations get politicized and executive–legislative relations are contentious – this could occur, for example, in Pakistan, South Korea, and even Iran – the legislature could influence nuclear negotiations. Fourth, the strength of the main bureaucratic actors – the nuclear establishment, the military, the foreign affairs bureaucracy, and the political leadership – and the degree to which they participate in nuclear negotiations varies across cases.

5   On Pakistan, see Kerr (2011); on past US talks with Israel, see Cohen (2010).

6   On South Korea, see *The New York Times* (2013). On Brazil, see Aronson (2012). This article mentions many domestic issues that were present in the Indian case. It notes that 'powerful…constituencies have a vested interest in continuing Brazil's enrichment program, and Brazilian nationalists would have to be mollified. Thus, it is vital that Brazil be perceived as acting on its own rather than yielding to pressure from Washington…Still, the United States could offer incentives behind closed doors.'

7   US policymakers recognized this pattern well before the nuclear agreement was announced. Thus, Ambassador Blackwill noted that the building of a strategic partnership 'does not mean that Washington and New Delhi will always agree on specific policies' because 'the Indian bureaucracy can be as maddeningly slow and recalcitrant as that in the United States' and because 'Indian domestic politics will sometimes constrain the actions of governments in New Delhi' (Blackwill, 2005). For a related discussion, see also Schaffer (2009).

8   For alliances and partnerships, see David (1991); Walt (1987). For domestic influences on alliance cooperation, see Moravcsik (1993). For studies on legislatures and foreign policy, see Martin (2000); Milner (1997).

Appendix
Energy, Military, and Non-proliferation Issues in the Nuclear Agreement

THIS appendix examines the military and energy aspects of India's nuclear program; it clarifies the extent to which civilian nuclear imports contribute to India's energy sector; it discusses whether such imports enable India to expand its military nuclear program; and it reviews the nuclear agreement's impact on Pakistan's nuclear decisions and on the non-proliferation regime.

By way of background, India began a small civilian nuclear program in the 1940s and, following its 1962 war with China and Beijing's 1964 nuclear test, embarked upon a subterranean nuclear explosive program.[1] New Delhi then remained outside the NPT and tested a nuclear device in 1974, thereby obtaining a non-weaponized nuclear option. Since the late 1980s, following military crises with Pakistan, Pakistan's own nuclear advances, and no positive superpower response to the Rajiv Gandhi action plan for nuclear disarmament, New Delhi more actively worked on and acquired a weaponized nuclear option. It also rejected the CTBT in 1996. Yet, Indian governments headed by the Congress Party and by centrist coalitions did not conduct further nuclear tests and did not overtly declare India to be a nuclear weapons state. In 1998, however, the BJP-led government authorized a series of nuclear tests and formally took India across the nuclear weapons threshold.

India's Nuclear Reactors and Energy Plans

India's DAE operates two nuclear programs. Its military program uses weapons-grade plutonium from the Dhruva and the now-closed Cirus reactor. Its civilian nuclear power program involves over 20 additional reactors, shown in Table A1. These include two 160 MW US-supplied light water reactors at Tarapur (operational since 1969 and operating under safeguards); two 100–200 MW Canadian-supplied Candu heavy water reactors (that became operational in 1973 and 1981, and operated under safeguards); and 16 Indian-built heavy water reactors derived from the Candu, that were outside safeguards until India agreed to safeguard eight under the nuclear agreement.

Table A.1 India's Nuclear Power Reactors

Reactor	State	Capacity (MW, electric)	Year of Operation	Notes
Tarapur 1 & 2	Maharashtra	2 × 160	1969	US-supplied (by GE), safeguarded
Rawatbhatta 1 & 2	Rajasthan	2 × 100	1973, 1981	Candu from Canada, safeguarded
Kalpakkam 1 & 2	Tamil Nadu	2 × 220	1984, 1986	Candu-based
Narora 1 & 2	Uttar Pradesh	2 × 220	1991, 1992	Candu-based, safeguards in 2014
Kakrapur 1 & 2	Gujarat	2 × 220	1993, 1995	Candu-based, safeguards in 2010
Kaiga 1 & 2	Karnataka	2 × 220	2000	Candu-based
Rawatbhatta 3 & 4	Rajasthan	2 × 220	2000	Candu-based, safeguards in 2010
Tarapur 3 & 4	Maharashtra	2 × 540	2005, 2006	
Kaiga 3 & 4	Karnataka	2 × 220	2007, 2010	Candu-based
Rawatbhatta 5 & 6	Rajasthan	2 × 220	2009, 2010	Candu-based, safeguards in 2009
Kudankulam 1 & 2	Tamil Nadu	2 × 1,000	2013–14	Russian-built, safeguarded

Reactor	State	Capacity (MW, electric)	Year of Operation	Notes
Breeder	Tamil Nadu	500	2014–15	Breeder reactor at Kalpakkam
Future Indian-built Plants			**Year of Beginning Construction**	
Rawatbhatta 7 & 8	Rajasthan	2 × 700	2011	
Kakrapur 3 & 4	Gujarat	2 × 700	2011	
Kaiga 5 & 6	Karnataka	2 × 700	2014–17?	
Gorakhpur 1 & 2	Haryana	2 × 700	2014–17?	
Banswada 1 & 2	Rajasthan	2 × 700	2014–17?	
Chutka 1 & 2	Madhya Pradesh	2 × 700	2014–17?	
Planned International Reactors				
Kudankulam 3–6	Tamil Nadu	4 × 1,000		Russian-built
Jaitapur 1–6	Maharashtra	6 × 1,600		Built by Areva
Mithi Virdi 1–6	Gujarat	6 × 1,250		Built by Westinghouse
Kovvada 1–4	Andhra Pradesh	4 × 1,300		Built by GE-Hitachi

Notes: The Candu reactors, and the Indian-built 220, 540, and 700 MW reactors, are all pressurized heavy water reactors (PHWR) that use natural uranium fuel. The foreign-supplied light water reactors (LWR) include: (a) boiling water reactors at Tarapur; (b) similar planned reactors at Kovvada; and (c) pressurized water reactors at Kudankulam, Jaitapur, and Mithi Virdi; all these use enriched uranium fuel.

In addition, DAE began building a 500 MW breeder reactor in 2004 and planned to complete it by 2010 (it was eventually delayed and is expected to be commissioned around 2014–15). The breeder is a bridge between India's heavy water reactors, which rely on India's limited uranium reserves for fuel, and future reactors that would use India's plentiful thorium reserves. This is part of DAE's three-phase nuclear plan, where, in the first phase, a 10,000 MW base in heavy water reactors would produce enough plutonium to fuel a chain of breeder reactors. In the second phase, these breeder reactors would produce a large amount of Uranium-233. In the third stage, this U-233 and thorium would fuel India's next generation of thermal reactors, such as the advanced heavy water reactors.

Finally, Russia began building two 1,000 MW light water reactors, at Kudankulam, in Tamil Nadu, in 2002; the first of these reactors was completed in 2012 and commissioned in 2013.

The International Technology Embargo

Three points are relevant to understanding the impact of international technology embargoes on India's nuclear program. First, India imported its first five major reactors: two US-supplied plants at Tarapur, the Canadian-supplied Cirus, and two Canadian-supplied Candu reactors. International suppliers then halted nuclear trade with India after its 1974 nuclear test. This international embargo slowed the installation of new nuclear plants, and also prevented India from acquiring high-capacity plants. Specifically, after the Canadian-supplied Candu in 1973, no further reactors entered India's energy grid in the 1970s, and only three reactors were completed in the 1980s (that is, the second Canadian-supplied Candu and two Indian-built clones of the Candu). Thereafter, although India completed eight new reactors from 1991 to 2000, these had small 220 MW capacities (compared with 1,000 MW plants in other countries). Subsequently, from 2001 to 2010, India completed six more heavy water reactors: four with 220 MW capacities and two with 540 MW capacities.

Second, as a result of this slow growth and low capacity of its reactors, nuclear plants generated only 3 per cent of India's electricity in the mid-2000s. The DAE then planned to build eight 700 MW reactors (these were scaled-up versions of its 540 MW plants), but it would still fall short of its goals of generating 20,000 MW of nuclear power by 2020. The DAE therefore sought to import eight 1,000 MW light water reactors to reach its 20,000 MW target: but it could not import such reactors until the US and the NSG changed their rules to allow such imports.

Third, DAE was not supplying enough uranium fuel for its reactors. It was not mining and milling enough natural uranium fuel for its heavy water reactors, which therefore operated at just 50–60 per cent of their capacity in the mid-2000s.[2] The civilian nuclear agreement helped DAE overcome this uranium deficit. Further, DAE imported enriched uranium fuel for the Tarapur reactors. The US had terminated fuel supplies for these reactors in the early 1980s, after which France, China (in 1995), and Russia (in 2001 and 2006) provided the fuel.

The given discussion clarifies how India expected to benefit from civilian nuclear imports. Proponents argued that India would benefit by importing: (a) natural uranium fuel for Indian-built heavy water reactors; and (b) light water reactors on a large scale, along with the enriched uranium fuel for such reactors. Opponents noted that imported nuclear reactors would cost two to three times more than indigenous ones. They added that India did not need to import reactors because it already had an indigenous three-phase nuclear program based on breeder reactors and advanced heavy water reactors. However, they recognized that since India would take at least 15 years to build four to five breeders, any industrial-scale three-phase program generating several thousand megawatts of electricity would not materialize for perhaps two decades. The more fundamental question was the extent to which nuclear energy contributed to India's electricity needs.

Nuclear Energy Projections

In the mid-2000s, India's government and analysts projected that nuclear energy would provide an estimated 3.7–4 per cent of India's electricity by 2010 (see Table A2). Thereafter, by 2020, after DAE completed eight new 700 MW reactors, India's nuclear power capacity was projected to be 14,000 MW, which could account for 5–7 per cent of India's electricity supply. And, if India imported light water reactors generating 10,000 MW of electricity, its nuclear power capacity would be 24,000 MW, contributing perhaps 9 per cent of India's electricity.

Table A.2 Projected Nuclear Share of India's Electricity

	PHWRs (MW) (Indigenous)	LWR (MW) (Imported)	Breeder reactor (MW) (Indigenous)	Total Nuclear Capacity (MW)	Nuclear Share of Electrical Capacity (%)
2007	3,800	320		4,100	3.2
2010*	4,460	2,320	500	7,200	3.7–4
2020	10,000	2,320	1,000–2,000	14,000	5–7
2020, with imports	10,000	10,000	1,000–2,000	24,000	~9
c. 2030	14,000	~40,000	2,000–4,000	~60,000	~12

Notes: (a) PHWR: pressured heavy water reactor; LWR: light water reactor. (b) *The table shows projections made during 2005–08 for India's future nuclear power expansion. In practice, the 2010 projections would only materialize around 2014 when the two 1,000 MW Russian reactors became operational. Similarly, the 2020 and 2030 projections depended upon international suppliers beginning reactor construction in India by the early 2010s; because such construction had not begun at this time, these projections would be delayed by several years.

India's government further projected that, by 2030, it could operate four nuclear parks, each generating about 10,000 MW of electricity, based on imported US, French, and Russian light water reactors. It could also complete 20 Indian-built 700 MW reactors. Its nuclear power capacity could then increase to 60,000 MW and nuclear power could be generating perhaps 12 per cent of India's electricity. However, India could only realize these projections if Indian and international suppliers overcame the political, logistical, and financial challenges to building nuclear plants on a large scale. In the early 2010s, they had not overcome such challenges; as a result, the projections, if they are eventually realized, would be delayed by a decade or longer.

Falling Short on the Projections

In the early 2010s – several years after the US–India nuclear agreement was finalized – international suppliers had not started constructing reactors in India, largely because of India's nuclear liability laws. India did advance its indigenous nuclear program, but at a rate much slower than projected.

First, domestic politics affected India's nuclear program. Specifically, protests against the Russian-built plants at Kudankulam delayed the completion of the first plant from October 2011 to mid-2012, and the plant was only commissioned in 2013. Similar protests in 2010 and 2011, against proposed French-built reactors at Jaitapur, did not affect the construction of the reactors because such construction had not begun. Finally, to address safety concerns (that gained prominence after the March 2011 accident at Japan's Fukushima reactors), India's government set up an independent regulatory authority in late 2011.

Second, India did safeguard the 14 reactors it had committed to safeguarding under its separation plan and it fuelled many of them with foreign-supplied uranium.[3] In 2012, the DAE observed that seven of India's reactors generating 1,400 MW of electricity were using imported fuel and working near their full capacity, while nine reactors generating 2,630 MW used domestically supplied uranium.

Third, India's nuclear establishment moved ahead with its indigenous reactor program. In 2011 and 2012, it began constructing four 700 MW heavy water reactors and expected to complete these by 2017 (they would increase India's nuclear power capacity from 4,780 MW in June 2012 to 10,080 MW by 2017). Beyond these, in June 2012, it affirmed plans to begin building 16 further reactors by 2020: eight Indian-built 700 MW heavy water reactors and eight light water reactors from international vendors.

Environmental Implications

Would India's increasing reliance on nuclear energy have positive environmental implications? It would, though the magnitude would initially be modest.

In general, every 10,000 MW of new nuclear energy capacity translates into a carbon dioxide reduction of 75 million tons. Thus, if India increased its nuclear capacity by 20,000 MW (which it sought to do by 2020), then these new nuclear plants, if they were to substitute for coal-fired plants, would lessen India's annual carbon dioxide emissions by 150 million tons. If India increased its nuclear capacity by 40,000 MW (which it planned to do by 2030–40), then the carbon dioxide savings would be 300 million tons. These reductions would be modest when compared with India's total annual carbon dioxide emissions, which were 1,680 million tons in 2010, and were projected to be 1,900 million tons in 2020 and 3,000 million tons in 2030.[4] However, they compare favourably with reductions planned by other states: for example, emission cuts planned by the EU under the Kyoto Protocol are 200 million tons per year.

Imported Uranium and India's Nuclear Weapons Program

To what extent would imported uranium for India's civilian reactors free up its limited domestic uranium for its military reactors? This question was a major non-proliferation concern with the nuclear agreement.

In general, DAE could use four sources of plutonium for its military program. First, the Cirus reactor, operational since 1960 and shut down in 2010, produced plutonium sufficient for about two nuclear weapons every year; and the Dhruva reactor, operational since 1986, produced plutonium sufficient for about five nuclear weapons each year. By 2010, these plants had produced weapons-grade plutonium sufficient for 100–125 nuclear weapons.[5]

Second, India could use reactor-grade plutonium from its heavy water reactors, most of which had operated outside safeguards in the 1990s and 2000s, for nuclear weapons. These reactors had produced about 10 tons of plutonium by 2010 (though less than half of this was reprocessed), and this would suffice for hundreds of nuclear weapons, with two limitations. One limitation is that reactor-grade plutonium is not well-suited for nuclear weapons. Another is that much of this plutonium would be required to fuel India's breeder reactors. India's first breeder reactor consumed an estimated 3–4 tons of this plutonium for its initial loading, and, if DAE builds four additional breeder reactors by 2025, these would require another 16 tons of plutonium and would consume much of India's inventory of reactor-grade plutonium.[6]

Third, DAE could produce weapons-grade plutonium from its heavy water reactors by operating them in a low burn-up mode (it had apparently attempted this in the late 1990s and early 2000s). A 220 MW reactor operated in this mode could produce 150–200 kg of weapons-grade plutonium each year, but would require a considerable 190 tons of uranium, in contrast to just 30 tons when operating in a normal mode.

Fourth, India could obtain weapons-grade plutonium from its breeder reactor. A few years after it is operational, say, around 2017, the breeder could produce about 130 kg of such plutonium annually, which would be sufficient for 25 nuclear weapons annually. Yet, as noted previously, DAE may require this plutonium to fuel additional breeder reactors, and it may not then use much of the breeder-derived plutonium for nuclear weapons.

In summary, India has four potential sources of plutonium for nuclear weapons (though the second to fourth sources have limitations). By 2015, these would have produced weapons-grade plutonium for perhaps 125–150 nuclear weapons (all from Cirus and Dhruva-derived plutonium) and reactor-grade plutonium for dozens more weapons. By 2020, they could produce weapons-grade plutonium for perhaps 250 nuclear weapons (that is, assuming about 150–175 from Cirus and Dhruva-derived plutonium and 100 from breeder-derived plutonium). If India's defence planners deem these inventories to be sufficient for a minimum deterrent, they may not significantly expand India's production of unsafeguarded plutonium: and the concern about foreign-supplied uranium enabling India to expand its military plutonium stock would not then arise.

Even if DAE wanted to considerably enlarge its stock of weapons-grade plutonium, its ability to do so using foreign-supplied uranium would be limited. First, while foreign-supplied uranium could free up India's domestic uranium for the Dhruva reactor, this reactor only produces plutonium sufficient for five nuclear weapons per year. Second, while foreign-supplied uranium could free up India's domestic uranium for its heavy water reactors operated in a low burn-up mode, this would require a large amount of uranium (190 tons annually for a typical 220 MW reactor) and would be detected. Since this would raise international concerns, DAE would likely refrain from such use of foreign-supplied uranium. Third, DAE could build an entirely new research reactor, fuelled by domestic uranium, for a military program as of 2013, however, it had not built any such reactor.

To summarize, foreign-supplied uranium could theoretically free up domestic uranium for India's military reactors, but this concern may also not materialize for reasons just noted.

Nuclear Testing Issues

One other issue concerning India's military nuclear program was whether New Delhi required additional nuclear testing, which would likely result in international suppliers terminating civilian nuclear cooperation with India. In May 1998, India announced that it had tested five nuclear devices: three subkiloton devices, a 12 kiloton fission device, and a 43 kiloton thermonuclear device that could be scaled up to 200 kilotons.

International observers noted that the actual yield of the thermonuclear device was much lower. Subsequently, DRDO officials stated that the second fusion stage of the thermonuclear device 'was not only far below the design prediction made by the Bhabha Atomic Research Centre (BARC), but that it actually failed'; such perspectives suggested that India needed more testing to establish a credible deterrent (Iyengar, 2009; Santhanam and Parthasarathi, 2009). India's government officially refuted this argument, noting that DRDO personnel were not privy to BARC's weapon designs and that DRDO had underestimated the test yields. Indian strategic experts also noted that India could maintain a deterrent based on proven fission devices (Subrahmanyam and Arunachalam, 2009). Thus, while there were technical doubts about whether India had reliably tested a thermonuclear device, India's government affirmed that it did not require further testing to maintain a nuclear deterrent.

The Impact on Non-proliferation

The US–India nuclear agreement gave rise to three non-proliferation concerns. First, it somewhat affected Pakistan's decisions to increase its plutonium production (Islamabad also took such decisions in response to India's 'Cold Start' strategy involving quick conventional military strikes against Pakistan during any crisis). Here, while Pakistan had begun constructing a second plutonium-producing reactor at Khushab in 2000–02, well before the nuclear agreement was announced, it began constructing a third Khushab reactor in 2006 and a fourth around 2011. The three new Khushab reactors could produce plutonium sufficient for 12–15 nuclear weapons per year and would augment Pakistan's prior capabilities of producing enriched uranium and plutonium sufficient for seven to 14 weapons per year (Albright and Brannan, 2011).

Islamabad took the position that the US–India nuclear agreement would enable India to enlarge its fissile material production (though the earlier discussion here clarified that such an increase did not actually occur in the early 2010s) and that it needed to close a potentially growing fissile material gap with India. Influenced by such thinking, it apparently took a decision to enlarge its plutonium production capability at an April 2006 meeting of its Nuclear Command Authority (Lavoy, 2008). In early 2010, it blocked talks on the FMCT. In late 2011, it stated that it could reconsider its FMCT position if it received a civilian nuclear agreement similar to the agreement with India (*Arms Control Today*, 2011).

Second, China advanced its civilian nuclear reactor sales to Pakistan. In 2010, Beijing formally announced plans to build 300–340 MW Chashma-3 and -4 reactors in Pakistan, arguing that these were grandfathered under contracts signed before it joined the NSG. Subsequently, however, Beijing sought to build a 1,000 MW reactor at Chashma and, because it was unclear as to whether such a plant was grandfathered under earlier contracts, this significantly tested the NSG's full-scope safeguards rule.

Third, North Korea argued that, because Washington bent non-proliferation rules for India, it should do the same for Pyongyang and accept Pyongyang as a nuclear weapons state (Cha, 2009).

To summarize, the US–India nuclear agreement set a precedent that Pyongyang, Beijing, and Islamabad sought to emulate, giving rise to the challenge of selectively accommodating these states without undermining the NSG's full-scope safeguards rule and the broader non-proliferation regime.

Endnotes

1   For the development of India's nuclear program, see Karnad (2008b); Koithara (2012); Perkovich (1999); Tellis (2000).
2   In the mid-2000s, India's 16 heavy water reactors and two military reactors required an estimated 600 tons of uranium annually (assuming 30 tons for each

of the 14 220 MW reactors; 70 tons for each of the two 540 MW reactors; and 35 tons for the Cirus and Dhruva reactors). Yet, at the time, DAE was operating just one uranium mill capable of supplying about 200–250 tons of uranium per year, while a second mill capable of supplying 300–350 tons per year was commissioned in 2009. Moreover, India was probably not mining enough uranium for these mills: its estimated annual uranium production was 230 tons in 2004 and 2005; 180 tons in 2006; 270 tons from 2007 to 2009; and 400 tons in 2010 and 2011 (as per the World Nuclear Association, available at http://www.world-nuclear.org/info/inf23.html). Therefore, India's reactors were operating at just 50–60 per cent of their actual capacity. On a related note, India's natural uranium ores are of a lower grade and more expensive than internationally supplied uranium.

3   By 2012, India had signed uranium supply agreements with Russia, France, and Kazakhstan (it received 800 tons of uranium from these sources), and also with Namibia and Mongolia.

4   These figures were noted in a study by the Energy Information Agency (2006). For comparison, the actual carbon dioxide emissions (in million metric tons) in 2010 were as follows: China (6,200), the US (5,600), India (1,680), Europe (4,700), and world total (29,500).

5   For these estimates, see a report by the International Panel on Fissile Materials, *Global Fissile Material Report 2010*. These calculations assume that about 5 kg of weapons-grade plutonium, or 8–10 kg of reactor-grade plutonium, is used for a nuclear weapon; that Dhruva had produced an estimated 410 kg of plutonium and Cirus had produced about 230 kg; and that DAE had used up about 130 kg of this plutonium for nuclear tests or other purposes.

6   For different perspectives suggesting that India would have much excess plutonium, see Ramanna et al. (2006).

References

Abraham, Itty. 1998. *The Making of the Indian Atomic Bomb: Science, Secrecy, and the Postcolonial State*. New York: Zed Books.

Abraham, Mohit. 2012. 'Defective Law on Nuclear Liability'. *The Economic Times*, 20 December.

Aiyar, Shankkar. 2008a. 'It's Dealtime, Folks'. *India Today*, 10 July.

———. 2008b. 'It is 275'. *India Today*, 22 July.

Albright, David and Paul Brannan. 2008. *Indian Nuclear Export Controls and Information Security: Important Questions Remain*. Washington, DC: Institute for Science and International Security.

———. 2011. *Pakistan Doubling Rate of Making Nuclear Weapons: Time for Pakistan to Reverse Course*. Washington, DC: Institute for Science and International Security.

Anderson, Robert. 2010. *Nucleus and Nation: Scientists, International Networks, and Power in India*. Chicago, IL: University of Chicago Press.

Arms Control Association (ACA). 2007. 'Ensure Nuclear Cooperation with India is Consistent with the Law'. 14 May.

———. 2008a. 'Rice's Pledge to Make Global Rules on Nuclear Trade with India "Consistent" with U.S. Law Requires Shift in U.S. Policy'. 14 February.

———. 2008b. 'Decision Time on the Indian Nuclear Deal: Help Avert a Nonproliferation Disaster'. 15 August.

———. 2008c. 'US–India Nuclear Cooperation Agreement: A Bad Deal'. 17 September.

Arms Control Today. 2011. 'The South Asian Nuclear Balance: An Interview with Pakistani Ambassador to the CD Zamir Akram'. December.

Aronson, Bernard. 2012. 'Can Brazil Stop Iran'. *The New York Times*, 3 April.

Asia Society. 2006. 'President Addresses Asia Society', Washington, DC, February 22.

Bagchi, Indrani. 2004. 'Changing the Nuke Order'. *India Today*, 15 March.

———. 2005. 'N-Separation Plan Ready'. *The Times of India*, 19 December.

———. 2006. 'India, US Fast Breeding N-deal'. *The Times of India*, 20 February.

———. 2008. 'Austria, Ireland against NSG Waiver for India'. *The Times of India*, 6 September.

Bagla, Pallava. 2006. 'The Fast Breeder Program Just Cannot be Put on the Civilian List'. *The Indian Express*, 8 February.

Bajpai, K. Shankar. 2008. 'Growing Up'. *Hindustan Times*, 8 September.

Baru, Sanjaya. 2009a. 'Can Indian Think Tanks and Research Institutions Cope with the Rising Demand for Foreign and Security Policy Research'. ISAS Working Paper No. 67, 16 June.

———. 2009b. 'The Influence of Business and Media on Indian Foreign Policy'. *India Review* 8 (3): 266–85.

Baumgartner, Frank R., Jeffrey Berry, Marie Hojnacki, David Kimball, and Beth Leech. 2009. *Lobbying and Policy Change: Who Wins, Who Loses, and Why*. Chicago, IL: University of Chicago Press.

Bhatt, Sheela. 2008. 'How the Trust Vote was Won'. rediff.com, 26 July.

Bhushan, Bharat. 2005. 'The Truth about the Indo-US Nuclear Deal'. *The Telegraph*, 14 November.

Blackwill, Robert. 2005. 'The India Imperative'. *National Interest*, 80: 8–16.

Boese, Wade. 2006. 'Reshaping U.S. Nonproliferation Strategy: An Interview with Undersecretary of State Robert Joseph'. *Arms Control Today*, 36 (5).

Boyle, David, Warren Miller, and Paul Nelson. 2007. 'U.S.–India Nuclear Alert'. *The Washington Times*, 15 July.

Brinkley, Joel. 2005. 'U.S. Nuclear Deal with India Criticized by G.O.P. in Congress'. *The New York Times*, 31 October.

Burns, Nicholas. 2007a. 'Heady Times for India and the US'. *The Washington Post*, 29 April.

———. 2007b. 'America's Strategic Opportunity with India'. *Foreign Affairs*, 86 (6): 131–146.

Bush, George W. 1999. 'A Distinctly American Internationalism'. Speech at the Ronald Reagan Presidential Library, Simi Valley, California, 19 November.

Carter, Jimmy. 2006. 'A Dangerous Deal with India'. *The Washington Post*, 29 March.

———. 2008. 'India Deal Puts World at Risk'. *International Herald Tribune*, 11 September.

Cha, Victor. 2009. 'What do They Really Want: Obama's North Korea Conundrum'. *Washington Quarterly* 32 (4): 119–38.

Chatterjee, Manini. 2007. 'Anguished PM to Left: If You Want to Withdraw, So Be It'. *The Telegraph*, 11 August.

Chaudhry, Pramit Pal. 2007. 'Peter Pan Syndrome'. *Hindustan Times*, 27 August.

Chellaney, Brahma. 2007. 'Nuclear Winter: U.S.–India Nuclear Contretemps'. *The Times of India*, 2 May.

———. 2008. 'A Flawed Safeguards Accord'. *The Asian Age*, 11 July.

———. 2010. 'Full Official Text and Key Features of U.S.–India Reprocessing Agreement'. 30 March.

Chengappa, Raj. 2007. 'How the Deal was Clinched'. *India Today*, 27 August.

Cigler, Alan and Burdett Loomis, eds. 2011. *Interest Group Politics*. Washington, DC: Congressional Quarterly Press.

CNN-IBN. 2008. 'US Envoy Says "Now or Never" for Nuclear Deal'. 9 February, http://ibnlive.in.com/news/its-now-or-never-for-nuclear-deal-mulford/58530-3-1.html.

Cohen, Avner. 2010. *The Worst-kept Secret: Israel's Bargain with the Bomb*. New York: Columbia University Press.

Cohen, Stephen. 2001. *India: Emerging Power*. Washington, DC: Brookings Institution Press.

Cohen, William. 2007. 'The Indian Giver'. *The Wall Street Journal*, 5 February.

Congress Sandesh. 2006. 'A Historic Deal'. Editorial, March, Page 4.

Council on Foreign Relations. 2005. 'Scheinman: New U.S.–India Agreement Undercuts U.S. Allegiance to Nonproliferation of Nuclear Weapons'. 3 November.

David, Steven. 1991. *Choosing Sides: Alignment and Realignment in the Third World*. Baltimore, MD: John Hopkins University Press.

Department of Commerce. 2003. 'United States and India Hold Talks on Stimulating High-technology Commerce'. 2 July.

Department of State. 2005. 'Background Briefing by Administration Officials on U.S.-South Asia Relations'. Washington, DC, March 25.

DNA. 2007. 'Brajesh Mishra Says Deal Can Be Rescued'. 22 October.

———. 2008. 'India Enters N-Club'. 6 September.

Embassy of India. 2005. 'Media Briefing by Foreign Secretary Shyam Saran'. Washington, DC, 14 April.

Emmott, Bill. 2008. 'New Life for the India Nuclear Pact'. *The Washington Post*, 7 July.

Energy Information Agency. 2006. *Annual Energy Outlook 2006*. Washington, DC: US Department of Energy.

Entman, Robert. 2004. *Projections of Power: Framing News, Public Opinion and US Foreign Policy*. Chicago: University of Chicago Press, 2004.

Evans, Peter, Harold Jacobson, and Robert Putnam, eds. 1993. *Double-edged Diplomacy: International Bargaining and Domestic Politics*. Berkeley, CA: University of California Press.

Ferguson, Charles and Michael Levi. 2006. *U.S.–India Nuclear Cooperation: A Strategy for Moving Forward*. New York: Council on Foreign Relations.

Frey, Karsten. 2006. *India's Nuclear Bomb and National Security*. New York: Routledge.

Friedman, Thomas. 2006. 'Letting India in the Club?' *The New York Times*, 8 March.

Fuhrman, Matthew. 2012. *Atomic Assistance: How 'Atoms for Peace' Programs Cause Nuclear Insecurity*. Ithaca, NY: Cornell University Press.

Gahlaut, Seema. 2008. *Indian Export Control Policy: Political Commitment, Institutional Capacity, and Nonproliferation Record*. Athens, GA: Center for International Trade and Security.

Gandhi, Sonia. 2006. 'Letter to Congress Workers'. *Congress Sandesh*, March, Page 1.

Gentleman, Amelia and Thom Shanker. 2006. 'India Welcomes U.S. Senate's Approval of Nuclear Pact'. *The New York Times*, 17 November.

George, Varghese. 2007. 'Behind PM's Isolation on Nuclear Deal: Wary Allies and a Nervous Party'. *The Indian Express*, 16 October.

Global Security Institute. 2008. 'Letter from the GSI and Middle Powers Initiative to NSG States', 13 August.

Gopalakrishnan, A. 2006a. 'A Question of Nuclear Separation'. *The Asian Age*, 14 January.

———. 2006b. 'Don't Compromise India's Dignity'. *The Asian Age*, 1 March.

———. 2006c. 'A Deal of Broken Assurances'. *The Asian Age*, 7 July.

———. 2006d. 'What PM Told Us on the N-Deal'. *The Asian Age*, 22 September.

———. 2006e. 'Bill Paves Way for Covert US Operations'. *The Asian Age*, 21 November.

———. 2006f. 'Was the Government Aware of Section 115?' *The Asian Age*, 28 November.

———. 2007a. 'PM Must be Careful about Nuclear Pitfalls'. *The Asian Age*, 1 June.

———. 2007b. 'N-deal: Parliament Must have Decisive Authority'. rediff.com, 20 July.

Gould, Harold and Sumit Ganguly, eds. 1992. *The Hope and the Reality: US–India Relations from Roosevelt to Reagan*. Boulder, CO: Westview Press.

Government of India. 2005. Press Release, 26 March.

———. 2006. 'PM Conveys Persisting Indian Concerns to US President'. Press Release, 21 December.

———. 2008. 'Statement by External Affairs Minister of India Mr. Pranab Mukherjee on the Civil Nuclear Initiative'. 5 September.

Grimmett, Richard. 2012. *Conventional Arms Transfers to Developing Countries 2004–2011*. Washington, DC: Congressional Research Service.

Gupta, Shishir. 2007. 'BJP Reserves its Comment on N-deal but Praises UPA Negotiators for "Superb Job"'. *The Indian Express*, 27 July.

———. 2008. 'Pokharan-III'. *The Indian Express*, 9 May.

Gupta, Shishir and Pranab Dhal Samanta. 2006. 'After Kakodkar Meets PM, Cabinet Secretary Steps in'. *The Indian Express*, 9 February.

Gupta, Smita. 2008a. 'All Hands on Deck'. *Outlook India*, 28 July.

———. 2008b. 'Well Begun, Half Done'. *Outlook India*, 4 August.

Haniffa, Aziz. 2007. 'Why Nicholas Burns Put off India Visit'. rediff.com, 23 May.

———. 2008a. 'N-Deal: Experts Urge Senate Leader to Act Soon'. rediff.com, 22 September.

———. 2008b. 'We Want the Agreement to Satisfy You, Bush Tells PM'. rediff.com, 26 September.

———. 2012. 'Explained: Why Indo-US Nuclear Deal is in Cold Storage'. rediff.com, 11 June.

Harrison, Selig. 2001. 'No More Sanctions'. *The Washington Times*, 5 April.

Hawkins, William. 2008. 'U.S.–India Nuclear Bond?' *The Washington Times*, 21 September.

Hibbs, Mark. 2007. 'Delays Expected in Closing on US–India Pact'. *Nucleonics Week*, 20 September.

———. 2008a. 'NSG Prepares to Set Specific Conditions for Lifting Sanctions Against India'. *Nuclear Fuels*, 14 January.

———. 2008b. 'New Zealand Floats Conditioning India NSG Exemption on Protocol'. *Nuclear Fuels*, 28 January.

———. 2008c. 'US Steps up Bilateral Diplomacy to Get India Safeguards Approval'. *Nucleonics Week*, 10 July.

———. 2008d. 'US Pressing for NSG Exemption for India by End of this Week'. *Nucleonics Week*, 21 August.

———. 2008e. 'NSG States Raise Compliance Issues on India Exemption'. *Nuclear Fuels*, 25 August.

———. 2008f. 'NSG States Seek Many Changes to US Draft Resolution Exempting India'. *Nucleonics Week*, 28 August 2008.

———. 2010. 'Moving Forward on the U.S.–India Nuclear Deal'. Issue Brief, Carnegie Endowment for International Peace, 5 April.

Hibbs, Mark and Daniel Horner. 2006. 'NSG Countries Not Prepared to Challenge US Over India Nuclear Trade'. *Nucleonics Week*, 29 June.

———. 2007. 'India-Specific Provisions may be Non-Binding Part of IAEA Agreement'. *Nuclear Fuels*, 3 December.

———. 2008. 'Pakistan, Other States Not Satisfied after Indian Briefing on IAEA Pact'. *Nucleonics Week*, 24 July.

Hibbs, Mark and Ann Machlachlan. 2007. 'NSG Members Asked France, Russia about Their Negotiations with India'. *Nuclear Fuels*, 3 December.

Hibbs, Mark and Sunil Saraf. 2008. 'Nuclear Deal with US Falters as Indians Head for the Polls'. *Nucleonics Week*, 5 June.

Hindustan Times. 1998. 'India Seeks Changes in Hi-tech Transfer Over CTBT'. 17 September.

———. 2006. 'An Opaque and Unequal Deal'. Editorial, 28 January.

———. 2007a. 'Hyde and Seek'. Editorial, 8 August.

———. 2007b. 'Don't Allow N-Deal to be Hijacked by Opponents: Scientists'. 30 August.

———. 2008a. 'The Nuclear Deal'. Editorial, March 23

———. 2008b. 'Actively Inactive'. Editorial, May 27.

———. 2008c. 'India Intrigued by Bush Observation'. 12 September.

Hymans, Jacques. 2006. *The Psychology of Nuclear Proliferation: Identity, Emotions, and Foreign Policy*. New York, NY: Cambridge University Press.

———. 2011. 'Veto Players, Nuclear Energy, and Nonproliferation: Domestic Institutional Barriers to a Japanese Bomb'. *International Security* 36 (2): 154–189.

Iida, Keisuke. 1993. 'When and How do Domestic Constraints Matter? Two-level Games with Uncertainty'. *Journal of Conflict Resolution* 37 (3): 403–26.

Institute for Defence Studies and Analyses (IDSA). 2006. 'Indo-US Nuclear Deal: The Bill and Apprehensions'. Occasional Paper, November.

Iyengar, P. K. 2008a. 'Ten Misconceptions about the Nuclear Deal'. 22 July.

———. 2008b. 'True Colors of the Nuclear Deal'. 30 September.

———. 2009. 'Non-Fissile Doubts'. *Outlook*, 26 October.

Iyengar, P. K., A. N. Prasad, A. Gopalakrishnan, and Bharat Karnad. 2009. *Strategic Sellout: Indian-US Nuclear Deal*. New Delhi: Pentagon Press.

Jaishankar, Dhruva. 2009. 'Chronicle of a Deal Foretold: Washington's Perspective in Negotiating the Indo-US Nuclear Agreement'. In *Indo-US Nuclear Deal: Seeking Synergy in Bilateralism*, edited by P. R. Chari, 99–122. New Delhi: Taylor and Francis.

Juster, Kenneth. 2003. 'Stimulating High-technology Cooperation with India'. Remarks at the US–India Business Council, New York, 2 June.

———. 2004. 'Keynote Remarks of Kenneth Juster, Undersecretary of Commerce, at the India–United States Conference on Space Science, Applications, and Commerce'. Bangalore, 22 June.

Kamdar, Mira. 2008. 'Risking Armageddon for Cold, Hard Cash'. *The Washington Post*, 7 September.

Karat, Prakash. 2006. 'Why Avoid Sense of Parliament?' *People's Democracy*, 13 August.

Karnad, Bharat. 2005. 'Remember the Tritium'. *Deccan Chronicle*, 7 August.

———. 2006. 'Nuclear Testing is the Crux'. *The Asian Age*, 19 December.

———. 2007. 'Is N-testing a Purely Political Decision?' *The Asian Age*, 9 January.

———. 2008a. 'Safeguards that Erode Security'. Mint, 14 July.

———. 2008b. *India's Nuclear Policy*. Westport, CT: Praeger.

Kelley, Donald. 2005. *Divided Power: The Presidency, Congress, and the Formation of American Foreign Policy*. Fayetteville, AR: University of Arkansas Press.

Kerr, Paul. 2011. *Pakistan's Nuclear Weapons: Proliferation and Security Issues*. Washington, DC: Congressional Research Service.

Kessler, Glenn. 2007. *The Confidante: Condoleezza Rice and the Creation of the Bush Legacy*. New York, NY: St. Martin's Press.

Kessler, Glenn and Peter Slevin. 2003. 'Washington Post Reporters Interview Powell'. *The Washington Post*, 3 October.

Khare, Harish. 2005. 'Team Manmohan at Work, at Last'. *The Hindu*, 8 August.

Khare, Harish and Siddharth Varadarajan. 2007a. 'NSA Interview: This is as Good a Text as One Can Possibly Get'. *The Hindu*, 28 July.

———. 2007b. 'For Nuclear Renaissance, the World Needs India'. *The Hindu*, 10 August.

Kimball, Daryll. 2007. 'Introductory Note: Henry J. Hyde United States/India Peaceful Atomic Energy Cooperation Act of 2006'. *International Legal Materials* 46 (March): 409–14.

Kimball, Daryll and Joseph Cirincione. 2006. *A Nonproliferation Disaster*. Washington, DC: Center for American Progress.

King, Gary, Robert Keohane, and Sidney Verba. 1994. *Designing Social Inquiry*. Princeton, NJ: Princeton University Press.

Kissel, Mary. 2007. 'Delhi Drama'. *The Wall Street Journal*, 4 September.

Knopf, Jeffrey. 1998. *Domestic Society and International Cooperation: The Impact of Protest on U.S. Arms Control Policy*. Cambridge: Cambridge University Press.

Koithara, Verghese. 2012. *Managing India's Nuclear Forces*. Washington, DC: Brookings.

Kollman, Ken. 1998. *Outside Lobbying: Public Opinion and Interest Group Strategies*. Princeton, NJ: Princeton University Press.

Krepon, Michael. 2008. 'Likely Consequences of the Nuclear Suppliers Group Decision'. The Henry L. Stimson Center, 8 September.

Kroenig, Matthew, 2010. *Exporting the Bomb: Technology Transfer and the Spread of Nuclear Weapons*. Ithaca, NY: Cornell University Press.

Kux, Dennis. 1993. *Estranged Democracies: India and the United States, 1941–1991*. Washington, DC: National Defense University Press.

Kumar, Vinay. 2008. 'Left Parties Reject Compromise Formula'. *The Hindu*, 25 June.

Lakshmi, Rama. 2008. 'In India, Outcry over US Letter'. *The Washington Post*, 4 September.

Lavoy, Peter. 2008. 'Islamabad's Nuclear Posture: Its Premises and Implementation'. In *Pakistan's Nuclear Future: Worries Beyond War*, edited by Henry D. Sokolski, 129–165. Carlisle, PA: Strategic Studies Institute.

Lawyers Alliance for World Security. 2007a. 'Can President Bush Refuse to Follow the Expressed Will of Congress Concerning Nuclear Exports to India?', 17 January.

———. 2007b. 'New U.S.–India Nuclear Agreement Delayed: Indefinitely?', 18 April.

Laxman, Srinivas. 2006. 'N-scientists Rubbish Compromise Formula'. *The Times of India*, 23 February.

Left Stand on the Nuclear Deal: Notes Exchanged in the UPA–Left Committee on India–US Civil Nuclear Cooperation. 2008. New Delhi: Progressive Printers.

Limaye, Satu. 1993. *U.S.–Indian Relations: The Pursuit of Accommodation*. Boulder, CO: Westview Press.

———. 2002. 'US–India Relations: Visible to the Naked Eye'. CSIS Issue Brief.

Lindsay, James. 2003. 'Deference and Defiance: The Shifting Rhythms of Executive–Legislative Relations in Foreign Policy'. *Presidential Studies Quarterly* 33 (3): 530–46.

Malik, V. P. 2007. 'Read 123 Fine Print and Rest Easy'. *The Indian Express*, 20 August.

Martin, Lisa. 2000. *Democratic Commitments*. Princeton, NJ: Princeton University Press.

McMahon, Robert. 1994. *The Cold War on the Periphery: The United States, India, and Pakistan*. New York: Columbia University Press.

Menon, Shiv Shankar and K. P. Nayar. 2008. 'How the Nuke Wall was Scaled in Vienna—Moves that Softened China, Austria, and New Zealand'. *The Telegraph*, 8 September.

Miller, Manjari Chatterjee. 2013. 'India's Feeble Foreign Policy'. *Foreign Affairs* (May/June) 92 (3): 14–19.

Milner, Helen. 1997. Interests, *Institutions and Information: Domestic Politics and International Relations*. Princeton, NJ: Princeton University Press.

Mishra, Brajesh. 2003. 'India, United States, and the New World Order'. Speech at the Council on Foreign Relations, New York, 7 May.

Mistry, Dinshaw. 2013. 'The India Lobby and the Nuclear Agreement with India'. *Political Science Quarterly* (Winter) 128 (4).

Mitra, Amit. 2010. 'Sabotaging India's Rise'. *The Times of India*, 10 April.

Mo, Jongryn. 1994. 'The Logic of Two-level Games with Endogenous Domestic Coalitions'. *Journal of Conflict Resolution* 38 (3): 402–22.

Mohan, C. Raja. 2006a. *Impossible Allies: The United States, India, and the Global Order.* Delhi: India Research Press.

———. 2006b. 'Half Reactions and Easy Solutions'. *The Indian Express*, 11 February.

———. 2006c. 'What? We Worry?' *The Indian Express*, 1 July.

———. 2009. 'The Making of Indian Foreign Policy: The Role of Scholarship and Public Opinion'. Paper prepared for the conference on Upgrading International Studies in India, Lee Kuan Yew School of Public Policy, Singapore, 26 March.

Moravcsik, Andrew. 1993. 'Armaments among Allies: European Weapons Cooperation, 1975–85'. In *Double-edged Diplomacy: International Bargaining and Domestic Politics*, edited by Peter Evans, Harold Jacobson, and Robert Putnam, 128–167. Berkeley: University of California Press.

———. 2003. 'Theory Synthesis in International Relations: Real Not Metaphysical'. *International Studies Review* 5 (1): 131–36.

Narang, Vipin and Paul Staniland. 2012. 'Institutions and Worldviews in Indian Foreign Security Policy'. *India Review* 11 (2): 76–94.

Nayar, K. P. 2008. 'Secret Nuke Talks with US—Madrid Mission brought Menon and Burns Together'. *The Telegraph*, 8 January.

New Zealand Herald. 2008. 'NZ Backs Nuclear Exemption for India after US Pressure'. 8 September.

Nuclear Fuels. 2007. 'NSG Not Prepared to Quickly Respond to US Pressure on Exemption for India'. 30 July.

Nucleonics Week. 2008. 'Scope of NSG Exemption for India Yet to be Defined by Member States'. 11 September.

Observer Research Foundation. 2005. 'India's Vote in the IAEA: The Balance Sheet'. Issue brief No. 5, November.

Pant, Harsh. 2011. *The US–India Nuclear Pact: Policy, Process, and Great Power Politics.* New Delhi: Oxford University Press.

Parsi, Trita. 2011. *A Single Roll of the Dice: Obama's Diplomacy with Iran.* New Haven, CT: Yale University Press.

Paul, T. V. and Mahesh Shankar. 2007. 'Why the US–India Nuclear Accord is a Good Deal'. *Survival* 49 (4): 111–22.

People's Democracy. 2005a. 'Unbalanced & Inequitable'. Editorial, 24 July.

———. 2005b. 'Discussion in Parliament on US–India Agreements: Statement by Nilotpal Basu in the Rajya Sabha'. 14 August.

———. 2006. 'US Legislation on Nuclear Deal Not Acceptable'. Editorial, 17 December.

———. 2007a. 'Reject US Terms for Nuclear Cooperation'. Editorial, 13 May.

———. 2007b. 'Nuclear Deal: Don't Hide the Hyde Act'. Editorial, 17 June.

Perkovich, George. 1999. *India's Nuclear Bomb.* Berkeley, CA: University of California Press.

———. 2005. *Faulty Promises: The US–India Nuclear Deal.* Washington, DC: Carnegie Endowment for International Peace.

Prasad, A. N. 2008. 'Remote Control in US Hands'. *Deccan Herald*, 13 July.

Putnam, Robert. 1988. 'Diplomacy and Domestic Politics: The Logic of Two-level Games'. *International Organization* 42 (3): 427–60.

Rajaraman, R. 2005. 'India–U.S. Deal and the Nuclear Ceiling'. *The Hindu*, 10 September.

———. 2006. 'Who's Afraid of the Nuke Deal?' *The Indian Express*, 14 February.

Rajghatta, Chidanand and Indrani Bagchi. 2007. 'US Hawks Slam "Greedy" India over Nuclear Deal'. *The Times of India*, 13 April.

Ram, N. 2007. 'The Nuclear Deal: Key Issues and Political Circumstances'. *The Hindu*, 22 August.

Ramachandran, R. 2005. 'Behind the Bargain'. *Frontline*, 30 July–12 August.

———. 2007. 'Long Haul Ahead'. *Frontline*, 16–29 June.

Ramakrishnan, Venkatesh and R. Ramachandran. 2008. 'Interview with Prakash Karat: Total Violation of Committee's Decision'. *Frontline*, 5–18 July.

Ramanna, M. V. 2009. 'India's Nuclear Enclave and the Practice of Secrecy'. In *South Asian Cultures of the Bomb*, edited by Itty Abraham, 41–67. Bloomington, IN: Indiana University Press.

Ramanna, M. V., Zia Mian, A.H. Nayyar, and R. Rajaraman. 2006. 'Fissile Materials in South Asia and the Implications of the U.S.–India Nuclear Deal'. *Science and Global Security* 14 (2–3): 117–45.

Ravi, N. 2005. 'A Persistent Irritant Goes with a Grand Bargain'. *The Hindu*, 30 July.

rediff.com. 2005. 'Don't Raise Iran at UNSC, Left Warns Govt'. 28 September.

rediff.com. 2006. 'Burns–Saran talks: Progress Made but Not Enough'. 24 February.

———. 2008. 'Let the Nuclear Deal Go through: Brajesh Mishra'. 27 February.

Rice, Condoleezza. 2000. 'Promoting the National Interest'. *Foreign Affairs* 79 (1): 45–62.

———. 2011. *No Higher Honor: A Memoir of My Years in Washington*. New York: Crown Publishing Group.

Rublee, Maria Rost. 2009. *Nonproliferation Norms: Why States Choose Nuclear Restraint*. Athens, GA: University of Georgia Press.

Rumsfeld, Donald. 2011. *Known and Unknown*. New York: Penguin.

Sagan, Scott. 1996–97. 'Why do States build Nuclear Weapons: Three Models in Search of a Bomb'. *International Security* 21 (3): 54–86.

Samanta, Pranab. 2007. 'Last Lap in Nuclear Deal Gets Slippery: India, US will Hardtalk in Ten Days'. *The Indian Express*, 18 March.

Santhanam, K. and Ashok Parthasarathi. 2009. 'Pokhran-II Thermonuclear Test, a Failure'. *The Hindu*, 17 September.

Sartori, Giovanni. 1997. *Comparative Constitutional Engineering*. New York: NYU Press.

Schaffer, Teresita. 2009. *India and the United States in the 21st Century: Reinventing Partnership*. Washington, DC: Center for Strategic and International Studies.

Scott, James and Ralph Carter. 2002. 'Acting on the Hill: Congressional Assertiveness in U.S. Foreign Policy'. *Congress & the Presidency* 29 (2): 151–69.

Sebenius, James and Michael Singh. 2012. 'Is a Nuclear Deal with Iran Possible? An Analytical Framework for the Iran Nuclear Negotiations'. *International Security* 37 (3): 52–91.

Sikri, Rajiv. 2009. *Challenge and Strategy: Rethinking India's Foreign Policy.* New Delhi: Sage.

Singh, Jaswant. 1998. 'Against Nuclear Apartheid'. *Foreign Affairs* 77 (5): 41–52.

———. 1999. *Defending India.* New York: St. Martin's Press.

Singh, V. P. 2006. 'Respect Concerns of Nuclear Scientists: Open Letter to the Prime Minister'. rediff.com, 21 February.

———. 2007. 'Parliament vs PM'. *India Today*, 19 October.

Sinha, Yashwant. 2005. 'Indo-U.S. Nuclear Deal is Unequal'. *The Asian Age*, 25 August.

Sokolski, Henry. 2008. 'Negotiating India's Next Nuclear Explosion'. *The Wall Street Journal Asia*, 10 July.

Solingen, Etel. 2007. *Nuclear Logics: Contrasting Paths in East Asia and the Middle East.* Princeton, NJ: Princeton University Press.

Squassoni, Sharon. 2006. 'U.S.–India Nuclear Cooperation: A Side-by-Side Comparison of Current Legislation'. CRS Report for Congress, 22 November.

Srinivasan, M. R. 2008a. 'Nuclear Ground Realities'. *The Indian Express*, 28 March.

———. 2008b. 'France, Russia Will Give Fuel if US Doesn't'. *The Economic Times*, 17 September.

———. 2012. 'A Liability for Our Nuclear Plans'. *The Hindu*, 15 October.

Subrahmanyam, K. 2005a. 'Vote in Vienna: A Correct Stand'. *The Tribune*, 26 September.

———. 2005b. 'India and the Nuclear Deal'. *The Times of India*, 12 December.

———. 2005c. 'Will Partisan Politics Nuke a Good Deal?' *The Times of India*, 22 July.

———. 2006. 'Costs of Rejection'. *The Times of India*, 25 July.

———. 2007. 'The Right to Test Again'. *The Indian Express*, 20 November.

———. 2008a. 'NDA Should Rise Above Parochial Concerns on Nuclear Issue'. 9 April.

———. 2008b. 'Unbound By the Rules'. *The Indian Express*, 9 August.

———. 2008c. 'We're Not a Rogue State'. *The Times of India*, 3 September.

———. 2008d. 'It's a Done Deal'. *The Times of India*, 29 September.

Subrahmanyam, K. and V. S. Arunachalam. 2009. 'Deterrence and Explosive Yield'. *The Hindu*, 20 September.

Subramanian, T. S. 2005a. 'Waiting, with Caution'. *Frontline*, 30 July–12 August.

———. 2005b. 'Identifying a Civilian Nuclear Facility is India's Decision'. *The Hindu*, 12 August.

———. 2007. 'It is a Practical Solution that Meets All Our Requirements'. *The Hindu*, 11 August.

Talbott, Strobe. 1998. 'U.S. Diplomacy in South Asia: A Progress Report'. The Brookings Institution, Washington, DC, 12 November.

———. 2004. *Engaging India: Diplomacy, Democracy, and the Bomb.* Washington, DC: Brookings Institution Press.

Tauscher, Ellen and Edward Markey. 2008. 'Don't Loosen Nuclear Rules for India'. *The New York Times*, 20 August.

Tellis, Ashley. 2000. *India's Emerging Nuclear Posture: Between Recessed Deterrent and Ready Arsenal*. Santa Monica, CA: Rand.

———. 2005. *India as a New Global Power*. Washington, DC: Carnegie Endowment for International Peace.

———. 2006a. 'The Evolution of US–India Ties: Missile Defense in an Emerging Strategic Relationship', *International Security* 30 (4): 113–51.

———. 2006b. *Atoms for War*. Washington, DC: Carnegie Endowment for International Peace.

The Economic Times. 2010a. 'Pressure Groups on Civil Nuclear Liability Bill Nullified'. 26 August.

———. 2010b. 'US Seeks Changes in Nuclear Liability Bill'. 9 September.

———. 2010c. 'Indian Firms to be Hit Hard by N-Liability Law Provisions'. 5 December.

The Hindu. 2006. 'Safeguards, End to U.S. Restrictions Must be Interlocking Actions'. Editorial, 27 July.

———. 2007a. 'NDA Briefed on Nuclear Agreement'. 27 July.

———. 2007b. 'A Sound and Honourable 123'. Editorial, 6 August.

———. 2007c. 'Put the Nuclear Deal on Hold'. Editorial, 20 August.

———. 2007d. 'Top Nuclear Scientists Take a Dig at Left Front'. 31 August.

———. 2007e. 'Basic Concerns of Various Sections had been Met: Srinivasan'. 2 September.

———. 2007f. 'Text of the UPA–Left Meeting Report; Government Can go to IAEA'. 17 November.

———. 2008a. 'Left Parties to Take All Steps to Stop India–U.S. Nuclear Deal'. 7 March.

———. 2008b. 'Bardhan: We Cannot be Party to Government Going Ahead with Deal'. 8 March.

———. 2008c. 'Congress–Left Near Break-up on Nuclear Deal'. 19 June.

———. 2008d. 'We Will go to IAEA Very Soon: Manmohan'. 8 July.

———. 2008e. 'It's a Privileged Document, Says Congress'. 8 July.

The Indian Express. 2007a. 'Atomic Atma'. Editorial, 28 August.

———. 2007b. 'Convince me N-Weapons Plan Safe, I'll Say go Ahead with Deal: Brajesh Mishra'. 25 October.

———. 2007c. 'UPA Talked to Me on N-Deal'. 5 November.

———. 2008a. 'N-Deal: Was India Misled? Left, BJP Say Yes; US Says No'. 3 September.

———. 2008b. 'India Gets NSG Waiver, Manmohan Calls it Historic Deal. 6 September.

———. 2010. 'N-Liability Law: Meeting Suppliers Midway, Govt May Fix Time and Cost'. 27 December.

The New York Times. 2005. 'Green Light for Bomb Builders'. Editorial, 22 July.

———. 2006a. 'President Bush Goes to India'. Editorial, 28 February.

———. 2006b. 'The Indian Nuclear Deal'. Editorial, 7 April.

———. 2007a. 'A Bad Deal Gets Worse'. Editorial, 5 August.

———. 2007b. 'Questions about the India Deal, Finally'. Editorial, 6 October.

———. 2008a. 'Let's Hear it for New Zealand'. Editorial, 31 August.

———. 2008b. 'A Bad Deal'. Editorial, 9 September.

———. 2008c. 'A Bad India Deal'. Editorial, 30 September.

———. 2013. 'Toward a Nuclear Deal with South Korea'. Editorial, 18 April.

The Telegraph. 2006. 'Taking the N-Train'. Editorial, 19 November.

———. 2007a. 'N-business & Pleasure Mix: Bush Aide on Indian Double Mission'. 28 May.

———. 2007b. 'There at Last'. Editorial, 25 July.

———. 2007c. 'BJP echoes Left on N-text'. 27 July.

———. 2007d. 'Deal of Triumph'. Editorial, 15 August.

———. 2007e. 'A Different Tune'. Editorial, 19 September.

———. 2008. 'Huddle to Amend Text as NSG Meet Drags on'. 6 September.

The Times of India. 2006a. 'Govt to Protect India's Interests on Iran Nuke Issue: Sonia'. 21 February.

———. 2006b. 'Power Agenda'. Editorial, 24 February.

———. 2006c. 'Unclear Policy'. Editorial, 15 March.

———. 2006d. 'No-Test Clause in Pact with US: MEA'. 17 April.

———. 2006e. 'Passage to America'. Editorial, 29 June.

———. 2006f. 'Left Almost Pulled Out Over N-Deal'. 4 November.

———. 2007a. 'A Really Big Deal'. Editorial, 21 August.

———. 2007b. 'It's Now or Never'. Editorial, 25 August.

———. 2007c. 'Government Blinks'. Editorial, 15 October.

———. 2008a. 'PM for Nuclear Deal Even without Left'. 19 June.

———. 2008b. 'Make or Break'. Editorial, 20 June.

———. 2008c. 'It's Now or Never'. Editorial, 27 June.

———. 2008d. 'India Reserves Right to Go Ahead with N-Tests: Kakodkar'. 8 September.

———. 2008e. 'Interview With Nicholas Burns'. 29 February.

The Wall Street Journal Asia. 2008. 'A Civil Nuclear Power'. Editorial, 21 July.

Varadarajan, Siddharth. 2004. 'US–India Negotiations Entering Crucial Phase'. *The Hindu*, 18 October.

———. 2005. 'Nuclear Cooperation with the US: Experts Urge Caution'. *The Hindu*, 18 July.

———. 2006a. 'Indo-US Nuclear Deal: Safeguards for Breeder Reactors a Key Obstacle'. *The Hindu*, 21 January.

———. 2006b. 'Question Mark Over Indo-US Nuclear Deal'. *The Hindu*, 7 February.

———. 2007a. 'Draft 123 Text to be Given to U.S'. *The Hindu*, 17 February.

———. 2007b. 'Reference to Indian Nuclear Test Unacceptable'. *The Hindu*, 17 February.

———. 2007c. 'No Place to Hide as Nuclear Deal Enters Last Lap'. *The Hindu*, 24 March.

———. 2007d. 'Major Obstacles Persist in Nuclear Deal'. *The Hindu*, 25 April.

———. 2007e. 'India will Stick to Rights-based Approach on Reprocessing'. *The Hindu*, 3 June.

———. 2007f. 'Manmohan Sent Strong Message through Burns'. *The Hindu*, 6 June.

———. 2007g. 'Taking Stock of the Indo-U.S. Nuclear Deal'. *The Hindu*, 17 August.

———. 2007h. 'Deal Breather, Not Deal Breaker'. *The Hindu*, 20 August.

———. 2008a. 'An Endgame with No Clear Winners'. *The Hindu*, 22 July.

———. 2008b. 'India Bracing Itself for American NSG Draft Guidelines'. *The Hindu*, 26 July.

———. 2008c. 'NSG Begins Talks on India Waiver'. *The Hindu*, 22 August.

———. 2008d. 'Conditions Mooted for Indian Nuclear Waiver'. *The Hindu*, 23 August.

———. 2008e. 'Looking Beyond the NSG Debacle'. *The Hindu*, 25 August.

———. 2008f. 'Waiver Enables Member States to Provide India Full Civil Nuclear Cooperation'. *The Hindu*, 7 September.

———. 2008g. 'India in Dilemma Over 123 Agreement'. *The Hindu*, 10 September.

———. 2008h. 'End of the Road for the 123 Agreement'. *The Hindu*, 16 September.

———. 2009. 'Ghost of Tarapur Haunts Reprocessing Agreement with U.S'. *The Hindu*, 16 December.

———. 2010. 'U.S. Can Suspend Reprocessing if "National Security" is Threatened'. *The Hindu*, 31 March.

The Washington Post. 2005. 'A New Nuclear Era'. Editorial, 20 July.

———. 2006. 'Talking Nukes with India'. Editorial, 26 February.

———. 2007a. 'Bet on India'. Editorial, 19 July.

———. 2007b. 'The Model that India Offers'. Editorial, 19 August.

———. 2008a. 'India's Outstretched Hand'. Editorial, 23 July.

———. 2008b. 'Yes for an Answer'. Editorial, 12 September.

The Washington Times. 2007. 'Nuking the Nuke Deal'. Editorial, 5 September.

The White House. 1998. 'Excerpts of President Clinton's Remarks on the Indian Nuclear Tests'. Washington, DC, 12 May.

———. 2002. 'The National Security Strategy of the United States of America'. September.

———. 2005. 'Joint Statement between President George W. Bush and Prime Minister Manmohan Singh'. Washington, DC, 18 July.

———. 2006a. 'Press Briefing by Secretary of State Rice and National Security Advisor Hadley'. Washington, DC, 28 February.

———. 2006b. 'Statement of Administration Policy, HR 5682, United States and India Nuclear Cooperation Promotion Act of 2006'. 26 July.

———. 2006c. 'Statement of Administration Policy, S 3709, United States–India Peaceful Atomic Energy Cooperation and U.S. Additional Protocol Implementation Act'. 16 November.

———. 2008. 'Statement by the President on the Occasion of Signing H.R. 7081'. 8 October.

Vickery, Raymond. 2011. *The Eagle and the Elephant: Strategic Aspects of US–India Economic Engagement*. Washington, DC: Johns Hopkins.

Walt, Stephen. 1987. *The Origin of Alliances*. Ithaca, NY: Cornell University Press.

Warburg, Gerald Felix. 2012. 'Lessons Learned from the US–India Nuclear Cooperation Agreement'. *Nonproliferation Review* 19 (3): 451–71.

Weaver, Kent and Bert Rockman. 1993. *Do Institutions Matter?* Washington, DC: Brookings Institution Press.

Weiss, Leonard. 2007. 'U.S.–India Nuclear Cooperation: Better Later than Sooner'. *Nonproliferation Review* 14 (3): 429–57.

Zuberi, Matin. 2005. *The Nuclear Deal: India cannot be Coerced*. New Delhi: Observer Research Foundation.

Index